Crisis Management in
the Tourism Industry

Crisis Management in the Tourism Industry

Dirk Glaesser

AMSTERDAM BOSTON HEIDELBERG LONDON NEW YORK OXFORD PARIS
SAN DEIGO SAN FRANCISCO SINGAPORE SYDNEY TOKYO

Butterworth-Heinemann
An imprint of Elsevier
Linacre House, Jordan Hill, Oxford OX2 8DP
200 Wheeler Road, Burlington, MA 01803

First published 2003

British Library Cataloguing in Publication Data
A catalogue record for this book is available from the British Library

Library of Congress Cataloguing in Publication Data
A catalogue record for this book is available from the Library of Congress

ISBN 0 7506 5976 9

For information on all Butterworth-Heinemann publications visit our
website at www.bh.com

Typeset by Newgen Imaging Systems (P) Ltd, Chennai, India
Printed and bound in Great Britain

To those who dedicate their lives to tourism

Contents

List of examples

Foreword

Tourism deals like no other sector with the pleasant and beautiful things of our lives. It is a steadily growing sector, more and more globally linked, in which many people of this planet already participate, whether as service providers or tourists.

In such an environment, it is difficult to think about Crisis Management. This subject, often neglected, is mostly considered as a task to be looked at only when a crisis actually occurs. However, in order for this approach to be effective, it needs to be designed with deep knowledge of the different mechanisms that are triggered by negative events. Consumers, competitors, governments, tour operators, and all the other service providers are heavily interlinked and must not be analysed on an individual basis but as a whole.

This was shown more than ever before with the terrorist attacks of September 11 on the United States of America, when the whole world was witness to the enormous sensitivity of this sector and its deep interdependence with all the other economic sectors. It proved the need to analyse crises in tourism thoroughly to be able to prevent and deal with them as efficiently as possible.

Crisis Management has become particularly important for those destinations and poorer countries heavily dependant on tourism as a source of income since they are the ones who suffer most when negative events occur.

In this book, Dr Glaesser examines the subject in a very systematic and consistent manner and shows that not every negative event must necessarily turn into a crisis. He analyses the fundamental relationships one has to be aware of to understand why a crisis in tourism might appear, how it can be prevented and coped with as well as the wide range of strategic and tactical possibilities and instruments linked to this question. Although this subject can cover an enormous variety of topics, he was able to prepare a comprehensive book, of vital interest to the sector and illustrated with a whole collection of actual case studies.

In an era where the well-being of tourists has become one of the primary concerns of the tourism industry, I sincerely hope that this book will help destinations and tourism enterprises to develop tourism in the most beneficial and sustainable way possible.

Francesco Frangialli
Secretary-General
World Tourism Organization

Acknowledgements

While preparing a book like this, which intends to offer a comprehensive approach to the topic of crisis management and, above all, tries to connect the bits and pieces that are so important for understanding why some situations occur, in ways that no one would have expected, I had the assistance of an excellent team.

In the first place, I want to thank my wife Matilde for supporting me and having the time to discuss all the facets of this book. My very good friend Ass. jur. Ute Meyer helped me with plenty of comments to improve the script. I am also very grateful to Prof. Dr Peter Keller, an authority on the issues of international tourism policy, and Prof. Dr Edgar Kreilkamp, a profound expert on strategic management, for their comments and advice.

I am also very grateful to cand. rer. nat. Stefanie Theuerkorn and lic. oec. HSG Philip Boksberger, who at the final phase of this book helped me to get it done in good time. I also want to thank Prof. Dr Guillermo Aceves, who provided me with valuable comments from a US point of view. Finally, a word to Bärbel, Dietrich, and Jens Glaeßer who were an iron grip of support in all the phases of this book.

Preface

Nowadays, travel is such an important part of daily life that it is hard to imagine that the roots of society's extensive participation in the tourism industry can be traced back to only a few decades.

The positive effects of tourism are varied. For tourists, a holiday means satisfaction as travel gives them the opportunity to bring their hopes and dreams to life. Furthermore, by holidaying outside their usual surroundings, tourists increase their knowledge of other cultures and ways of life, be it knowingly or unknowingly. This changed view of things helps to foster greater acceptance and tolerance among the human race.

As far as the national economy is concerned, the tourism industry has, in many countries, achieved such a leading position that it counts as one of the most important sources of income and foreign exchange. This growth will continue in the future and will contribute to make tourism the most significant industry in the world. Besides, tourism is, like no other industry, in a position to create prosperity and economic development opportunities even for places that would otherwise be considered as difficult to develop.

However, the positive development of the tourism industry is gradually being threatened by negative events. Incidents, which have taken place in the recent past, had economic consequences that were previously unheard of in other economic spheres. According to estimates, the tourism industry's profit loss in the wake of the Pan-Am disaster was between 4 and 7 billion US dollars. In the first 2 months of 1991, the drop in turnover for airlines alone as a result of the Gulf War was estimated at 2 billion US dollars. Terrorist attacks in Egypt also caused tourists to stay away, which meant that, in the space of a year, the revenue from the international tourism industry for this destination dropped by 1 billion US dollars. But all this was topped by the events of September 11 in the United States of America, which caused not only the worst impact on the worldwide tourism industry since World War II but also illustrated that those effects were able to trigger a slowdown of the whole world's economy. This was until now unknown. Nevertheless, these events were not the first ones to affect hard the tourism industry.

Even indirect effects like, for example, the rise in transport and travel costs across the globe, which threaten especially the competitiveness of long-haul tourism destinations, have a considerable impact. At the same time, a number of other effects are becoming apparent such as image damage and the limitation on entrepreneurial room for manoeuvre from which businesses are still affected in both the medium and long term.

Two fundamental areas can be identified that influence these developments. On the one hand, environmental conditions are becoming more and more complex for businesses. There is a variety of factors that contribute to this problem: first, the continuously increasing competition pressure, which arises from growing and constantly improving tourism facilities; second, highly flexible transport facilities, increasing travel intensities accompanied by simultaneously decreasing durations of stay and more spontaneous booking behaviour.

On the other hand, the sensitivity with which the general public and the individual consumer assess life risk is intensifying. The increase in individualistic ways of life means that the individual rather than the family unit must cope with a sense of insecurity. Therefore, replacement institutions or organizations, which could be used to reduce this sense of insecurity, were looked at more intensely. Risks, which were previously taken on and accepted by the individual, have recently been assigned to businesses as risks for which they can be made responsible. Nowadays, businesses must tackle the problems of claims that earlier could only be addressed to the state. Frequently, they must assume liability for services that were neither promised nor contractually agreed. Therefore, organizations are evaluated from a political and moral point of view by the general public to a degree unknown before.

This means that the tourism industry as an economic sector is challenged by negative events more than any other sector. Meanwhile, its above-average sensitivity towards these events has given it such an exposed position that it already serves as an early warning indicator of critical situations for other sectors.

The businesses that now face these challenges are confronted with two fundamental difficulties: first, to completely avoid risk is virtually impossible. Even organizations that rely exclusively or predominantly on risk management for their existence cannot completely control or avoid risk (this applies, e.g. to the military or the police). Second, the costs associated with the theoretical aim of totally avoiding risk are considerable. Product saleability sets the limits on these costs.

Under these circumstances, it is becoming more and more important to analyse negative events from every angle, to systematically identify critical success factors, to integrate them and take them into account when considering the strategic corporate orientation.

That is the aim of this book, which examines crisis management as an exception to the rules of marketing. This subject has, until now, been extensively neglected in literature because scientific research into marketing concentrated predominantly on a positive type of marketing, which could, in turn, create or extend the markets for the respective goods. The few analyses of negative events, which could be attributed to marketing, had mainly to do with the press and public relations. Even the possibility of using marketing to exert influence over negative events by taking preventive measures was only occasionally dealt with and, if so, concentrated too much on operative measures or their preparation.

Due to the complexity of the subject, it would be unrealistic to try to deal with it exhaustively in one single investigation. Therefore, this book concentrates on central aspects of crisis management in the tourism industry in order to fill in the gaps in literature, at least as far as the important points are concerned.

The book is presented in six chapters. In Chapter 1, an overview of the scientific discussion related to the term 'crisis' is given. In particular, it explores aspects that demonstrate that the reasons for a crisis must not necessarily lead to a change-oriented form of crisis management. A consequence of this is the further development of the term 'crisis', which is useful when considering the purpose of crisis management. Above all, a revaluation of the activities of crisis management considers that preventive measures are of great value. The purpose of crisis management in the tourism industry is then presented taking the peculiarity of the tourism product into consideration.

In order to better analyse the processes that trigger negative events, various spheres of activity are introduced in Chapter 2 using system-theoretic thinking as a basis. This way, the book differs from other investigations that previously dealt with those influences that bring about a crisis. Within the consumer's sphere of activity, not only the actual and potential customers but also the wider social environment of the organization is considered. Regarding the product sphere of activity, this book concentrates on the core tourism product: the destination. To analyse the effects in this sphere, a system for determining the basic and additional benefits of the tourism product is introduced. Competitors, state and other spheres of activity are also considered.

Using the findings as a basis, Chapter 3 looks at the question of which analysis tools are available for determining the critical areas within a company and promptly identifying negative events. It also examines to what extent they are appropriate for situations that arise within the tourism industry. New in this context is the consideration of image transfer and the evaluation of its implementation possibilities within the framework of crisis management. Subsequently, both indicator early warning methods and those based on detection of weak signals are examined with regard to their suitability for crisis management in the tourism industry.

In Chapter 4, the necessities and opportunities demanded by a preventive form of crisis management are investigated. In particular, findings made within the product sphere of activity are analysed within the context of corporate strategies. That which has also been neglected until now, that is, strategic opportunities of action which exist due to business configuration, contractual structuring of company relations and actual company appearance and which can influence the onset and effects of negative events, are also examined. Finally, various forms of crisis management strategies are also considered in view of their specific merits and problems.

The focal point of Chapter 5 is the peculiarities of crisis planning and the preparation of organizational measures related to negative events.

In Chapter 6, the findings are finally transferred to the marketing instruments. The importance of the timing aspect for crisis management is considered as well as the important question of budget calculation. Furthermore, the four marketing instruments (product, price, distribution and communication policy) are, in addition to their design ability, assessed according to their suitability, availability and restrictions.

1

Introduction to crisis management

1.1 What is a crisis?

1.1.1 Defining crisis

The word crisis comes from the Greek 'krisis', which means differentiation or decision. Within the legal sphere, the term was used to describe the differentiation between just and unjust whilst, in theology, it described the separation of salvation and damnation. Medical terminology used the expression for the break in a development that had before been continuous. In the sixteenth century, with the revival of classic medicine the word became part of everyday language. The use of the term crisis became evident in all areas of politics, society and the economy and, by the mid-nineteenth century, people were already complaining about its overuse.

The increase in the linguistic use of the term crisis was accompanied by a renewed scientific discussion of the 'crisis' phenomenon. Various scientific findings can be classed as either referring to persons/institutions or as contributions to the individual/collective model depending on their focal points.

As a rule, the human being is the focal point of considerations concerning individual models. In this case, the individual experiences the crisis as an intensification of the actual situation, which, in extreme cases, can lead to his or her end. Contributions to the individual model come from medicine and psychosomatics, psychosocial development theory and crisis intervention (crisis intervention is a collective term for theories about human behaviour in exceptional circumstances and therapy concepts). For collective models, on the other hand, social systems are analysed under certain circumstances that could be described as a crisis. Economics, political science and communications research all contribute to the collective model.

Furthermore, by using the subdivision practised in political science, system- and decision-oriented approaches can be distinguished. Within the framework of decision-theoretic approaches, crisis is understood as a dangerous and extraordinary situation in which a decision must be made under time pressure. Investigations carried out from this angle concentrate on the state of an acute crisis and acquire knowledge on the work flow organization in a crisis.

In systemic approaches, crisis is seen as a critical change in important variables that endanger or destroy either parts of or the entire system. The majority of the contributions to this area come from political science and the aim is the development of early warning systems (for the use of the term early warning, see Section 3.2). Due to their analysis of actual use and overuse, the results are especially useful for the organizational structure of the company in situations of crisis. Diagram 1 shows the areas of knowledge within crisis research.

1.1.2 The meaning of the term crisis within the economic sphere

National economics was the first to look into crises. The approaches understood as crises predominantly as cyclical economic problems. Business administration only started to take an interest later and this was prompted by the conditions that accompanied the crude oil shortage of the 1970s. The limitations that were, until then, unknown and the ever more frequent insolvency of companies prompted an economic

	System-oriented approaches	Decision-oriented approaches
Individual models	Medicine • Turning point is the decision between life and death during the course of an illness Psychology • Perception of an occurrence or situation as an intolerable difficulty that exceeds a person's resources and coping mechanisms • Failure of behavioural patterns • Danger of identity loss	Individual cognitive problem-solving qualities of decision makers in crisis situations

Collective models	Social sciences
	• Crises as phenomena of societies: endangered national interests during conflict due to a threatening escalation towards war (e.g. Cuban crisis)
	• Crises as phenomena of societal subsystems:
	  • Politics: real changes to political relations pattern (e.g. coup, revolution)
	  • Economy: exogenous economic shocks; phases of downward trend in the economic cycle
		Collective decision behaviour in crisis situations

Source: Based on Linde (1994).

Diagram 1 Areas of knowledge within crisis research

investigation, the consequence of which was the emphasis on coping with crisis.

Business administration predominantly terms crisis as a process that negatively influences the development of a company to a considerable extent (Krystek, 1987; Schulten, 1995). In this sense, the crisis either endangers or makes the survival of the affected company impossible. To determine a crisis situation, the question must be asked as to whether the organization still has the ability to achieve important corporate goals. However, only those goals that exert considerable influence over the future survival of the company are of significance. According to Burtscher (1996, p. 31):

> ... a company crisis should only be spoken of when the achievement of existential or dominant goals, which are decisive factors in the survival of the entire system, are seriously endangered.

The initial specifications of these high-ranking goals include solvency, that is, the ability to fulfil business payment obligations, and success expressed through minimum profit or return on investment. The advantage of this narrow version of the term crisis was the simple definition of crisis conditions within a company. Its financial base allows the simple derivation from accounting through a target/actual comparison. This approach can be traced back to the fact that a clear definition criterion was sought for to distinguish crisis management from normal management. Thus, crisis management was seen as separate from normal management activities.

However, this advantage of a simple definition was confronted with the disadvantage that the actual causes of the deviation from corporate goals, which occur earlier, were not covered (as it will also be discussed later, this also leads to crisis management concentrating on the area of coping). For this reason, further developments included the protection of the company's success factors that form the basis of solvency and success as a further criterion important for survival (Krystek, 1987; Gälweiler, 1992; Schulten, 1995). However, the inclusion of the concept of success factors, that is, factors that determine the present and, more specifically, future success of the organisation – presented by Porter (1998a) as competitive advantage – also brings difficulties with it. In particular, the missing quantification and generally difficult precision of the factor not only make a prompt and comprehensive analysis of competitive advantage necessary, they also make it more difficult to determine a situation of crisis.

Another characteristic of a crisis is the development possibility over the course of time. This process character is marked, on the one hand, by its temporal limitations, on the other, by its ambivalence. The latter is a prerequisite for the actual crisis management, that is, the sensibleness of the use of countermeasures (if ambivalence is missing, a catastrophic situation is present, see also Section 1.1.4). Only after the so-called turning point of the crisis can it be decided whether the previously ambivalent crisis situation will take a clearly positive or negative course (it has been a particular achievement of Pohl, 1997, to define, besides its starting and end points, the turning point of a crisis).

In addition, the fact that it is not possible to determine the onset of a negative event implies immediacy in view of the prior warning time and the available reaction time. Because crises, considered as processes, progressively limit opportunities of action, a need for decision and action is triggered, which is perceived by the participants as time pressure. The intensity of the time pressure can essentially be broken down into the following three components:

- limitation on the time available, that is, the decision time;
- individual sensitivity of the participants towards external pressure;
- the magnitude of the problem.

Crises are also characterized by extremely badly structured decisions that can be traced back to information deficit or even too much information, restrictions on information processing, complexity, etc. The conclusion often reached in this context, that crises are unplanned processes, proves to be imprecise. As crises in certain areas can, with planning, be easily anticipated and, therefore, influenced, the term 'unwelcome development' in relation to the formulated corporate goals is more precise. (Both exceeding and falling short of goals can be undesired. Activities described as demarketing, which are of use in the undesired exceeding of corporate goals, should not, however, be the object of further considerations.)

At the same time, a crisis is an exceptional situation, the onset of which is uncertain. Consequently, all preparations with regard to negative events have only eventuality as a characteristic. The number of theoretically possible events and the accordingly considerable expenditure demand restrictions and concentration of the precautions. Even organizations such as armies or the police whose exclusive task is the identification and planning of such processes cannot prepare for every event. On the one hand, this has to do with the number of influential factors that contribute to complexity and, on the other hand, with their continuous change. The opportunities for companies are, in comparison, even more limited because the preparation for and the coping with crises are never seen to be corporate goals.

5

1.1.3 New aspects of the term crisis

Normally, within the sphere of business administration, corporate developments that led to a crisis have been traced back to adaptations and changes the organization failed to do. The continuation of the organization in its previous form was, therefore, not deemed to be sensible. An active countermeasure in the sense of a neutralization of the destructive effect of negative events was scarcely taken into consideration (one of the exceptions is Pohl, 1977, p. 87, who sees the 'mere negation of the undesired condition . . . and the re-establishment of the status quo' to be possible as an objective). Zahn (1983, p. 196), for example, makes this clear, by acknowledging the existence of this type of negative events and describing the consequential crisis as 'a business crisis directly caused by sudden and unforeseeable changes in the environment'. At the same time, however, he was of the opinion that it would hardly be possible to counter these occurrences and that that they are, therefore, not worth taking into consideration. He concentrated more on the 'homemade' crises that 'can be traced back to problems within the company' and, which, in his opinion, are the results of 'objective and more continuous' environmental changes such as 'changes of consumer behaviour' that were ignored by the management.

However, such an opinion is no longer up-to-date. Markets with intense competition, which can be traced back to the interchangeability of services and an offer surplus, demand different marketing strategies from businesses. Competitive advantage is built up, maintained and defended to a considerable extent by marketing activities. Because of this, not only are products becoming more susceptible, but maintaining the status quo can also be a thoroughly worthwhile objective. This situation also applies for the tourism market.

Consequently, the term crisis must be defined in a wider sense. The following comment from Gee and Gain (1986, p. 3) makes the use of the term 'tourism crisis' clear:

The term 'tourism crisis' is now being used with increasing frequency by destinations whose economy has suffered from an immediate drop in visitor arrivals . . .

Sönmez, Bachmann and Allen (1994, p. 2.2) define 'tourism crises' in even more concrete terms as

> ... any occurrence which can threaten the normal operations and conduct of tourism related businesses; damage a tourist destination's overall reputation for safety, attractiveness, and comfort by negatively affecting visitors' perceptions of that destination; and, in turn, cause downturn in the local travel and tourism economy, and interrupt the continuity of business operations for the local travel and tourism industry, by the reduction in tourist arrivals and expenditures.

Approaches that examine events, which can be traced back to sudden, negative environmental changes and which do not preclude the maintenance of the company status quo, can be found in communications research. Scherler (1996, p. 17), for example, defines the term crisis management as:

> ... measures of all types which allow a business to cope with a suddenly occurring danger or risk situation in order to return as quickly as possible to normal business routine.

Initially, crisis communication concentrated only on the communication with the environment during the phase of crisis coping. Over the course of time, it was successively widened to include preventive communication as well. The long-term consequence of negative events on the competitive position of businesses, predominantly determined by their marketing–political activities, was recognised as it is made clear in the following quote (Mathes, Gärtner and Czaplicki, 1991, p. 16):

> ... the significance of a crisis is that one unlucky incident can destroy the good image of a company which has been built up by years of Public Relations work.

It is obvious from the depicted examples that it has, above all, to do with the seriousness of events when it comes to promptly determining a crisis situation. It must be assessed whether actual or potential events within the company or its environment influence its competitive advantage or other important business goals (Pohl, 1977, describes identities

7

of an organization and sees the beginning of a crisis as being when a premise on decisions that no longer agrees with the company's fundamental goals has to be accepted). Advantageous in such a contemplation of crisis is the early opportunity to analyse these events within the framework of preventive crisis management. Moreover, the crisis situation can thereby be better determined than through the previously demanded 'survival threat' to the organization (Murray, 1995, views seriousness as well as immediacy as essential factors in a crisis). The objection to the latter is that, as a rule, it is only possible to determine this threat correctly when the crisis is already in an advanced state. It is then already too late for the introduction of crisis management countermeasures.

Furthermore, concentrating on the seriousness of events takes into account that certain areas never face a threat to survival. In tourism, for example, destinations are organizational units, which, despite a considerable number of negative influences, are not threatened in their existence. The risk of a threat to survival would apply to businesses active within the destination but it would not necessarily have to be so.

For the purpose of this book, a crisis is defined as an unwanted, unusual situation for an organization, which, due to the seriousness of the event, demands an immediate entrepreneurial response.

1.1.4 Catastrophes, turnarounds and clashes

The term crisis should be disassociated from various other terms that are also connected with negative events or are used instead of it, in order to ensure its standard use within the framework of the rest of this book.

Catastrophes are negative events, which, in contrast to crisis, have a clear inevitable outcome. Consequently, the catastrophe is missing the crisis' ambivalence towards development opportunities. A connection or a simultaneous occurrence of a catastrophe and a crisis can be found especially in tourism, where catastrophes that occur in the environmental sphere trigger a crisis for the affected organization.

Turnaround is understood as countermeasures used to cope when a organization falls short of its goals. These activities, which concentrate, in part, on an acute crisis, aim for an abrupt reversal of the development. Thus, they concentrate on a particular part of the crisis, the object of which is coping with the crisis. Turnaround, consequently, portrays a special case within crisis management.

Clashes between personal groupings, which can take place inside or outside the company, are described as conflicts. In contrast to crisis, conflicts can be of an unlimited duration and can even be desired. Thus, they must not necessarily have negative consequences. It is, however, possible that conflicts are the cause of a crisis.

1.1.5 Classification of crises

Typologies of crises found in literature are extensive and thorough, for which reason only those important for the further contemplation of this book should be entered into.

It has already been shown that crises go through a development process. This leads to a phased subdivision of the crisis process becoming practice. As a rule, it is possible to differentiate between two to four phases of a crisis. The presently predominant three-phase crisis process is used as a basis in this book. Using time pressure as a characteristic, this divides the phases of a crisis into potential, latent and acute crises.

Potential crises are characterizing a phase in which the crisis is only an imaginary construct. They are, as such, neither ascertainable nor existent, for which reason this situation is described by Krystek (1987, p. 29) as the 'quasi normal condition of the company' in which it constantly finds itself.

Latent crises describe the phase in which the crisis has already broken out but is not yet identifiable with the normal quantitative instruments available to the company. Countermeasures in this phase are not yet subject to noticeable restrictions.

The phase of an acute crisis is the period of time in which the destructive effect of the crisis is perceived and the company strives to cope. The symptoms apparent in the acute crisis phase (which should not, however, be confused with the causes) are, as a rule, recognized as an indication of crisis within a company. The perception of a crisis situation is revealed by means of company reporting.

The differentiation between natural and human-induced crises is particularly significant in tourism. Crises triggered by negative events in nature, for example, natural catastrophes (tropical cyclones, storm tides, floods, avalanches and earthquakes are seen to be the most important natural disasters within the realm of tourism; WTO, 1998b) differ considerably in their effect from human-induced crises; that is, events triggered by humans. As a rule, negative events attributed to humans as a trigger lead to a much longer loss of faith and, therefore, to more negative consequences than natural crises that can be traced back to inevitable causes. This could be observed, for example, in the consequences of the events in Los Angeles and San Francisco in 1992. Racial unrest in Los Angeles had an effect not only in terms of immediacy but also in long-term tourism losses, more than for the earthquake in San Francisco. There, arrivals actually increased in the 12 months following the earthquake (Hollinger and Schiebler, 1995; Santana, 1995).

If the temporal distance between the onset of a negative event and the perception of the critical situation is considered, it is possible to distinguish between crises with fast and slow onset speeds. Crises with fast onset speeds are due to the sudden change detected quicker than is the case with slower onset speeds.

1.2 What is crisis management?

1.2.1 Management

The term 'management' usually describes the leadership of an organizational unit. It is possible to differentiate between an institutional and functional way of thinking. With regard to the former, management is a description of those groups of people who carry out management tasks, their activities and functions.

As far as functional thinking is concerned, management is a term for all tasks and processes connected with the running of a working organization. In particular, these are planning, organization, implementation and control. The functional perspective of management can be extended to include a person- or material-related consideration.

1.2.2 Crisis management

The first use of the term crisis management is normally attributed to the political sphere. Accordingly, it is said that US President J.F. Kennedy used the expression during the Cuban Crisis of 1962 to describe the handling of a serious, extraordinary situation.

Continuing the subdivision into function and institution, common in management, there is also a differentiation between crisis management as a function and as an institution. Crisis management as an institution refers to groups of persons who are responsible for crisis management activities. They are the dominant bearer of the functional crisis management. Middle- and lower-level employees and external forces join with members of upper management levels as actors in a crisis.

Crisis management as a function refers to changes of tasks and processes when a crisis occurs. Different types of crisis management and corresponding activities are distinguished with regard to the process character of the crisis and the differentiation between its various phases.

In literature, the division of an active from a reactive form of crisis management predominates (Höhn, 1974; Krystek, 1979; von der Oelsnitz, 1993). The former stands for the proactive anticipation of a negative event, both mentally and in terms of preparation. The latter, reactive crisis management, concentrates on activities of crises that have already occurred and been detected.

Viewed chronologically, this approach goes back to Höhn (1974), who differentiates between crisis precautions and crisis care. In his analysis, crisis precautions include preparing for potential crises whilst the objective of the latter is to cope with acute crises.

Röting (1976) distinguishes further and makes the activities dependent on the phases of the crisis process. He comes to the differentiation of preventive crisis management, which should anticipate and compensate future crises; active crisis management, which should allow the prompt identification of events; and reactive crisis management, which should deal with compensating active crises.

Krystek (1987) names four areas of crisis management. An anticipative form of crisis management applies for potential business crises. The aim of this activity is an increase in reaction capability through the formation of prognoses or scenarios and the implementation of alternative plans. Within preventive crisis management, an existing but not yet recognized crisis should be tracked down with the help of an early warning system. The planning, implementation and control of preventive strategies and measures are also the object of this analysis. Repulsive crisis management should be viewed as crisis management aimed at maintaining the business and refers to crises that have already occurred. If there is no chance of survival for the company, a liquidating form of crisis management, the central task of which is the planned liquidation of the company, takes place. The ambivalence missing in this phase makes the classification as crisis management seem doubtful.

Müller (1986) calls for a division between strategic, success-ensuring and solvency-protecting forms of crisis management. In this way, strategic crisis management concentrates on the protection of the company's success factors. Success-ensuring crisis management should avoid existence-threatening shortfalls of success goals such as profitability and turnover. With a solvency-protecting crisis management, the aim is to overcome the dangers of insolvency and excessive debts. In this context, the exclusion of crisis avoidance and the limitation to coping activities should be seen as problematic within the area of crisis management.

Schulten (1995) distinguishes actions of crisis identification and crisis handling. Whilst he equates the former with early recognition, he reformulates crisis handling and no longer sees it as coinciding with crisis coping. He believes that coping with a crisis only requires coping actions and, therefore, assigns both avoidance and coping activities to crisis handling. This finally leads him to differentiate between strategic and operative crisis management in which the transition between the two lies where avoidance tactics are relinquished in favour of coping activities.

1.2.3 Conclusion

Although the term crisis management has gone through various attempts of definition, no standard one has been found. At least its subdivision into two main activities, crisis prevention and crisis coping, has proved unproblematic.

For the following analysis this division should be kept. In addition, three crisis activities that correspond to the three phases of the crisis process are distinguished (see also Section 1.1.5). An ideal type of development assumed, Diagram 2 portrays the progress of such activities.

Crisis prevention should be understood as preparation for uncertain future damage or negative events. In contrast to crisis coping, crisis prevention is characterized by continual occupation with the subject. It is comprised of the two areas, crisis precautions and crisis avoidance, in which both parts should not be viewed as temporally succeeding. They are rather independent parts, which, in practice and from a time

Crisis prevention				Crisis coping
Crisis precautions		Crisis avoidance		
Planning	Implementation	Early warning	Adjustment	Employment of instruments

Diagram 2 Phases of crisis management

perspective, can find themselves used one after the other or at the same time.

Crisis precautions describe planned precautionary activities and measures for more effective crisis coping, which are carried out with the aim of lowering the extent of damage. This area is consequentially of a strategic nature and includes risk policy, but also prepares operative crisis plans.

The object of crisis avoidance is to take measures that hinder the development of crisis out of identified crisis potentials. This is primarily the task of early warning, which deals with scanning and evaluation. The aim of early warning is to detect events in time and to estimate their seriousness in order to quickly undertake countermeasures.

The fundamental assumption, by which the sensibleness of avoidance crisis management is justified, is the possibility to advance the use of instruments. This is confirmed by observations of crises where, with the *ex post* contemplation, a cause or causes can be identified as the crisis trigger.

At least theoretically, an ideal point in time for early warning can be determined. On the one hand, it is known that the destructive effect of a negative event increases with time, on the other, the number of possible countermeasures decreases until the affected organization is no longer in control of the situation. At the same time, the cost of early warning cannot be viewed as a fixed cost but as an additional expenditure that is mainly connected to the realization in good time. This expenditure decreases over the course of time because the assessment of developments becomes simpler and, therefore, cheaper. By the time a crisis is detected using conventional instruments, the cost is zero.

It becomes clear, therefore, that it is not the realization 'at the earliest stage' but 'early enough' in the sense of giving sufficient time for reactions that must be the objective of early warning system to avoid crises. This 'early enough' varies depending on the endangered area and the possible negative event.

Apart from early warning, crisis avoidance deals with the adjustment of the organization to the situation in that it increases the reaction speed. Because this adjustment can be triggered by a negative event, the lines between preventive and coping activities become blurred.

Crisis coping has a defeating character. It is suddenly initiated and portrays an active and intended exertion of influence over the situation that can be carried out by the affected organization or others. It starts with the identification of a crisis situation. Apart from dealing with the causes of the crisis, crisis coping covers the employment of all management instruments in order to bring the crisis situation to an end. The goal is the management of a crisis in such a way that no more present or future negative consequences can occur.

Considering the process of crisis management as a whole, a fluid transition from prevention to actually coping with the crisis is revealed. Previously seen limitations of crisis management to coping activities in the sense of a coping crisis management do not make much sense now. Rather are the particular challenges laying in the preventive area of crisis management. This corresponds to the way the praxis is dealing with negative events, where all management areas within a company become involved. Therefore, the activities of both prevention and coping should be subsumed to crisis management just as crisis management should be understood as an extensive management problem.

This form of crisis management is dependent on the crisis phases, both part of regular corporate planning and also independent from it. The former is the case if it concerns preventive crisis management. The latter is the case if it concerns coping crisis management that is not only independent from regular corporate planning but can also change or replace its results.

1.3 Crisis management in the tourism industry

Anywhere where competitive advantage is easily open to attack or can be destroyed by negative events, preventive crisis management plays a particular role. This applies, in general, for tourism, which, like no other sector, works with imaginary values and making dreams come true. The early identification of negative events is, consequently, the particular task of crisis management. However, not only well-known events should be observed as they occur but potential events should also be analysed and their consequences assessed. For this, the attempt to use research knowledge from the sphere of risk technologies such as chemical or nuclear technology, which were long ago forced to extensively assess negative events, can be profitable for tourism.

As a general discussion about crisis and the necessity for the adjustment of the term crisis management were brought to the fore in the preceding remarks, a general concept for crisis management in tourism should be developed in the following. For this purpose, the tourism system is presented, the classification and description of units participating in tourism is looked into and the types and effects of negative events in tourism are investigated.

1.3.1 Tourism

Tourism is a phenomenon of the modern era and describes, in general terms, everything connected with travel. Generally, there are three constitutive characteristics: change of location, temporary stay and the existence of a motive. According to the definition of the World Tourism Organization and the United Nations, tourism should be understood as 'the activities of persons travelling to and staying in places outside of their usual environment for not more than one consecutive year for leisure, business or other purposes' (WTO/UN, 1994, p. 5).

Reverting to system-theoretic knowledge offers the most extensive portrayal of tourism possible, which is characterized, in particular, by interpersonal contact and numerous relations with the environment. Thus, the company is defined as a productive social system that maintains relations with its environment as an open structure. The different sections of the system are so much linked with one another 'that no section is independent of the other sections and the behaviour of the whole is influenced by the combined effect of all sections' (Ulrich and Probst, 1995). All elements outside of the company's system belong to the environment, which can be subdivided into dimensions and institutions. Taking a dimensional view on the environment, it is possible to differentiate between ecological, technological, economic and social spheres. If need be, this can also be extended to the political–legal sphere.

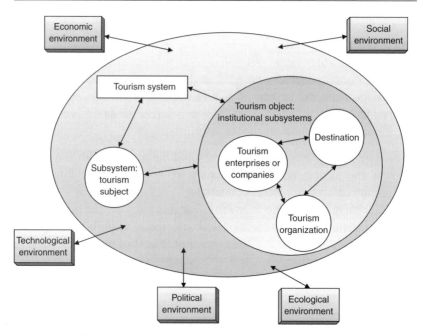

Source: Adapted from Kaspar (1998).

Diagram 3 The tourism system

Taking an institutional view on the environment, it is possible to separate institutions or groups from individuals, such as the state, customers,
competitors, capital investors, suppliers and employees. As a subsys-
tem of tourism, the tourism subject – the tourist – can be distinguished
from the institutional subsystems 'destination', 'tourism company' and
'tourism organization' (see Diagram 3).

1.3.2 The tourism product

The tourism product is varied and complex and is often constructed with
the cooperation of a number of people and organizations. In tourism,
even if those units that participate in service construction produce their
own tourism products, according to predominant opinion, only the marketable service bundle is understood as being the actual tourism product
because the respective service parts are barely saleable on their own
(Kaspar, 1991; Bieger, 1996a; Doswell, 1998).

Because, as with other service products, the tourism product is predominantly immaterial, this makes the service that is to be provided difficult to assess. This uncertainty increases due to the distance between the location of purchase and where the service is provided. Expressed in information–economic terms, the tourism product is a belief or trust product that demands that the supplier is able to reduce uncertainty and risk, above all, in relations with potential customers. Because quality can be checked, three kinds of goods can be distinguished: search goods (product quality can be easily checked before purchase), experience goods (checking is only possible on demand) and trust goods (impossible to acquire information due to prohibitive or high costs) (Haedrich, 1998a; Kaas, 1990).

The tourism product on offer is often divided into an original and derived offer (Kaspar, 1991, Müller, Kramer and Krippendorf, 1991; Freyer, 1995). Whilst natural factors, general infrastructure and social–cultural relationships, which characteristically have no direct relation to tourism, count towards the original offer, the derived offer incorporates factors that were knowingly created for the satisfaction of tourists' needs, for example, the tourism infra- and superstructure (Kaspar, 1991; Müller, Kramer and Krippendorf, 1991).

1.3.3 New aspects of the tourism product

Recently, it was demanded that the tourism product and the consumer goods product are treated the same way as well as the product components, 'original' and 'derived offer', were extended by the 'software' part of the offer (WTO, 1994a; Bieger, 1996a). Where original and derived offer refer to the hardware characteristics of the product, software describes the so-called soft characteristics such as experience.

From the demand perspective, the product can be characterized, generally, as a number of features that are combined and allow one or more of a prospective client's needs to be satisfied. By satisfying this need, the product provides the consumer with a benefit. Building on the benefit gauge developed by *Vershofen*, which differentiates between basic benefits, that is, the material–technical side of a product, and additional benefits, that is, the emotional–spiritual side, Kotler (1984) developed three levels of the term 'product'. He describes the first level as the core product that is the actual core service of the product, therefore, that 'which the customer actually purchases'. The second level is the actual product that is identified by a unit understood by the customer as an object and that includes five characteristic features: quality standard, features, styling, brand name and packaging. Other services and advantages that accompany the product form a third level and describe the augmented product.

This system was transferred to services (service describes, amongst other things, a combination of factors such as living things, material goods and nominal goods) by Bruhn and Meffert (1995) and the material and immaterial components of the product were also divided into three levels. In its first level, the model describes the core product as a fundamental service or mandatory component called for by customers. In the next level, the quality product incorporates those elements that stand for services expected by the customer as fundamentally desired components. Both services together refer to the so-called basic benefit, which can, therefore, also contain immaterial components and can be further understood in terms used by *Vershofen*. Separated from this is the additional benefit that forms the final level and describes discretionary services. Whereas those services provided as basic benefits correspond to customer expectations, activities that create additional benefits are useful in product differentiation and, eventually, the creation of competitive advantage (see, e.g. Diagram 4).

If this system is applied to basic tourism services, the core product describes, for example, overnight stay and catering services with regard to accommodation companies (the constitutive element is only the accommodation service itself that incorporates the granting of accommodation) or transport services as far as transport companies are concerned (Kroeber-Riel, 1986a, uses the example of airlines which limit their advertising to experience dimensions and no longer refer to interchangeable sevices). Destinations can incorporate many types of core services of which swimming and golf are examples for activity-oriented holidays and cultural buildings or history are examples of core services for regional holidays (for an analysis of a destination's core services that are of interest in this book, see also Section 2.2).

In general, the majority of products on offer are so well developed that objective differences in quality are scarcely perceived by the customer. This dematerialization of consumption can also be observed in tourism. Even here a change towards a buyer's market took place and the fulfilment of the 'fundamental physical need to travel' is already

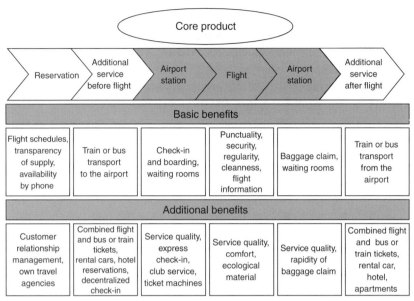

Source: Adapted from Bruhn and Meffert (1995).

Diagram 4 Basic and additional benefits of a flight service

seen as a foregone conclusion (Kroeber-Riel, 1986a; Wachenfeld, 1987; Haedrich, 1993; Opaschowski, 1995; Kreilkamp, 1998). The objective functional quality of a product is a necessary, but by no means sufficient, prerequisite for market success. On the contrary, a product's competitiveness is determined by its ability to impart consumption or holiday experience.

The value of experience becomes, therefore, the focus of considerations. Defined by Weinberg and Konert (1985, p. 85) as ' . . . subjectively experienced through the product, the service, . . . the contribution made to the consumer's quality of life . . . ', it conveys experiences that are embodied in the world of feeling and experience. Examples of frequently used experience values are: relaxation, security, love, luck, leisureliness, holiday romance, self-confidence, elegance, risk, warmth, technology, nature, liveliness, freedom, sensuality and adventure. At the same time, we must also be aware that words are only infrequently used to relay human feelings. Therefore, pictures are frequently used for the portrayal and conveyance of experiences.

Schulze (1996, p. 427) uses the differentiation between interior- and exterior-oriented consumption to make the function of experience in today's society clear. 'If glasses are bought in order to see better, a car for transportation, flour as food, etc., this is exterior-oriented behaviour.' Consequently, the quality of the product is not seen to be dependent on consumers because it concerns the product's objective features. This is different, however, for interior orientation. 'The interior-oriented consumer looks for glasses for which he already feels something, a car which fascinates him, a type of flour with which he can experience something: experience flour.' Finally, he concludes that, nowadays, holiday travel is 'called for exclusively due to interior-oriented motivation'.

Schrattenecker (1984, p. 61) also addresses the issue of the strong influence emotional criteria have on the selection process. Regarding the choice of destination, for example, she said:

> It should be assumed that the formation of a preference or a choice between target countries does not take place on an exclusively rational basis, but, in fact, an emotional analysis of the countries, which is predominantly based on the complexity of the assessable object, also takes place: there is, therefore, both rational and emotional content. For example, emotional criteria such as 'international flair' and rational criteria such as 'the existence of the opportunity to undertake water sports such as sailing, surfing and water skiing' could be a decisive factor when choosing a target country. These criteria are not mutually exclusive but complement one another: both the one – emotional – and the other – objective offer – are looked for.

This is expressed in more concrete terms by Fesenmeier and MacKay (1996, p. 42) who refer to the considerable significance of this experience value in the initial phase of travel decision:

> As such, destination decisions may be based on the symbolic elements of the destination (as conveyed in visual imagery) rather than the actual features.

This quote makes it clear that the creation of competitive advantage within the sphere of core benefits is scarcely possible for the tourism product if the products are no longer unique and, as a result, their objective functional features are no longer discernible. If the two basic types of competitive advantage are used as a basis, the missing opportunity for material differentiation means that the choice remains between a cost leadership or immaterial differentiation strategy, which is also known as an experience value strategy. Bieger (1996b) also confirms this: he regards only the possibility of software differentiation, under which he understands culture, systems, experiences, ambience and lifestyle, as useful for a destination with interchangeable resource getup, under which he subsumes capital, infrastructure and nature. Seen in the medium to long term, emotional consumer experience provides a larger contribution to consumer quality of life in many markets, including the tourism market, than the basic actual and functional features of the product that are regarded as trivial. Therefore, it is the task of strategic and operative marketing to generate, impart and maintain these additional benefits that decide the purchase decision. These new aspects are, at the same time, the particular challenge of the strategic crisis management.

1.4 What are negative events?

The critical conditions of the form of crisis management considered here can be traced back to the onset of certain negative events. This is voiced by Steger and Antes (1991), who use the term interference potential in this context and define it as follows: 'interference potential – that is to say events which lead to the plans of the company going unfulfilled and negative effects occurring instead . . . '. This shows that is it principally an event, that is, an accumulation of individual phenomena, which is the cause that a stable situation turns critical. The use of the term 'interference potential' can be disadvantageous, however, due to people misinterpreting it as meaning an endangered area.

In general, a particular, extraordinary incident is defined as an event. If this particular, extraordinary incident is extended to include its negative consequences, a negative event could be spoken of. Putting negative events in concrete terms should not, however, lead to the assumption that the consequences of every event can be assessed as soon as it occurs. For the following analysis, negative events will be defined as all incidents pertaining to the organization's environment, which, in their way, are able to cause lasting damage from the perspective of the respective organizational unit. This means that they can threaten, weaken or destroy

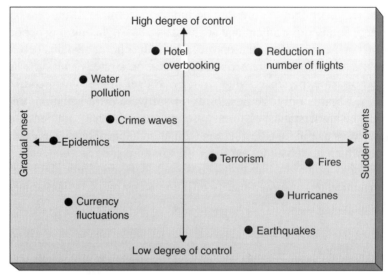

Source: Based on Gee and Gain (1986).

Diagram 5 Negative events

competitive advantage (an analysis of events that would not cause lasting damage falls under the area of normal management and is covered by risk management). Therefore, the most extensive point of view possible will be striven for, that is, one that does not just incorporate negative events in the sense of a security problem.

Diagram 5 gives a brief overview of potential negative events that could trigger tourism crises, subdivided according to how easy they are to control and their onset speed.

1.5 The dissemination of negative events

Negative events must to be realized and in order to cause an effect they must be either directly experienced or at least communicated (primary and secondary experience could be spoken of here). Experience shows that direct perception is of minor importance. Thus, the analysis of the communication of negative events is given here a particular importance as well as to those participating in the communication process.

Regarding forms of communication, it is normally possible to distinguish direct communication, which takes place between people on a personal level, and mass communication, the central characteristic feature of which is the involvement of technical media. The latter occupies a central position for the bridging of the gap between the wider environment (the recipient's family, friends and acquaintances are described as being part of the closer environment whereas the wider environment is characterized by groups, organizations, social stratum, etc., to which the recipient belongs) and the recipient of news. Today, mass media is used, on average, for more than 5 hours a day (Berg and Kiefer, 1992).

Within the communication process, mass media fulfils two fundamentally different functions. The first is the conveyance of information, the second, the changing of attitudes (attitude is described as a person's learned and relatively stable readiness to behave more or less consistently towards an object or situations) and opinions. The high importance of the role as information provider is confirmed by empirical investigations. For example, 95 per cent of the American population get their information about the wider environment from the mass media (Kroeber-Riel, 1992). Contrary to the supposition that often prevails, it is, above all the print media that determines the information status of the recipient. Television, to which this function is frequently attributed, actually performs rather an initiating function especially for events of emotional importance.

1.5.1 Dissemination influence variables

Various factors exert influence over the dissemination of an event by the media. Galtung and Ruge (1965) drew up a catalogue of news factors as selection guidelines that have since repeatedly been empirically investigated. All agree that it is important that the news communicate something new. It must, therefore, be topical. Besides, it must deal with an event of value. As a result, newsworthiness could be spoken of and implies, therefore, that the event must be of interest from the point of view of the recipient. It is indeed clear to see that the interests of the recipients are of an extremely differing nature; nevertheless, some similarities can be identified:

- The consequence that the event has for the recipient of the information, that is, one's own concernment, counts as well as the extent of the event, which means the scope of those primarily affected, as news value. Both can be summarized to describe the significance of the event (Weischenberg, 1990). Due to this significance, it is possible to differentiate between hard and soft news. Whilst hard news places the aspect of the information at the fore, soft news fulfils the recipient's entertainment needs.

■ The proximity of the event to the recipient is also an important criterion when assessing the value of news. Proximity stands, on the one hand, for the location of the event, on the other, for the importance of the information for the recipient. This applies both for hard and soft news. Skriver (1990) examined the significance of geographical proximity: he found that, for a report of not less than 10 cm in local newspapers, thirty-nine deaths are required for an event that took place 10 000 km away, seven for an event 1000 km away and only one death is required for an event that took place 100 km away.

Another characteristic is cultural proximity. According to an investigation by Adams (1986), US news coverage of non-American natural disasters fluctuates depending on the cultural proximity of the dead to the American cultural circle. Accordingly, the extent of news coverage for a dead West European with that of three East Europeans or nine Latin Americans compared with that of eleven inhabitants of the Middle East or twelve Asians.

Psychological proximity is another influential factor. This is understood as the event's relationship to the recipient's realm of experience. It is this factor that has particularly significant consequences for tourism. Whilst, in the context of cultural proximity the number of dead is responsible for 3 per cent of news coverage, the tourism popularity of a country accounts for 33 per cent of this coverage (Adams, 1986). Moreover, this is intensified by tourists being the declared focus of attacks as Tscharnke (1995) proved on the basis of German Press Agency coverage.

■ Even the human emotional aspect determines the value of news. Some examples of a number of factors that determine the value of an event are: drama, tension, romance, love and sex, humour and fun, adventure and risk, sympathy, tragedy, prominence, age, curiosity, struggle and conflict. For soft news, in particular, it is the triggering of emotions that determines interest in the news (Pürer, 1991).

■ Furthermore, the terms of reference, which are developing over a longer period of time, contribute to the selection of events (Mathes, Gärtner and Czaplicki, 1991). Journalists and other groups from the social environment see current events, which can be the object of news coverage, in the context of a cognitive scheme made up of previously collected knowledge and existing attitudes. This corresponds to the findings of behavioural science according to which man's ability to understand relationships and the essential characteristics of a situation determine the selection of environmental signals. This process is influenced by structures anchored in memory, which follow the rules of repetition and attentiveness.

The terms of reference, which influence the journalists' perception and assessment, develop, as a rule, over a long period of time. Many topics, classified as sudden and unexpected, can with the knowledge of those terms of reference be put into perspective regarding their degree of surprise. Luhmann (1991, p. 11) also confirms this saying ' . . . that risk assessment and the readiness for risk acceptance is not only a physiological but mainly a social problem. We behave as it is expected by the relevant reference groups or as we – whether in accordance with or against the general opinion – are socialised'.

If the various individual values and factors are aggregated, they form a total news value that determines the selection. Consumer interests are clearly at the fore in the definitive value assessment as they determine with their consumption, respectively, their purchase of the news, the economic success of the news supplier. Nevertheless, other factors of news selection must also be considered such as the specific interests of the publishing houses, editors and journalists, the relevant statutes and press legislation and social, political and democratic interests. It is these last-named factors that often lead us to see the media apart from its infrastructure function, that is, the dissemination of news, as an independent factor that is forming the public opinion, and an organisation that is able to change attitudes and opinions.

1.5.2 The role of the mass media

The effect of information and assessments disseminated by the mass media on public opinion were examined in mass communications research. Within the various explanatory attempts, it is possible to distinguish the approaches of strengthening, conviction and agenda-setting (Kroeber-Riel, 1992).

25

Conviction assessment assumes that mass media is in a position to influence the recipient's attitudes and opinions contrary to his own views and in a direction desired by the media. Nowadays, this approach tends to be mostly rejected. Exceptionally, this effect tends to be attributed to themes that indirectly affect the recipient, in other words, which are of a more general social relevance and the influence, however, is only superficial or temporally limited (Dunwoody and Peters, 1993).

According to the strengthening hypothesis, the mass media confirms and strengthens existing attitudes and opinions by means of conveyed information. Because the recipient extensively avoids contradictions, he or she not only selectively takes on the numerous pieces of existing information but also assesses them just as selectively. Thus, news presented through the media have especially an effect on attitudes if information is sought for opinion-forming or opinions are formed for the first time.

A continuation of the strengthening effect approach is the agenda-setting approach, which is dominant in media research. Accordingly, by making certain events a subject of discussion, the media decides whether there is a place for them in public discussion. This is awarded a selection function, which applies, above all, if it concerns topics outside of the recipient's personal sphere of experience. Once this selection takes place, the media structures the themes that are subjects of the discussion by assigning them preferences.

1.5.3 Conclusion

To summarize, the mass media generates awareness and has a certain influence on the selection of topics for public debate. How far they bring about concrete changes in attitudes and opinions depends on a number of factors. What is important is that they trigger a process of information search, especially when dealing with topics of personal relevance. Therefore, the recipient uses a number of information sources and, as explained by the multi-stage communication process, uses both the means of personal and media communication.

The deviation from daily routine is responsible for negative events having an increased communication probability and a quicker dissemination process. Therefore, the significance of a negative event should be rated higher than that of a normal event. The globalization of communication services is finally responsible that events, once selected, have a quasi-unlimited audience. In addition, globalization means that another phenomenon can be observed that is of significance for tourism. Increased possibilities to communicate a negative event worldwide causes that the probability of incidents increases where publicity is sought. This applies for terrorist attacks, which stand a good chance of being staged spectacularly if they are aimed at tourists.

On the other hand, localization of news reporting contributes to events being detected that were previously paid no attention. Above all, when there is a news vacuum, these can spread in a kind of snowball effect until they are picked up by larger media.

It should, therefore, be assumed that, once negative events occur, they are difficult to hide, which makes it necessary for every responsible entrepreneur to understand their functions and how to deal with them.

Crises' spheres of activity

How do negative events function, once they have been experienced or communicated? This is the core question that the assessment of preventive and coping management techniques is faced with. Initially, the question of primary interest is which areas of consideration should be meaningfully distinguished in order to carry out a precise effect analysis with particular reference to the affected organization. The following two investigations should be described as examples that deal with negative events in tourism.

Hultkrantz and Olsson (1995) examined the effect of the nuclear fall-out at Chernobyl on Swedish tourism. A result of their analysis was the determination that this negative event had various effects on tourism. Whilst inbound tourism was noticeably affected by the event, no changes to domestic tourism could be observed.

The WTO (1991a) examined the consequences of the Gulf War on tourism. In addition, it undertook a sectional and regional separation of the observed areas. As a result of its analysis, various significant developments were defined within regional considerations. These varied, not only in their intensity, but also in their direction. They incorporated not only downward trends but also stagnation and increases in international arrivals and journeys.

Furthermore, sectional considerations observed that various market segments also reacted very differently to the same event. Whilst airlines, in general, suffered from the effects of the war, differences could be noted with long-haul journeys, which, in comparison, underwent a more intense reaction. This was the same for certain types of travel and hotel categories, which displayed more sensitive behaviour, and smaller businesses, which were affected more than larger ones.

Both investigations confirm that a different effect to the same event is possible. The foundation for a successful form of crisis management lies in this observation. It not only opens the opportunity to concentrate on and plan coping measures, but also indicates that the negative after-effects of a negative event can be can be diminished by strategic preparations.

Using system theory as a basis, the following spheres of activity are distinguished: consumers, tourism units, competitors, state and supplier, capital investors and employees (Diagram 6, see also Diagram 3).

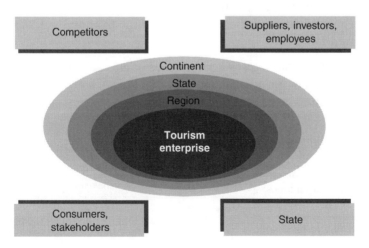

Diagram 6 The various spheres of activity

2.1 The consumer as a sphere of activity

The tourism product takes the presence of tourists for granted. The potential or participating consumer 'tourist' can, without doubt, be identified as the most important part of this consideration. It is the tourist's perception of and reaction to negative events that dominates the activities of crisis management.

2.1.1 The social environment of organizations

Traditional marketing concentrates on a company's current customers and target groups that are viewed as potential customers. In this case, the aim is the creation of sales markets for the products on offer.

The disadvantage of such behaviour is that other social groups within the environment of an organization, which are not considered as customer or potential customer, are neglected. These, however, prove to be an important influential factor for the company in a complex and rapidly changing environment. Haedrich (1998a) proved that, in 1991, only 40.6 per cent of the companies interviewed were in a position to implement their planned competitive strategies unhindered by social demands. The onset of a negative event will increase this number even further.

Other social groups have differing interests in the organization. Reference, public interest and stakeholder groups can be distinguished on account of the will to exert power and the possibility of sanctions (Diagram 7).

According to Janisch (1992), reference groups are social groups that have an actual or potential, direct or indirect relationship with the company as well as little will to exert power but a modest possibility of

		Will to exert power	
		Little	Great
Possibility of sanctions against the company	High	Stakeholders	
	Low	Reference groups	Public interest groups

Source: Adapted from Scherler, 1996.

Diagram 7 Reference/public interest/stakeholder groups

sanctions. This applies, for example, for the various organizations of the United Nations and the Church.

Public interest groups are described by Zwyssig (1995) as those social groups that boast an actual, direct or indirect relationship with the company and, therefore, display a direct interest in the company and its behaviour. In spite of their will to exert power, they have only few sanction possibilities at their disposal.

Finally, stakeholders are social environment groups who announce their interests to a company as concrete expectations and claims and who are in a position to influence, either by themselves or through their representatives, corporate goals, their implementation and industrial activities, as well as themselves being influenced by corporate goals, their implementation and industrial activities. Environmental and consumer organizations, trade unions, development organizations and citizen initiatives are specified as generally important stakeholders (Dyllick, 1992).

The significance of stakeholders within the context of negative events is subject to some peculiarities that depend on the distance from the product and the type of product. For example, massive breakdowns at a former chemical plant of Hoechst plc in Frankfurt am Main (Germany) in 1993 mainly led to reactions within the stakeholder sphere and less on the part of customers (Schönefeld, 1994). In spite of waves of protest amongst residents and company stakeholders, the company's trade results showed a higher profit at the end of the financial year than in previous years. On the one hand, this is explained by the nature of the company's products that can scarcely be perceived by sanctioning end users. Therefore, Hoechst plc, for example, is scarcely recognized as a manufacturer of artificial fertilizers and insecticides in the case of the end product. On the other hand, buyers of insecticides or artificial fertilizers are not overly interested in the manufacturer's social reputation as long as it does not affect their own product sales.

The events surrounding the attempt to sink Shell's Brent Spar oil loading platform in 1995 can be cited as a further example from the production branch of industry. For weeks on end, the company was the focus of public interest and suffered immensely from the pressure of end users who boycotted Shell products (in this way, sales loss is averaged at 20 per cent, in individual cases at more than 50 per cent, N.A., 1995a).

At the same time, however, the company had no problems at all with aviation fuel and lubricant oil sales.

This makes it clear that the significance of stakeholders is greater, the closer the end consumer feels to the product and the clearer the ascent of concessions in the interests of the end product. This applies, in particular, for tourism. On the one hand, product components, although generally paid little attention, can easily be detected for the individual. As a rule, a negative event that occurs here can be identified and sanctioned without too many difficulties. On the other hand, tourism services can scarcely be used otherwise and, furthermore, cannot be stored for later use. Consequentially, the social tourism environment is especially sensitive for destinations and businesses. Immediate effects at the onset of a negative event should also be assumed.

2.1.2 The significance of negative events in the purchase decision process

Purchase decisions are complex processes that are influenced by a number of variables. Basically, there is a variety of individual knowledge to explain purchase decisions. This is translated into total and partial models of purchase decision. Total models, which attempt to draw all determinants together, have not, until now, been in a position to unequivocally copy the purchase decision process. Therefore, the majority of considerations are based on partial models that consider only a few necessary influence variables.

This also applies for the tourism decision process. Moreover, because this spans a long period of time, the use of total models is made more difficult. Despite the peculiarities of tourism services, which underlie particularly complex information behaviour, knowledge transfer of consumer goods marketing is seen as something positive (Datzer, 1983a; Bieger, 1996a).

2.1.2.1 Determinants and types of purchase decision

According to the experiences of modern consumer research, consumer behaviour is influenced by psychological as well as social determinants. (In accordance with the number of those participating in the decision, it is possible to differentiate consumer and family decisions for the non-organizational sphere. The latter are not analysed in the following in order to reduce the complexity of the considerations and because it can be supposed that negative events will principally function in the same way.) If psychological processes are considered, it can be seen that emotions, motivations and attitudes, known collectively as activating processes, have an effect on consumer decisions. They describe processes that are linked to the internal excitement and tension of the consumer and form the driving force behind their actions.

Motives form a hypothetical working model made up of fundamental driving forces, emotions, impulses and cognitive processes structured to determine objectives. Motives, through which the 'why' question of a journey should be explained, are significant in explaining visitor behaviour (Schrattenecker, 1984; Frömbling, 1993).

Frömbling (1993) points to the suitability of differentiating the quality of motives into higher and lower motivations according to their type of driving force. Nowadays, this separation, which can be traced back to motivation research according to which lower needs are satisfied before higher ones, are used to explain experience-oriented consumption (Kroeber-Riel, 1992; see also the transfer to tourism by Scherrieb, 1992). From this point of view, motives play an important role within the context of negative events.

Values are, on the one hand, seen in close relationship to motives, on the other, equated with attitudes. They stand for fundamental moral concepts independent of short-term influences, which, moreover, are characterized by the social environment. (Previously, values were not used in tourism research. Segmenting exclusively on their basis did not prove to be successful because visitors could not be significantly differentiated from non-visitors; Frömbling, 1993.) The high temporal stability of values leads to them being of little significance as far as negative events are concerned.

Attitudes are differentiated from motives by their additional object assessments, for which reason they are seen to be relatively stable and consistent regarding their reaction to stimuli in the environment. If a destination is used as the reference point, attitude describes the subjectively perceived suitability of a destination for satisfying a motivation. (Specific and unspecific attitudes are distinguished. With the help of unspecific attitudes that convey the general attitude towards holiday travelling, such as travel forms, no great explanation effect can be proved for visitor behaviour in a region. It is only with the help of specific attitudes that refer to the marked forms of a region can visitor behaviour be analysed Frömbling, 1993; Nieschlag, Dichtl and Hörschgen, 1997.)

Using the A–B hypothesis, attitude is of relevance in the prediction of consumer behaviour. Frömbling (1993) also comes to this conclusion regarding travel behaviour: she points to the significance of the attitude towards the natural offer. Situative and personal factors along with economic restrictions put this into perspective in that we speak less of purchase behaviour indicators than purchase probability indicators. That no general validity applies becomes clear by means of the converse B–A hypothesis whereupon attitude towards the object is a result of the use or purchase and, consequently, is a result of this behaviour.

The mechanisms of mental information processing form the second part of the psychological process in connection with the decision process. The reception, perception and learning of information count towards these activities described as cognitive processes. In addition, the consumer is influenced by social determinants: the family and reference groups, which have an effect on the consumer in the closer environment, and the membership of cultural circles, which determines the wider environment, count towards this.

With the help of various amounts of cognitive and emotional participation in selection behaviour, five different types of consumer behaviour are distinguished by Kroeber-Riel (1992). They are simple models of purchase behaviour that make the fundamental mechanisms clear (processes with little cognitive control are described as behaviour and not as decisions in the narrower sense). In comparison to comprehensive structural models, they have the advantage of only containing those variables necessary to explain behaviour. Their general usefulness in tourism is confirmed by Mühlbacher and Botschen (1990) and Frömbling (1993).

Characteristic of habitual behaviour is either the upholding of decisions, which lead to repetition, or the adoption of certain behavioural patterns. These quasi-automatic processes require little need for information, the consequence of which is quick information processing. In the tourism sphere, this behaviour can be found, for example, in loyalty to the destination.

Impulsive behaviour is driven by affective reactions: this almost automatic behaviour can be traced back to situative and personal factors. This behaviour can be neglected in the tourism decision process because it is barely significant (Mühlbacher and Botschen, 1990; Kleinert, 1993).

Simplified and extensive decisions are distinguished by high cognitive participation and are described as the only real decisions. Both types of behaviour dominate travel decision (Frömbling, 1993). Extensive decision is characterized by extensive intellectual control, which triggers a need for information. The consumer uses this in an attempt to recognize his alternative scope and assess the various possibilities. A consequence of this is lengthy decision duration. Typically, this behaviour is only useful in tourism if the tourist has no experience of the product at all. But even decisions with high risk, for example, of a financial kind as well as products that have already suffered from negative events lead to extensive decisions (Weinberg, 1981; Frömbling, 1993; Kleinert, 1993). This shows that comprehensive and detailed information, provided either in written form or by means of recommendations, should be made available to tourists when making extensive purchase decisions.

As far as simplified decisions are concerned, the consumer has experience of the alternatives at his disposal. Cognitive, emotional and social restrictions ensure that the consumer concentrates on the alternatives already known to him, that is, the 'evoked set'. The evoked set incorporates the amount of products that the consumer neither negatively assesses nor relates a particular risk with them. They are principally classed as suitable for satisfying the need. The consequentially restricted efforts to obtain information are more related to brand than product: this is the same in tourism (Kleinert, 1993). In this context, expressive key information such as test results or product recommendations by opinion leaders, which incorporate a number of individual pieces of information, are of great significance. Negative events could lead to a change in the important assessment criteria of simplified purchase decision if schematized spheres were previously of little significance in times of crisis (see Example 1).

2.1.2.2 The involvement aspect

Falling back on the involvement construct offers an extensive analysis of the consequences of negative events on the decision process. The involvement describes the internal commitment a consumer devotes to an object or activity. It is possible to differentiate, according to cause, between personal, object-specific and situative involvement.

Example 1 Old patterns changed so fast

For many years, consumers did not care too much about the different service providers within the package tour they bought. The airplanes that were actually used were paid little attention to when it came to purchasing more economic tour packages.

This changed in 1996 when a charter airline flight from the Dominican Republic crashed a few minutes after its departure leaving all passengers dead. The flight was supposed to have been carried out by an Alas Nacionales Boeing 767. However, as the originally earmarked plane was not ready to use, it was replaced with a Boeing 757 from the Turkish airline Birgenair.

The immediate reaction of many travellers who were planning to take holidays was to look carefully and extensively into the different components of their package tour. They especially evaluated the part of the charter airline on which they requested detailed information including the aircraft model finally used. Such a habit was until then quite unusual. Even the detailed information that was available for the general public in the United States on accidents and incidents of airlines and their aircraft was not used by many tourists.

The Birgenair accident demonstrated clearly how a simplified decision process can turn into an extensive decision process.

A detailed database on aviation accidents can be found at http://www.ntsb.gov/ntsb/query.asp

2.1.2.2.1 Personal involvement

Personal involvement is the extent of a person's concern for a circumstance. It is based on personal motives, attitudes, experience and knowledge. Over the course of time, this circumstance becomes relatively stable and independent of situation. In tourism, this form of involvement can be observed frequently, especially in the case of younger consumers. It is normally related to the activity, like skiing or diving, that a tourist is practising.

This means that information about negative events, even if the level of diffusion is generally low, will be received with high attention, in segments where they affect, for example, enthusiastically practised activities. As a result, a quick diffusion of news amongst similarly interested groups of people is to be reckoned with. At the same time, negative events are constantly noticed and remembered for a long time by those involved at a personal level. This is independent of the decision situation.

The concrete effect of an event is dependent on the extent to which important product characteristics are affected. Subjective user assessment on the part of the tourist is decisive here. A tourist involved at a personal level assesses the circumstances in view of his experiences and knowledge more objectively (Kroeber-Riel, 1993a) (see Example 2).

Example 2 A different assessment

Personal involvement plays a very important role in tourism market segments that are more specialized.

Following the tragic attack on tourists in Luxor in 1997, Egypt's tourism sector suffered enormous losses. However, those interested in diving in the Red Sea did not react as normal sun and beach tourists. Most tour operators specialized in diving reported that after only a short phase of some 3 months of cancellations and absence, divers returned much faster and in higher proportions to Egypt than the normal tourist. In fact, since then, the arrivals of divers to Egypt increased annually in the higher two-digit range.

The same was observed in the case of the worldwide recognized and famous marathon event in New York City, which took place less than 2 months after the September 11 terrorist attacks in 2001. Although travel at that particular moment was reduced to the absolute minimum, and that planes were especially avoided, highly involved participants, both national and international, did not stay away from the event regardless of their feelings about security.

In the case of the ship accident of the tanker Jessica in early 2001, its 600 000 l of diesel fuel and 300 000 l of heating oil, threatened the natural reserve of the Galapagos Islands (the islands are on the equator in the Pacific Ocean, 960 km west of Ecuador, South America). Although the unique natural reserves and wildlife were affected by this accident and that worldwide news reported the incident, tourist arrivals at the end of 2001 remained unchanged at 70 000 persons. Since most of the visitors in this case had high personal involvement because of their scientific and ecological interest, the effects of this accident have been judged differently to most other cases.

2.1.2.2.2 Object-specific involvement

Object-specific involvement stands for the interest shown towards a product or service by the consumer. Functional–technical and social risk count towards its influential factors in the same way as frequency of use and the product's emotional appeal.

Depending on the perceived differences in travel products of a particular category, the tourist feels a different functional–technical risk. If these differences are great, a high functional–technical risk exists, which gives rise to high object-specific involvement because the tourist endeavours to weigh advantages and disadvantages up against one another in order to avoid negative consequences in the future (Jeck-Schlottmann, 1987). If a high degree of object-specific involvement exists, it can be assumed that a negative event will have a more disadvantageous effect due to the greater load and a strong discrimination effect in comparison to positive stimuli (Romeo, 1991).

Object-specific involvement varies depending on the frequency with which the product is used by the consumer. This can be related to a destination as well as to an activity (Jeck-Schlottmann, 1987; Weiermair and Gasser, 1995). In this context, it becomes clear that tourists, who already have experience with the destination or type of holiday at their disposal, perceive the same event differently to inexperienced tourists.

Tourism products also assume social risk because they are of symbolic value. On the one hand, this symbolic value can be located in the membership of a particular reference group. On the other hand, 'going on vacation' is a status symbol that implies a higher standard of living. This aspect is of great significance and is subject to the particular danger of its value being put into perspective by a negative event.

In addition, the travel product has an internally defined emotional value that bring to the tourist feelings of pleasure. Adapting this experience value to travel ensures that the tourist – assuming little cognitive control – wants to have the product in order to enjoy the product experience. Interference in this experience or its destruction would ensure that this product is paid fairly little attention.

2.1.2.2.3 Situative involvement

Situative involvement is understood as a temporal component. This means that the tourist, depending on the decision situation in which he finds himself, analyses information related to his travel decision differently. The nearer the time for decision, the higher the related activation through which he is encouraged to intellectually or emotionally assess the variables related with his decision.

2.1.2.2.4 Conclusion

Personal and object-specific involvement are more stable in the long term and independent of situative events, like negative events. Thus, both are described as continuous involvement. The degree of attention paid by the consumer to a certain amount of travel products due to object-specific or personal determinants is, therefore, stable.

Situative involvement, however, proved to be the most influential factor on the total involvement, dominating the object-specific and personal involvement. This is also of considerable significance from the point of view of negative events. Depending on the point in time at which a negative event occurs, the tourist boasts a varying degree of involvement. As a result, various consequences must be reckoned with. This must be considered when analysing effects, developing strategies, implementing instruments and also with regard to timing (also the media and message involvement exert influence over tourists as it has already been indicated; see Section 1.5).

2.1.2.3 The risk aspect

Risk-theoretic investigations within the framework of consumer behaviour concentrate on the risk of false purchase decision with regard to economic and social risk. By doing so, however, only some of the risks and their consequences are considered. In particular, the important area of the consequences of a negative event, which does not require a purchase decision, is not taken into consideration (Jungermann and Slovic, 1993b; Standop, 1996b).

For this purpose, the obvious thing would be to consider and fall back on research knowledge within the area of risk technologies. In the past, technologies particularly fraught with risk, such as nuclear power, caused the necessity to analyse the mechanisms of risk, unfavourable developments and the risk perception deeper. The continuous aim of these investigations was to find a risk acceptance threshold and develop strategies and instruments, in order to increase the acceptance of these risks.

Initially, the studies were the basis of a rather abstract relationship field, in which it was possible to differentiate between service providers and normative institutions, which, therefore, required a monopolistic offer structure. It was only later investigations that entered into the differentiated social environment of the organisation already described (see Section 2.1.1).

In the majority of uses of the term risk, two fundamental points of view can be distinguished (an overview of the various risk concepts can be found in, e.g. Kupsch, 1973; Fasse, 1995; Jungermann, 1991). Using a risk expectation model, it was attempted to describe, free of any value, judgement courses of events based on rationality axioms. According to this approach, found mostly in insurance mathematics, risk is defined as 'expected damage'. It is a product of magnitude of damage and probability of occurrence.

The consideration of personal factors, which influence consumer risk perception, leads to a subjective risk assessment and to descriptive models being used as a basis (Jungermann, 1991; Jungermann and Slovic, 1993b). Particular attention is given to this knowledge that goes beyond the implied objective determinability of probabilities and consequences (see Example 3).

Example 3 Driving is safe but flying so risky!

Many mistakes made while coping with crises are the result of a lack of understanding of risk perceptions. The crisis following the attacks of September 11 clearly demonstrated that this deficit is still existing. The attempts by many airline officials and politicians to convince the general public to board airplanes by simply arguing that flying is safe failed and was even seen as not trustworthy.

Understanding risk perception is the first step towards an effective crisis management. Airline professionals, like in this case, tend to use objective ways to assess risks. They are using odds like the ones on the following table, which clearly show that the chances of dying from a car accident in 1998 in the United States were much higher (1 in 6212) whereas the odds of dying from an airplane accident were much lower (1 in 390 532). In the framework of this information, officials were right in arguing: flying is safe.

Odds in the United States

Type of accident	Deaths, 1998	One-year odds
Motor vehicle	43 501	6 212
Air and space transport	692	390 532
Water transport	692	390 532
Railway	515	524 753
Fall on or from stairs or steps	1 389	194 563
Fall on same level from slipping, tripping or stumbling	740	365 200
Struck by falling object	723	373 787
During sport or recreation	685	394 523
Electric current	548	493 153

Source: Based on US National Safety Council data for the year 1998 for the American population.

Even the results that are achieved by looking at the passenger deaths per passenger mile of travel do underline their argumentation; as in 1999, the passenger death rate in the United States of America in automobiles was 0.83 per 100 million passenger-miles. In other words, much higher than the rates for buses, trains and airlines, which were 0.07, 0.10 and 0.003, respectively.

But why do these argumentation techniques fail? Consumers do not accept them, particularly for situations following a negative event. Consumers assess risks in ways that are best described by subjective risk perception. They consider at these moments a flight far more dangerous than a ride with a car. A well-thought crisis management has to understand well the mechanisms of these perceptions and must take them into account. Otherwise the efforts have to be multiplied to be, if so, successful.

2.1.2.3.1 Risk perception

Generally, risk is described as the possible negative consequences of the consumer's behaviour as perceived by the consumer. Seen from this point of view, risk during the travel decision is the deviation that can exist between the expected and the final, subjectively experienced tourism product. If this perceived risk exceeds a certain tolerance value, the consumer tries to reduce this risk using reduction techniques. Normally, this threshold value is reached quicker for a tourism product than for a material product (Kreilkamp, 1998).

This fundamental knowledge of risk perception in the purchase decision process obtains an extended significance under the particular conditions of a negative event. It is recommendable, therefore, in the further analysis to go back to the knowledge of fundamental risk perception and assessment. Thus, subjective risk perception is dependent on quantitative risk factors, qualitative characteristics of risk sources and individual consumer determinants (Jungermann and Slovic, 1993b; Wiedemann, 1994). In addition, particular risk factors exist due to criminal or terrorist threat (see Example 4).

Example 4 Sharks and coconuts

When it comes to sharks, most people remember in the first place the attacks of swimmers and surfers in Australia. Even for the Olympic Games in Sydney, the organizers were forced to take special measures to protect the swimmers, surfers and sailors from possible attacks from sharks and to communicate these actions to a sensitive world-wide audience.

Coconuts and coconut palm trees, on the other hand, are perceived as the symbol for beach and sun holidays. Every child knows how coconuts taste, coconuts are available in every supermarket – people don't fear coconuts, neither at home nor while on holidays.

However, the perceived risk is contrary to reality. Every year around 150 people die due to falling coconuts while the number of shark attacks was exactly 79 in 2000, which was slightly higher than the average from previous years. The number of those finally dying from sharks attacks was in fact, even lower. In 2000, it reached ten persons and varies normally between ten and twenty persons a year. Of the ten fatalities in 2000, only three were from Australia (from a total of seven attacks), two from Tanzania and single fatalities from Fiji, Japan, New Caledonia, Papua New Guinea and the USA.

Based on this information, Club Direct, a UK-based travel insurance, launched in 2002 a special press campaign warning tourists not to stay or camp under coconut trees, but also pointed out that their travel insurance would cover not only the risk to be exposed to coconut falls, but also to shark attacks.

2.1.2.3.1.1 Quantitative risk factors

Both damage probability and magnitude of damage count as quantitative risk factors. Both components are subject to a distorted perception that is dependent on various influences.

The use of mental heuristics on the part of the consumer is, above all, responsible for the distortion of damage probability, which is oriented towards the susceptibility and availability of the event (Tversky and Kahnemann, 1974; Jungermann and Slovic, 1993a). In part, the aforementioned supposition confirms that, within the sphere of preventive crisis management, concentration on the type of event enables a considerable contribution to the prompt identification of threatening situations.

All heuristics prevent the paralysis of the decision process and help to reduce search costs. Moreover, they are close to reality because they align themselves to experiences, but are also stable, which enables outside observers, with their knowledge, to hypothesize on possible behaviour. Among the important heuristics are the representativeness, availability and anchoring and adjustment heuristics.

Representativeness heuristics describe the judgement of risk due to a perceived affiliation of an object or activity to a certain risk category or type. In doing so, a conclusion for the risk is drawn from well-known cases. The units or groups subject to this generalization know no boundaries (Holzmüller and Schuh, 1988). They can concern branches as well as destinations or holiday categories amongst others. In this generalization phenomenon, an important approach can be seen to explain why negative events have such different consequences.

According to availability heuristics, the probability of occurrence of an event increases depending on how easily it is remembered or can be imagined. 'If an airplane has recently crashed, then we concentrate on the event and disregard all successfully run flights when it comes to deciding whether or not to fly somewhere' (Perrow, 1992, p. 370). These heuristics, which, in principle, lead to thoroughly appropriate and justifiable behaviour, are, above all, subject to the particular influence of the media. On the one hand, this points to the possibility of being able, under consideration of the terms of reference, to promptly assess the event with regard to its possible development. On the other hand, this finding also implies danger. This comes from the fact that extreme and unlikely improbabilities are judged with an unequally high probability by just pointing to their risk (as an example, Jungermann and Slovic, 1993a, cite a doctor's obligation to explain even in extremely rare cases so that the patient's freedom of choice is ensured). This condition must, above all, be taken into account with regard to preventive risk communication, the fundamental sensibleness of which is confirmed in tourism (Hellenthal, 1993).

According to anchoring and adjustment heuristics, orientation entities, the so-called perception anchors, are used to determine the probability of total system failure from the failure of a single entity (Tversky and Kahnemann, 1974). These heuristics become useful if related complex events are to be assessed.

Above all, two areas influence the subjective assessment of damage: the potential for catastrophe and personal dismay. The potential for catastrophe of an event increases with the consequences that the event has. The likelihood of the event is of minor importance. The frequent death of smokers shocks, therefore, less than one airplane crash in which many die (Jungermann and Slovic, 1993a). It can be assumed that this assessment is deeply embodied in the consumer and can only be changed by a long-term change of values, if at all.

Personal dismay has, like the potential for catastrophe, already been looked at. They are both essential features for the mass media when selecting news (see also Section 1.5). Geographic, cultural and psychological proximity determine how strongly the consumer feels the damage. This is to be expanded by a temporal component that expresses proximity to the actual decision and exerts considerable influence over dismay (see also the explanations of situative involvement in Section 2.1.2.2).

2.1.2.3.1.2 Qualitative characteristics of a risk source

The assessment of risk is, moreover, influenced by a number of qualitative characteristics. Among them is the fact that voluntarily undertaken risk is classified and accepted as less tragic than imposed dangers (Jungermann and Slovic, 1993a; Avenarius, 1995). This aspect is important for two main reasons: on the one hand, the tourist must be given the opportunity to voluntarily take on risk. Daring and contrived publicity messages that conceal known risks not only have dissatisfaction as a consequence due to the deviation of the actual from the desired image, these also do not give the tourist the opportunity of deciding to take on that risk himself. Even if this opportunity is given, it does not necessarily mean that it is perceived. As a rule, consumers tend to avoid making risky decisions (Jungermann and Slovic, 1993a). Nowadays, this fundamental behavioural characteristic of avoiding risky decisions known as 'omission bias' is helped by a number of legal norms (activities not carried out and through which damage could have been avoided are valued less than activities that finally lead to damage; Jungermann and Slovic, 1993a). Therefore, it must be made absolutely certain that the obligation to take a decision is enforced as frequently as possible for the tourist so as to keep the consequences of a negative event as low as possible.

A further element close to the voluntary aspect is responsibility. Whereas the deciding criterion in taking risk on voluntarily is that it concerns the consumer's own decision, this is now about another area that we are exposed to, namely natural events. In order to make this point of view clear, Luhmann (1991) always speaks of risk, if decision is the basis, and of danger, if the responsibility is attributed to the environment, that is, one is exposed to the event. Considerable importance is attached to this division when assessing negative events. In general, human-induced negative events are perceived more threatening and tragic as the following quote demonstrates (Jungermann and Slovic, 1993a, p. 100):

Whilst natural risks are classed as involuntary, uncontrollable, not attributable to society and, therefore, as more or less unavoidable – and obviously not as bad – civilian risks are seen as voluntary, controllable, attributable and avoidable – and, therefore, obviously worse.

In addition, it is also important to observe that there is a fundamental tendency to look for the culprits of a negative event (Luhmann, 1991). This fact, which can be traced back to psychological attribution research, illustrates a reason why people attempt to view more and more dangers as risks and to look for those responsible for them (Hilton and Slugorski, 1986). If this is extended to the aspect that risky decisions are sought to be avoided, it is possible to understand why tourists, often only with hindsight, have a particular interest in, for example, the duty of the organizer to provide explanations, whereby they retroactively have the opportunity to avoid responsibility.

Events that can be controlled by the individual are also subject to a fundamentally more favourable assessment, which stands outside of that particular sphere of influence (Jungermann and Slovic, 1993a). An example of this is an airplane crash that, with the same damage probability, is seen to be more tragic than a car crash because the latter is subject to the control of the driver. It was after the September 11 attack that attempts were made to strengthen cockpit doors, to tighten the security control or to give, for example, the simple and practical advise to throw books and shoes at highjackers before trying to overpower them. Besides their objective value, travellers perceived these measures valuable, logical and sensed having an influence on the risk. In other words, these measures reduced the subjectively perceived risk.

Negative events, which are well-known and the frequent onset of which people are used to, are more likely to be accepted than new risks. Essentially, this can be traced back to the fact that no one has experience of an unknown risk, so the effect is hard to estimate and less easy to calculate. It is the consequence of this incalculability that everything possible is undertaken in order to place the event into an explanation pattern with the aim of understanding it.

A not inconsiderable potential for crisis is established for the affected organization here. It no longer only concerns the organization's plausible and serious efforts to explain the background of the concrete incident. Rather, the 'signal potential' of the event must be assessed, by which the potential danger that this event gives notice of is meant (Jungermann and Slovic, 1993a). Only by this way can we estimate how strong public interest will be.

If the explanation is not successful and, apart from the fact that it is the first time such an event has occurred, a bad assessment of the companies' behaviour is reached, this incident can easily become a negative example and will, in the future, be used as a comparison (well-known examples of this are the oil loading platform Brent Spar and the tanker Exxon Valdez).

2.1.2.3.1.3 Individual risk factors

Risk perception and assessment are influenced by a number of personal determinants. On the one hand, they vary depending on demographic variables such as age, sex and education. Therefore, a higher risk perception on the part of female tourists in comparison to men is ascertained just as a lower risk perception in young tourists aged 18–24 in comparison to older tourists is reported (the investigation that forms the basis of this referred to the United States and the United Kingdom; WTO, 1994b).

On the other hand, expert or lay status is also of considerable significance regarding risk assessment. Where experts rely on quantitative characteristics in order to assess risk, laymen prefer qualitative features. (Perrow, 1992, speaks of absolute and limited rationality; see also Sections 2.1.2.3.1.1 and 2.1.2.3.1.2). In addition, experts tend to overrate probable but momentous events. Laymen, on the other hand, tend to rate improbable but momentous events higher from a risk point of view (Kemp, 1993; Wiedemann, 1994).

A further factor can be seen in cultural circle membership (see Example 5), which contributes to people perceiving and assessing events in a different way. This can be traced back to various social, behavioural and development forms (Kemp, 1993; Sönmez and Graefe, 1998). This is confirmed by the events of the mid-1980s in Europe at which time the number of US arrivals decreased considerably due to terrorist attacks whereas, at the same time, internal European arrivals increased (Hurley, 1988; Ryan, 1993). A similarly sensitive attitude towards negative events was reported for the Japanese as a consequence of news coverage about sex tourism in Hong Kong and the Philippines as well as for Europeans as a reaction to the nuclear fallout at Chernobyl (Gee and

Example 5 Cultural circle membership

The brutal massacre of fifty-eight foreign tourists and four Egyptians in Luxor by Islamic extremists in November 1997 destabilized Egypt by destroying its tourism industry, the mainstay of Egypt's economy. Before the November massacre, with some 4.2 million visitors, the tourism industry was set to generate in 1997 nearly $4 billion in revenue for Egypt, making tourism the country's most important source of foreign exchange.

The Luxor attack triggered an immediate cancellation reaction and a sustainable downturn of bookings to Egypt as a holiday destination in 1998. The overall development of international tourists' arrivals in Egypt dropped by 12.8 per cent. Tourist executives estimate the Luxor incident cost Egyptian tourism about 50 per cent of its annual revenues. 'By any account, it was a catastrophe. I myself lost something like 85 per cent of my business', said Ilhamy el-Zayyat, head of Egypt's Chamber of Tourism and owner of a major travel agency.

While most of the important European source markets had similar forms of decline after the attacks, Switzerland and Japan have to be looked at more closely. In both cases, the dismay of the respective national group played a part because thirty-five Swiss and ten Japanese fell victim in the attack. However, the unusually abrupt and long-term slump has to be traced back to culturally caused risk adversity. This was repeatedly confirmed for the Japanese.

Monthly arrivals and overnight stays of all tourists

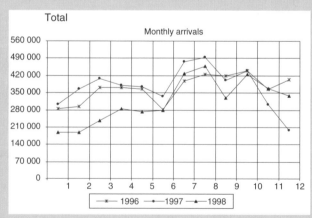

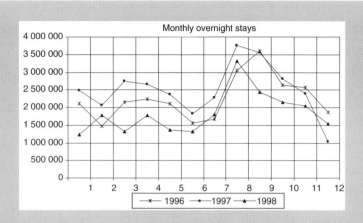

Monthly arrivals and overnight stays of the Swiss

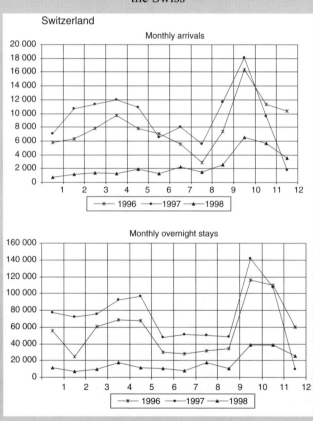

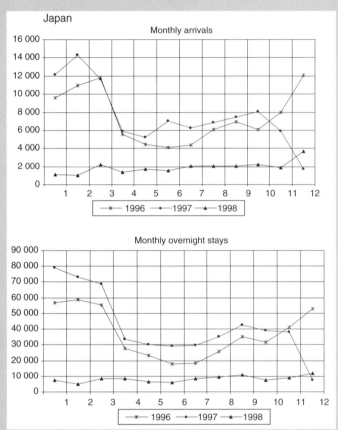

Monthly arrivals and overnight stays of the Japanese

Source: Based on unpublished data from the WTO.

The observation of the development of the Russian source market is particularly interesting. Due to a cultural circle membership, which makes them perceive these events less important and risky, tourist arrivals and overnight stays to Egypt have increased tenfold since 1991. As the following diagrams of monthly arrivals and nights from 1996 to 1998 show, this growth trend continued even after the Luxor attack.

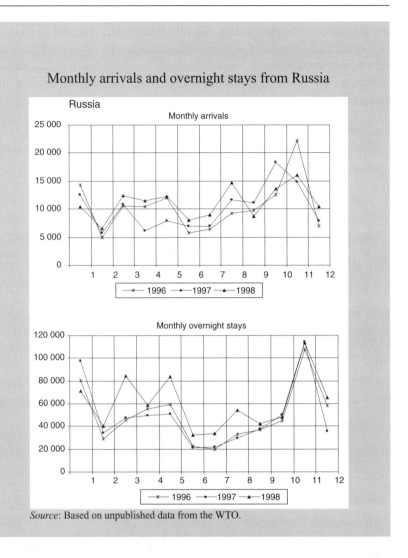

Monthly arrivals and overnight stays from Russia

Source: Based on unpublished data from the WTO.

Gain, 1986). This particular risk aversion has even stronger consequences in comparison to other cultures since, after the consequential
absence from the destination, a recuperation process only occurs very
slowly (Gee and Gain, 1986).

In addition, the dismay of a national group is of great significance
for tourism. Miami, for example, was long known for having an above-
average rate of violent crimes, but it was the murder of a German tourist
in April 1993 that caused a sharp decline in the number of German
visitors. It indicates that, for tourists, there is a differentiation between

general threat and becoming victims themselves. The former is perceived and accepted in the sense of a backdrop but does not have any further consequences. A perceivable reaction only takes place if a person from the national group to which he belongs is threatened (see Example 6).

Example 6 It happens only to others, until ... – the thing with the nationals

In the beginning of the 1990s, Florida gained an inevitable reputation of being home for serious crimes committed against residents and tourists, who seemed to be lucrative targets for petty criminals. In 1992, in Dade county alone, over 12 000 crimes against visitors were reported. Despite this, tourism grew as foreign tourists did not feel affected or concerned by this violence.

However, things started to change when the first tourists from important foreign source markets were subject of these attacks. In 1993, the number of attacks against tourists peaked as more than ten tourists from Canada, Great Britain, Germany and Venezuela were killed. These attacks, some of them quite brutal, received heavy national and international media coverage. Emotions ran high and the *British Sunday Times* even titled the Sunshine State as the 'State of Terror'. The European tourists' acceptance of crime changed as from this moment rapidly. Once they learned about their countrymen's destinies, they suddenly felt related and endangered to become victims of murderers and serious robberies themselves. As a result, Florida's image as a sunshine and holiday destination became the place of occurring tourist nightmares. Tourist arrivals declined heavily. In particular, the number of German visits to Florida dropped by one-third from 608 000 in 1993 to 411 000 in 1994. This meant a severe economic loss for its tourism industry, which counted in 1993 with $US 28 billion and was the most important source of revenue of the state's economy.

Numerous federal and local initiatives aimed at improving the security for tourists were established after these incidents. They not only reduced the crime rate to its lowest level in 25 years but also helped the number of tourism arrivals to grow once again.

It is not a question of threat aimed at citizens from a particular country but, seen from the point of the cause, rather a coincidental fact. Whilst the former is explained by the fact that criminal or terrorist activities are carried out against tourists because of their nationality, here it concerns a general threat that is only seen to be more tragic because a representative of the tourist's own group is affected.

The different individual risk factors discussed give an overview of the most probable and most important influence variables. In practice, several of these factors will influence the situation at the same time. For example, the peculiarity that conflicts in which US Americans are involved are causing a general decline in international trips of US tourists (Wilkinson, 1993) always occurs due to national group and cultural circle membership factors. However, the circumstance that negative events cannot be classified due to a lack of geographical knowledge and, therefore, have greater effects also plays a role (Leaf, 1995).

2.1.2.3.1.4 Particular risk factors – criminal or terrorist threat

The security aspect as a subsection of negative events occupies a special place (thus, security is defined as the fear of becoming a possible victim of violent crime, flight safety, terrorist acts, etc.; WTO, 1994b; Smith 1998). Criminal activities are indeed a continuous component of daily life but, in the context of tourism, they increase in significance (the great significance of security during the travel decision process is confirmed by the Longwood's study carried out by Kemmer, 1995, which places the security of a destination in second or third place when selecting a destination). Above all, the fact that the tourism activity as such is strongly related to such things as discovering new areas and taking risks makes tourists especially vulnerable targets (WTO, 1994c). In the light of their relationship to tourism, criminal activities can be classified as shown in Diagram 8.

Provided that it concerns a general criminal act, the victims of which are tourists, no effect on general tourism development must be reckoned within the short term (Wilkinson, 1993). This must, however, be put into perspective inasmuch as that it can cause a complete change of attitude in the long term. This leads, if not to a change of destination in the sense of another country, to a re-orientation when choosing a region and resort.

Type 1	Tourists are incidental victims of criminal activity that is independent of the nature of the tourist destination
Type 2	A venue that is used by criminals because of the nature of the tourist location, but the victims are not specifically tourists
Type 3	A location that attracts criminal activity because tourists are easy victims
Type 4	Criminal activity becomes organized to meet certain types of tourist demand
Type 5	Organized criminal and terrorist groups commit specific violent actions against tourists and tourists facilities

Source: After information from Ryan (1993).

Diagram 8 Classification of criminal activities

In addition, these activities are only accepted to a certain extent: as soon as they bring serious injury or the death of a person in their wake, tourist behaviour suddenly changes. Despite a continuing attractive image, a destination is then classed as dangerous (Ahmed, 1996).

It follows that a systematic encounter with criminal acts cannot be avoided, it must be a permanent component of product policy for the destination manager (Ritchie and Crouch, 1997). On the one hand, the remedying of causes by which it is clear that criminal activity can scarcely be completely prevented belongs to this class, on the other, the enlightenment of tourists. It is important for the tourist to know the dangers that exist in a destination in order to adjust their behaviour and, secondly, to set these in relation to the usual danger at the location (Ritchie and Crouch, 1997). That way, the tourist is in a position to undertake his contribution towards preventing a dangerous situation.

Terrorism occupies a special position within the sphere of negative events. Seen from a general point of view, terrorist activity causes only a slight decline in tourist arrivals provided that tourists are not explicitly defined as the target. This situation changes suddenly, however, if tourists are expressly declared as the object of attack and systematic aggression leads to injury and death (Wilkinson, 1993; Sönmez, 1998a, gives an overview of terrorists attacks that affected tourism in the respective countries). Here, two different situations can be distinguished in which the tourist is understood either as a symbol of the sending state or as a part of the economic system of the destination. Whilst, in the first situation, the group of endangered people can be clearly defined, this is more difficult in the second case. Here, almost every tourist can be the target of an attack.

In the first case, threat probability for tourists grows in direct relation to how politically exposed the country of origin is, that is, its activity and siding in international conflicts and crises. The aim of the attack is to communicate something to the sending state, which is disregarded under normal circumstances. This exterior-oriented activity has a greater effect, the more serious it is, the more exposed the place is in which it takes place with regard to tourism and the greater the related potential for catastrophe is. The latter explains attacks on airplanes that makes use of the potential for catastrophe and, therefore, the deterrent effect. They also make use of the circumstance that approximately one-third of international tourists use the airplane as a mode of transport (Diagram 9).

In the second case, tourists are used against the recipient state, region or destination, that is, interior oriented. The importance of tourism as an economic sphere and source of foreign currency for the recipient state contributes to this. Also, this sphere is made interesting by its extraordinary sensitivity.

The Basque terrorist organisation ETA, which has made tourism objects the target of its attacks since the 1980s, is referred to as the founder of such activities. It is not the tourist but the state of the target country, in this case Spain, which should be affected. In contrast to their usual tactics, advance warning of the tourist attacks were given and

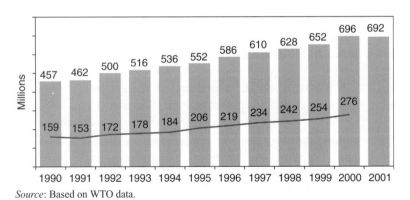

Source: Based on WTO data.

Diagram 9 International tourist arrivals and arrivals by air

times were chosen when only few tourists would be present. This solution, which was the only one accepted by the supporters of the terrorist organisation, was also the reason why tourism was scarcely affected. ETA's behaviour has since frequently been copied, for example, by Sendero Luminoso who has, since 1989, defined the tourism sector in Peru as a target and the PKK, which has also attacked tourism targets in Turkey since 1991 (Smith, 1998).

As well as this purely interior- or exterior-oriented direction of terrorist activity, a mixture of the two can also occur. This is the case, for example, with the IRA's bombings that have persisted since the mid-1980s and have targeted both the economic system of the United Kingdom and British tourists in Northern Ireland.

2.1.2.3.2 Risk acceptance

Despite the influences described, it should not be overlooked that the tourist is prepared to accept a certain amount of risk. The effort to avoid risk actively applies to the exceeding of a particular tolerance threshold (Kroeber-Riel, 1992). The level of this individual threshold value is determined by, apart from the aforementioned influence factors, the credibility of the affected organization, the speed of its actions and the repetition of the events.

Whilst the credibility of the organization and the speed of its actions will be dealt with in detail later, attention is paid here to the repetition of negative events (see also Sections 4.3 and 6.6.1.2). By dealing with issues of public concern, it has become known that the sensitivity threshold, therefore, the willingness to accept a certain event, reduces if the event is repeated. This is the same when products are recalled. Events otherwise perceived over the course of time as unrelated are felt, due to repeated call-backs, to be related and as such more attributable to the responsibility of the affected company (Standop, 1996a). It should also be considered that, events perceived at a stage of high involvement, need much less repetition to be remembered than with low involvement. Thus, it can be seen that the repetition of an event has a negative effect on the tourist's tolerance threshold.

Seen as a whole, negative events scarcely have an effect on consumer behaviour as long as they remain within the relevant individual tolerance threshold (Schrattenecker, 1984; Gu and Martin, 1992). The intention to visit or purchase a tourism product only starts to decrease once this threshold has been exceeded (see Example 7).

Example 7   Mountains – a dream without limits

The Mont Blanc Massif

Source: PGHM.

Most of them came as tourists, spending their holidays hiking and climbing in the mountains, some of them will never return. Despite the fact that every year more than seventy hikers die in the Mont Blanc massif (Europe), there is no impact on those to come. It is a well-known fact that this massif produces a lot of incidents and that some hikers have lost their lives, but it is seen by most of them as their greatest challenge to climb the legendary Mont Blanc, with its 4807 m, the highest peak of Western Europe. Even if they return injured, they do not leave the country with bad memories, as it was and is their dream for which they are prepared to forget everything they are concerned about normally and accept the highest risk you can run: your life!

The more than 900 rescue interventions of the specialized mountain rescue service 'Peloton de Gendarmerie de Haute-Montagne' (PGHM) in the past years proved the risks but also demonstrated that

57

there is no impact on the enormous attraction this massif continues to play for many hikers.

Interventions from 1996 to 2001

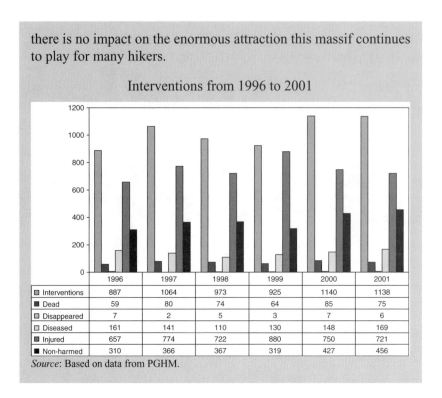

	1996	1997	1998	1999	2000	2001
Interventions	887	1064	973	925	1140	1138
Dead	59	80	74	64	85	75
Disappeared	7	2	5	3	7	6
Diseased	161	141	110	130	148	169
Injured	657	774	722	880	750	721
Non-harmed	310	366	367	319	427	456

Source: Based on data from PGHM.

2.1.2.4 The legal aspect – behavioural restrictions

In order to assess the reaction of tourists to negative events, it is also necessary to consider the legal implications of these events to the tourist. The following evaluations will use the German legislation as an example because it is considered to be one of the strictest of its kind in the world. The respective legal sources will vary from legal system to legal system. However, they all form an additional framework that has to be considered when analysing the consumers' sphere.

With reference to legal consequences, considerable differences exist in German law between individual tourists and package holiday tourists.

2.1.2.4.1 Possibilities for the individual tourist

Individual tourists can terminate various types of contract directly with the service provider. According to German law, these are, for example, accommodation contracts (§§ 535 ff CC; CC stands for German Civil Code), hospitality contracts (§§ 651, 433 ff CC) or transportation contracts (§§ 631 ff CC). These types of contract are of considerable significance for domestic tourism.

However, the individual tourist has no particular opportunity to terminate a contract on the grounds of a negative event. In exceptional cases, the right for an extraordinary notice of cancellation may exist. The prerequisites shall not be discussed here. If the contracts are agreed abroad, it is possible that the individual tourist will have to validate his claims in front of a foreign court. This entails considerable expense and various judicial difficulties.

2.1.2.4.2 Possibilities for the package holiday tourist

The situation for package holiday tourists is different. They conclude a contract directly with the tour operator that includes various services (a detailed appreciation of contractual relations applicable to tourists is given by WTO, 1985). According to the guidelines of the German law for package holidays (§§ 651 a to l CC), German law and German jurisdiction apply for this legal relationship as long as the holiday was booked with a German tour operator.

Various legal opportunities are open to the package holiday tourist. They are explained in brief here:

- Before the start of the holiday, package holiday tourists have the right to withdraw without cause (§ 651 i CC). In this case, the tour operator can claim appropriate compensation (the cancellation fee for a package holiday with flight can be 4 per cent of the holiday price 30 days before the start of the holiday and up to 50 per cent, 6 days before; (Strangfeld, 1993; Führich, 1995a; Niehuus, 1996). Based on their General Travel Conditions, tour operators also allow the tourist to change his or her booking given that the tourist has to cover the cost of that change. From the legal point of view, the originally concluded travel contract is still in force. This serves, in particular, the interests of the tour operator.
- If the holiday has already begun, warranty claims due to shortcomings (§ 651 c CC) and the right to withdraw due to considerable shortcomings (§ 651 e CC) or as a result of acts of God (§ 651 j CC) are valid. (When a shortcoming becomes considerable and entitles the consumer to withdraw is defined by the reason for travelling, the character of the holiday, duration and the extent

of the shortcoming; Führich, 1995a.) The shortcomings of the contractually agreed service package with the tour operator can be of a varied nature. Every year, this list is extended by judicial decisions (Strangfeld, 1993; Führich, 1995a). Generally, the tour operator has to guarantee, regardless of negligence and fault, the success of a holiday and they bear the risk of failure (Führich, 1995a). The tour operator is not liable if the interference lies outside of his area of influence; that is, it does not concern a risk that could have been managed by the tour operator.

2.1.2.4.3 The term 'act of God'

The term 'act of God' is not defined either in § 651 j CC or in any other similar regulation. An exemplary listing of relevant causes of interference, as was included in a previous governmental draft of a law about tour operator contracts, is also lacking (Bundestongdruksache, 1977). Within the framework of the right to withdraw, the term 'act of God', according to personal liability law, is understood as an '. . . event coming from the outside, showing no operational relation and not averted even by the most extraordinary diligence' (Führich, 1995a, p. 361; Niehuus, 1996, p. 216). Acts of God do not belong to the area of risks of either the tourist or the tour operator. Just based on the occurrence of such an event, it cannot be concluded, however, that there was an act of God in the sense of § 651 j CC. Rather, it must always be examined whether, in the case assessed, the conceptual characteristics of an act of God are given. The event must interfere considerably with the holiday, questioning the contractual benefits of the trip as a whole but not necessarily the holiday's feasibility (Führich, 1995a). According to legal practice, problems with the providing of holiday service (e.g. destruction of or damage to accommodation), impairment by environmental pollution within the destination (beach pollution due to an oil spill) or personal threat (war, terrorist attacks, radioactive contamination) are examples that belong here (Führich, 1995a). Other indisputable examples of acts of God are:

- war or the threat of war due to civil war conditions;
- if tourists are systematically attacked as a named target;
- impairment by environmental pollutions of a catastrophic nature that are serious and out of the ordinary (e.g. epidemics, natural disasters, radiation danger from Chernobyl).

As a rule, courts draw upon the respective assessments of the Foreign Office (FO) when deciding what is an act of God. The FO gives, for example, a general travel warning for a particular region or declares a destination to be an area of crisis (see also Section 3.2.1.3.1.2). In this case, the existence of an act of God can be assumed. Being aware of the economic significance of its assessment, the German Foreign Office, for example, emphasizes the information character and rejects all legal consequences.

What is important in the classification of certain incidents as acts of God is that it concerns unforeseeable events. For this reason, political unrest and general political crises in a destination – like, for example, Sri Lanka, China, Turkey and Egypt – were not viewed as acts of God (Strangfeld, 1993; Führich, 1995a; Nies and Traut, 1995). Decisive in the assessment of predictability is whether the tour operator could reasonably be informed about the conditions at the destination when the contract was concluded and whether there is a 'concrete probability' and not just a conceivable possibility. This has to been done by using all modern means of communication available to the tour operator. The tour operator's duty to enquire and to inform exists until the start of the holiday. If this obligation is not carried out, there is a shortcoming that the tour operator is responsible for and entitles the customer to claim for indemnification (Führich, 1995a; Seyderhelm, 1997).

From the point of view of crisis management, this duty to enquire and to inform may conceal an explosive situation: a tour operator undertaking particular efforts, using preventive measures, to remove the possible crisis character from negative events is constantly faced with the decision as to what information should be made available to the tourist. At the same time, warning cannot be given of every unlikely event. As has already been illustrated (see Section 2.1.2.3.1.1), as risk perception increases, the more improbable the event is. Nevertheless, the danger exists that important information is not relayed to the customer. Therefore, a compromise should be found, which must be accompanied by a good understanding of the various effects and their contexts.

The legal consequences of acts of God is the mutual and extraordinary right to withdraw from the contract. By this, the tour operator will be relieved of the consequences of extraordinary and incalculable events (Niehuus, 1996). After an effective withdrawal, the holiday price already paid must be paid back by the tour operator after the cost of services provided has been deducted. In addition, the tour operator is obliged to return the tourist home although half of any additional costs must be covered by the tourist (Niehuus, 1996).

In contrast, the individual tourist in the same type of crisis situation must undertake a return journey at his or her own risk and expense.

2.1.2.4.4 No 'act of God' with regard to general life risk

Disturbances that are assigned to the tourist's general life risk or impairment of the environment in the destination are not subsumed under the heading acts of God (Führich, 1995a). Areas that concern normal, natural risk to the tourist and are not travel specific (e.g. muggings, theft) are not understood as general life risks (Strangfeld, 1993; Führich, 1995a). However, as soon as this risk becomes a specific risk for the tourist, the tour operator is obliged to inform the tourist (Führich, 1995a; Niehuus, 1996).

Also in the case of the impairment of the environment, the tourist must take on the risk for himself or herself. It is assumed that the tourist can gain a picture of the conditions by consulting generally accessible information sources. However, if the tour operator makes concrete promises concerning the environment, he or she has to accept liability. Moreover, all risks that have a negative effect on the particular purpose of the holiday must be observed by the tour operator and conveyed to the tourist. If this does not happen, the reason for liability comes, not from the risk itself, but from the fact that this information was not given to the tourist (Führich, 1995a; Niehuus, 1996).

It becomes clear that, when negative events occur, the package holiday tourist is entitled to considerable reaction opportunities even after the start of the trip.

2.1.2.5 The temporal aspect – phases of travel decision

The majority of travel decisions are not made at short notice but take place over a longer period of time. As a consequence, negative events may affect consumers at different phases of their travel decision. This influences the effect that the onset of the event has on the consumer (see Example 8).

Example 8 Rimini and the algae effect

Since the establishment of the first bathing resorts by the mid-1800s, the Romagna Coast in Italy profited from growth of tourist arrivals and tourism-related infrastructure. Tourism development was traditionally based solely on the resources of sea and beaches. Domestic tourists as much as foreigners, among these predominantly Germans, found it an ideal destination for relaxation and family holidays.

The effect of a temporal aspect can be illustrated by two similar negative events, namely the increased algae build-up, which happened at different times of the year in Rimini (Italy) and were each followed by different consequences.

In June 1989, the growth of algae in the Adriatic Sea and the appearance of patches of mucilage caused a serious crisis for tourism. Exactly on 28 June, shortly before the high point of the bathing season and the start of holidays in Germany, which share the biggest part of foreign tourists to the coast, the first patches of the new algae were reported. The phenomenon continued throughout the month of July and it was not until 6 August that the algae started to disappear. The press covered the situation intensively and amplified the negative image of the destination. Hoteliers put immediately heavy efforts in combating the loss of the season. Various actions such as mobile swimming pools on the beaches, floating barriers against the mucilage and price discounts tried to remedy the crisis. However, foreign tourists, in particular, preferred not to book their summer vacations in the Romagna Coast and cancelled existing reservations in order to spend their summer vacation at other destinations that could guarantee them sea, beaches and sun without any pollution. After all the crisis revoked, a chain reaction followed: the negative image of the destination was not only tied to the pollution of the sea but also to all those negative aspects that had been latently present before, such as chaos, crowds, noise, criminality, etc. Furthermore, the negative image was extended even to those areas that originally had not been affected at all by the phenomenon.

The total number of tourist arrivals decreased by more than 25 per cent with respect to the previous year. In particular, the sector of intermediate- and large-scale tourism with the highest quality standards and greatest attraction to foreign tourists suffered with a loss of 50–60 per cent more than any other sector. In fact, the smaller and more familiar residences and boarding houses could rely on their loyal clients and repeaters, because of their personal relationships and more domestic guests. Also, there were hardly changes concerning the second-home system, while the number of rented accommodations went down by 40–50 per cent.

It is interesting to note that an earlier growth of algae in the Adriatic Sea had appeared a year before, exactly on 15 August 1988. But at that time tourism was not affected much as the late season had already begun and most visitors had already completed their holidays at the seaside. The media also paid only little attention to this phenomenon.

Source: Becheri, E.: Rimini and co – The end of a legend? *Tourism Management*, Vol. 12, No. 3, September 1991, pp. 229–235.

For a more detailed and differentiated analysis, four essential periods of time in which a tourist can be confronted with the occurrence of a negative event are distinguished in the following evaluation.

2.1.2.5.1 Orientation and decision phase

In the orientation phase, the tourist can be described as being absolutely free in his or her decision choice. Fundamentally, he or she knows neither personal, social nor legal restrictions of the concrete travel decision. Information about holiday activities and destinations is constantly absorbed, assessed, rejected and learnt (Datzer, 1983b; Kroeber-Riel, 1992; Frömbling, 1993). Expressed in general terms, impressions are gathered in this phase that form the tourism image of the product. (A destination's tourism image is a refinement of the general image of a destination. The latter is established over a long period of time and does not necessarily include tourism information; see also Section 2.2.4).

Unlike other products, the consumer pays greater attention to the tourism product in this phase. Two influences, in particular, are responsible for this: on the one hand, travel is strongly influenced by the tourist's desire for adventure and curiosity, the consequence of which is frequent changes not only of destination but also of activities. On the other hand, travelling must be classed as fundamental need, which encourages the tourist to constantly search for information.

As well as this fundamental interest, the development of various involvement components becomes important. Situative involvement is the least developed in this phase. The actual determining influence on the current overall involvement level comes from the consumer's personal involvement (see also Section 2.1.2.2.1). This means that events that affect objects of personal interest to the tourist will be disseminated quicker and paid more attention.

In addition, it can be assumed that in this subphase, mass media coverage is of comparably little consequence. This applies, above all, if it concerns well-known events. Nevertheless, extraordinary events with a high potential for catastrophe and a crisis management that is carried out badly can contribute to these incidents being remembered in later travel decisions, especially if they are discussed for a long time.

Within the orientation phase, there comes after this time span, one point as from which the normally passive position of the consumer to search for information becomes active. At this point, the decision process, which is actually difficult to define, begins and can last from one to several months (Hahn and Hartmann, 1973; Freyer, 1995).

Situative involvement increases to its highest value and dominates total involvement from then on. Generally, prominent characteristics of this active and targeted search for information are that they are practised more by younger tourists than older ones, in the same way as first-time visitors ask for and lay claim to more information on the social environment than people returning to a destination. (Datzer, 1983b; Sönmez and Graefe, 1998a; this can be explained by the high purchase risk that the tourist experiences in this situation; Kroeber-Riel, 1992.) In this way, it becomes clear that young people and first-time travellers, who are extremely dependent on reference groups, are especially dependent on the public attention that is paid to a negative event. It can, moreover, be concluded that negative events, the consequence of which is unfavourable public attention, particularly influence these groups and the tourism products dependent on them in this phase.

In addition, it generally applies that information searches are dependent on educational level: a tourist with a higher school education takes stock of more neutral information sources and processes the information more cognitively (Datzer, 1983b).

Regarding negative events, active information search can, however, be identified by the threshold value of personal risk acceptance. This is confirmed, on the one hand, by the generally high interest of tourists to be informed about the probability and extent of negative events (Sönmez and Graefe, 1998a). On the other hand, by the fact that this information is not always actively sought, 65 per cent of the interviewed persons of the German 'Reiseanalyse', a well-known regular survey, claimed not to consider information about negative events or only in simple circumstances.

To the question, had they considered reports of unrest, natural disasters or crises when making travel decisions, they answered as shown in Diagram 10.

Generally, this phase is particularly critical. Because a far greater amount of alternatives is available to the tourist, smaller well-known events ensure that the products become excluded from further considerations. The danger of this early exclusion from the evoked set lies in the fact that this takes place at a point of time when, as a rule, no travel agency has been visited yet (WTO, 1994b; for the importance of destination selection in the decision process, see Braun and Lohmann, 1989). Moreover, the consumer has not yet articulated a desire and potentially explanatory information cannot yet be given in a targeted manner.

Experience has shown that this critical period of time for planning summer holidays lies somewhere between the beginning of December of the previous year and the end of March and, for winter holidays, sometime in September/October. However, this is moving more and

Answers	Respondents (%)
No, I don't take any notice	24.2
Yes, I think about them and consider them but don't put too much effort into it	41.0
Yes, I take such reports very seriously and consider them when travelling	28.8
No answer	5.9

Source: Based on Braun and Lohmann (1989).

Diagram 10 Consideration of crisis reports

more to the point of travel due to a tendency towards travel decisions at short notice. Besides the need to take particular precautions for these sensitive times, it remains to emphasize that, from the customer's point of view, the value of crisis management fluctuates over the course of the year. It is important to recognize this temporarily changing value of crisis management and take it into account when reacting.

2.1.2.5.2 Post-decision phase

This period of time begins once the travel decision has been made. This phase can also be subdivided into a period of time that begins when the inner decision is made and a time span that begins with the contractually agreed travel decision. It cannot be determined exactly when this inner decision has been made unless it is documented. Fundamentally, however, its existence is confirmed. After it has been made, the sought after and perceived information is basically used to confirm the choice that has already been made (Braun and Lohmann, 1989). This behaviour, as explained by the dissonance theory, is confirmed for decisions based on great efforts as it is the case for the travel decision, which is normally an extensive or limited decision. A consequence of this is the unequally favourable evaluation of the choice made in comparison to the rejected alternatives (Raffée, Sauter and Silberer, 1973; see also Section 2.1.2.1).

Braun and Lohmann (1989) also point to this circumstance of edging out alternatives. They found that 86.6 per cent of the tourists questioned within the survey claimed after the realization of their holiday that no other destination had come into question as a alternative. This high value irritates and was even classed by the authors as 'very improbable' because, under such circumstances, it could not have anything to do with a decision any longer. They reported similar doubts with regard to the results of the survey because only 3.7 per cent of the tourists questioned claimed that they had changed their travel plans once decided (Braun and Lohmann, 1989). On the other hand, these numbers illustrate that, after a travel decision is inwardly made, a higher acceptance threshold for negative events exists.

It is also of interest in the circumstances at hand that this threshold value is influenced by the cognitive overlap of alternative products (Mazanec, 1989). If selection possibilities lie closer to one another, reorientation is easier for the tourist and his decision process is hardly lengthened at all. This insight, which will be dealt with further under the destination sphere of activity, already suggests the disadvantage of a similar perception of products that makes reorientation considerably easier for the consumer.

The signing of the contract means that the tourist's actions are – as already illustrated in the legal discussions – restricted in various ways (see also Section 2.1.2.4). If it is not related to the right of the package holiday tourist to withdraw due to considerable shortcomings or as a result of acts of God, then the tourist is subject to the peculiarities of the right to terminate a contract. The latter, however, incorporates cancellation costs. (At the same time, however, the company is also very interested in satisfied customers who they also wish to serve in the future. The probability of a long-term customer relationship and the extent of economic loss determines the company's reactions.)

2.1.2.5.3 The holiday phase

In this phase, the tourist has already started his holiday. Confronted with a negative event at this point, the tourist is a direct participant and will react depending on the personal threat to himself or herself. In this phase, the individual tourist can make no further claims provided that they are not in direct connection with the service provider or are covered by specific risk insurance. The package holiday tourist, on the other hand, can refer to the circumstance that the tour operator must, regardless of negligence or fault, take responsibility for the success of a holiday and the danger of failure and, in addition, has the right to withdraw if an act of God takes place (see also Section 2.1.2.4).

In both cases, it can be assumed that holidays cannot be repeated. Holidays once applied for and approved cannot be credited back. (An exception arises if the employee becomes ill on holiday and the sick days are, therefore, not calculated as holiday. Moreover, compensation guidelines as stated in § 651f CC, which can form the basis for compensation due to untaken holiday, are useful to the package holiday tourist; Führich, 1995a.) As a result, the only alternatives for those affected, apart from remaining at the destination, are a return home or an improbable and costly redirection to a new destination. The latter is accordingly connected with considerable additional financial effort.

Important in this phase, also towards to customer, is the credibility of actions the organization carries out. Their significance increases the more long-term the service provider's interest is and the more intense the multiplying effect the tourist can exert.

2.1.2.5.4 The post-holiday phase

The post-holiday phase is different from the orientation phase in that a close reference to the holiday exists and the tourist still has a very clear picture of the holiday in his or her head. His or her attitude towards the destination and the service provider is based on direct experience and is more stable in contrast to attitudes based on experience indirectly made. The consequence of this is a higher behavioural relevance. How much this applies also to travel behaviour depends, above all, on the tourist's basic motivations. Trips undertaken with the aim to discover something seldom lead to a repetition, whereas other motivations more often will (Frömbling, 1993).

However, this phase also increases in significance where experience values are used to sell the tourism product. For the tourists, it is as important as for other consumers, to reflect on the experiences made and to be able to share this with other people (Boltz, 1994). If this reflection and stabilization is not successful, dissatisfaction can set in. This can no longer affect the trip undertaken but can affect the person's future travel decisions.

In all cases, the tourist, as the observer of the negative event or as the qualified assessor who knows the destination or has carried out the activity, is asked for his opinion. As a result, he essentially influences the future value of the product (for the significance of this type of information in travel decision, see Braun and Lohmann, 1989).

2.1.2.5.5 Conclusion

Viewed in brief from the temporal point of view, two variables dominate the effect a negative event has in the consumer sphere of activity: situative involvement and legal restrictions. Influences on the previously described phases are brought together in Diagram 11.

The assessment of consequences is also dependent on a number of individual aspects as was previously indicated. Even if the majority of tourists visit destinations in seasonal peak periods, it should be observed that not all tourists are in the same phase of travel decision when a negative event occurs. The consequentially different situations

Aspects	Phases			
	Orientation	Post-decision	Holiday	Post-holiday
Situative Involvement	■ Low ■ High	■ High	■ High	■ Low
Legal limitations				
• Right to withdraw		Package holiday tourist		
• Extraordinary right to withdraw		Package holiday tourist		
• Shortcomings			Package holiday tourist Individual tourist	
Expected consequences from visitors and consumers	Strong decline to be expected	Depending on contractual terms	Low, depending on the long-term interest the service provider has	Not existing, if no regular guest

Diagram 11 Phases of travel decision

and the differing reactions of tourists should be taken into account for later use and mix of the instruments.

2.2 The tourism product as a sphere of activity

The destination can be described as the most essential tourism product for crisis management. In the past, destinations were frequently affected by negative events. Therefore, the following discussion focusses mainly on this tourism product. Nevertheless, the discussions, findings and conclusions are useful for tour operators as well as for other service providers whether from the tourism industry or not.

2.2.1 The destination as a competitive unit

Destinations can be rated differently: continents and states are described as destinations. The WTO's Silk Route project, which incorporates countries along the 12 000-km long Silk Route in the Euro-Asiatic area, or the Slave Route, which supposedly unites fifteen states on the African continent, are examples of this. But individual states, regions or even individual hotels are also considered to be destinations (WTO 1993, 1994a; Bieger, 1996a; Doswell, 1998; Haedrich, 1998b). Kotler, Haider and Rein (1993) make less of a differentiation and speak about towns, regions and nations. Regarding the size of the geographical area, there exist no fundamental upper or lower limit at all.

However, this list should not give the impression that it has to do with a hierarchical overlap-free gradation of levels, between which there is a clean dividing line. Rather, it is only a form of today's product understanding in line with market requirements. It replaces the traditional order of tourism responsibility that is oriented towards political areas of influence. Only the consumer's perception decides what is understood as a destination and how big this is.

With this understanding of the tourism product, it becomes clear that a geographical area can be a component of more than one destination. For example, it can also be an integral part of the smaller destination of a beach holidayer just as it is at the same time an element of Europe as a destination for an American tourist on a round trip.

2.2.2 Factors influencing the determination of a destination

The factors that help determine a destination is predominantly influenced by tourist motives and distance. (When considering what a destination is, the same criteria are of use in the selection as those that are used for market segmenting. This means that, as well as efficiency, the temporal stability of the concept is also important in the same way as decisions should come to a potentially heterogenous distinguishing, which, however, should be as homogenous as possible.) Motives are the focal point of the considerations. An activity holiday ensures that 'activity' is the core of the offer around which further services are grouped. They determine at the same time the activity radius of the destination for the tourist, that is, its geographic dimension. The riding holidayer understands destination as a larger area than a beach holidayer, the pilgrim as a larger area than a business traveller.

Motives as influential factors in determining a destination are complemented by the distances that lie between the traveller's departure location and his destination. Depending on the distance, a destination is described as a greater geographical unit if they lie further away from the hometown of the tourist. This effect, known as the distance hypothesis, according to which the image of a destination is more facetted the closer it is, has since been confirmed as empirical (Mayerhofer, 1995).

This assertion corresponds with findings made that, with increased distance, the media pursues the event with simultaneously decreasing attention (see Section 1.5). The following has an effect for a negative event: news value decreases with increasing distance, which means that the less probable incident receives public attention. In addition, image is defined by few factors by which the number of events that have a direct relationship with these factors decrease.

Increasing distance can, however, also be disadvantageous. If negative events can no longer be precisely assigned to a geographical area, neighbouring regions can also suffer the effects of the events although they probably were not affected by them at all.

Nevertheless, changes happen over years, which make a temporal dimension necessary when assessing destinations (see Example 9).

Example 9 Appalling Africa

Africa is one of the world's regions most affected by these effects, as the former Secretary-General of the World Tourism Organization, Enriquez Savignac, once pointed out. Although the continent is composed to date of fifty-four different countries, Africa is often perceived as one region when it comes to negative effects.

Many tourists classify the whole of Africa as a risky location. European travellers first visit destinations in the Americas, then Asia and finally South America. Only those who have seen already most of the world start considering Africa as a destination. Carter (1988) analysed why so many tourists desist from visiting Africa. He found that the image of Africa that holds sway in the major source markets of tourism is dominated by the belief that African destinations are risky because of a perceived lack of social stability within the region. Tourists could rarely explain this perceived disorder in causal or historical terms. They rather express it as an inherent characteristic of the region as a whole as if it would be part of the geography.

Carter also found that most of the tourists classified destinations in Africa as risky because they were all seen as locations of illnesses and particularly infection diseases. Tourists generally associate news reports on HIV/AIDS (which reached in some countries infection rates of more than 20 per cent of the adult population), the cholera or the Ebola virus, with the whole region of Africa rather than to the dangerous area. Africa is viewed as a marginal region that is alien and, by and large, this feeling of alienation is a source of fear and evasion for these travellers. Many of these defined Africa as a single undifferentiated territory that was dangerous. Even in the estimations of different countries, the same equivalence was drawn between the political instability of the rest of Africa and danger.

The common perception of Africa as a continent wracked by conflict, famine and HIV/AIDS are key obstacles to the wider success of its tourism industry. Neither is the continent a land of unrelenting disaster nor is Africa a single country, as it is often portrayed by the media. These perceptions need to be dispelled. Discerning tourists would never consider cancelling their holidays to France or the United Kingdom over conflict in the Balkans, but would likely abandon holiday plans in an African country over the outbreak of a conflict in another country thousands of miles away.

Source: Carter, S. (1998): Tourist's and traveller's social construction of Africa and Asia as risky locations. *Tourism Management*, Vol. 19, No. 4, pp. 349–358.

2.2.3 Competitive advantage of destinations

Like other products, destinations rival each other. They must develop special advantages that are as unique as possible in order to be competitive. To assess these advantages and, therefore, be able to better estimate the consequence of negative events, the destination's services must be closely viewed.

2.2.3.1 The definition of relevant competitive factors

Tschiderer's (1980) approach is already classical. He defines the holiday location products as a bundle of market services. In his opinion, these are made up of a constant core part and a derived variable offer. He describes the natural offer as a core service of the service bundle, 'which, with few exceptions, is the core of holiday tourism and, therefore, the deciding element of the service'. It is this focus on the natural offer that functions in a restricting manner and is no longer appropriate.

Frömbling (1993, p. 121) holds a purchase-oriented perspective to define the service characteristics of the tourism product and uses the previously discussed terms, basic and additional benefits (see also Section 1.3.2).

> After deciding to go ahead with a holiday or journey, a tourist is confronted with many tourist areas and holiday offers. These are especially similar in their basic benefit characteristics and, inasmuch, can be described as homogeneous.... The satisfaction of holiday requirements which go beyond the basic benefits can, therefore, following the general benefit theory, be defined as additional benefits which are strived for when holidaying or travelling. Only these secondary requirements (the need for experience) lead to a differentiated perception of the . . . offers supplied by tourist regions.

To define competitive advantage, Frömbling (1993) divides the motivations of tourists into primary and secondary needs. Whilst she sees the primary motive for travel as being the need for a holiday, she believes the following, amongst others, to be secondary needs: active health aspirations as a need for security, socializing and social contact as a social need, prestige and status as a need for recognition, experience and spontaneity as a need for self-realisation. As a result, Frömbling (1993, p. 119) uses Maslow's motivation hierarchy to which she remarks:

> The Maslow model makes it clear that, in tourism, there are obviously certain basic needs which must be satisfied to a certain extent for everyone.

Here, it should be established that, when using the Maslow needs hierarchy, it should be observed that – apart from the lowest level, the basic needs – the sequence is different for most people (see also further criticism in Kroeber-Riel, 1992). Ahmed (1996) also points to the geographical aspect that exerts influence over motivations and the satisfaction felt. This is explained, for example, by people for whom prestige is more important than love.

Further – and this is where the essential criticism of Frömbling's behaviour is declared – it can be assumed that there is no doubt that a holiday provides recreation for holidayers. Moreover, the general classification of relaxation as a primary need is not helpful. The important question is rather what the individual understands by recreation. A person from a large and crowded city perhaps sees this as being a beach

holiday whilst someone from the country relates this to a city break. A manager who spends hours in meetings sees recreation in the seclusion of a cruise whilst an assembly-line worker might be attracted by the nightlife of Majorca. The more clichés that are hidden in these examples, the more, however, they bring the fundamentally different understanding of recreation to the fore.

The knowledge that what tourists understand by recreation can be completely different, and is reflected again in the approach of Gutiérrez and Bordas (1993), who speak of the tourist's basic needs in this context. In Diagram 12, they assign a few chosen basic needs to the corresponding type of tourism.

Basic need	Type of tourism
Resting under the sun	Sun and beach tourism
Discovering other cultures	Cultural tourism
Practising sports	Sports tourism
Facing nature	Adventure tourism

Source: Adapted from Gutiérrez and Bordas (1993).

Diagram 12 Examples of the tourist's basic needs and the corresponding tourism offers

Essentially different to the usual definitions of holiday motivations is the fact that it attempts to define primary needs. These help to identify the basic services of a product. It is only then discernible who should be considered as a competitor at all as the following example shows (Gutiérrez and Bordas, 1993, p. 118):

Rio de Janeiro, for instance, competes in the markets of 'sun and beach' and 'conventions'. In each of these markets, it has different competitors. It probably competes with Cancun in the market of 'sun and beach' but not on the one of 'meetings' where it maybe has Mexico, D.F. as a competitor, among many others.

If we follow this approach further, there opens a possibility to define the basic and additional services of the tourism product. If we consider, for example, a golf player, his primary need in a holiday is golf. The

75

destination that interests him as a golfer must, consequentially, consider all other golfing destinations as competitors. Golf forms, therefore, the basic benefit of the holiday, the additional offer of the destination represents the additional benefits. This is different for a study trip. In this case, the aim of the holiday is probably the broadening of knowledge about a particular country or an analysis of the culture. The required basic service can, therefore, only be provided in this country.

For an in-depth analysis, these basic and additional benefits are combined with competitive advantage. According to Porter (1998a), it is possible to distinguish two basic types of competitive advantage: cost leadership and differentiation. From the customer's point of view this means that the customer is offered either a higher value – material or immaterial – in comparison to the competing suppliers or a comparable service for less money.

2.2.3.2 Differentiation advantage in basic benefits

Attaining competitive advantage over the basic benefits of holiday travel is becoming increasingly difficult. An essential reason for this is the progressive globalization of tourism, which extends the tourism offer and demands the fundamental interchangeability of services. (Keller and Smeral, 1998, give a detailed list of the most important factors of supply and demand that influence globalization and increase competitive pressure in the sense of interchangeability.)

On the one hand, it can be seen that the number of destinations that offer interchangeable basic services such as the beach holiday has increased. It is also clear, on the other hand, that some services are unique and cannot be imitated. The pyramids of Egypt are an example. A tourist, who, motivated to undertake a cultural holiday, wishes to analyse these testaments to contemporary history, has no opportunity to substitute them. Pyramids or the cultural dimension of Upper Egypt are, therefore, a competitive advantage in the basic benefits of the destination that cannot be imitated.

This is similar for pilgrims whose destination, a holy site, can be substituted by other holy sites but only to a certain extent because each of these locations is characterized by a unique cultural object. Every year, this is spectacularly repeated in the eyes of the world public when Mecca is the aim of innumerable pilgrims although the risks due to the massive crush take on considerable dimensions and the results, time after time, are death and injury.

After seeing these examples, it is easy to understand that some destinations, seen from the primary need, cannot be substituted. (Examples of competitive advantage within the immaterial area of basic benefits are *emotional tourism* when war veterans, for example, return to war locations and *military tourism* by which soldiers formerly stationed abroad return to those locations; Smith, 1998.) This does not mean, however, that destinations with competitive advantage in their basic benefits are immune to every type of negative event. Rather, this points to a generally higher acceptance threshold as far as negative events are concerned. At the same time, this type of competitive advantage allows us to conclude that holidays in these destinations can certainly suffer from negative events, which means that the number of tourists who tour the destination will decrease. However, this effect will only last for a short time. The latter can be explained by the fact that potential tourist's needs have not been satisfied. It is in this case not so much the general desire to take a trip which inspires the tourist but the much more concrete travel motives. Therefore, travel to this destination is not suspended as soon as it is affected by a negative event but only postponed until the conditions are more favourable.

For this reason, it can be concluded that greater crisis resistance and a quicker opportunity for recuperation can be obtained through competitive advantage in the basic benefits of the destination.

2.2.3.3 Differentiation advantage in additional benefits

The situation changes enormously if this advantage of non-interchangeability of the core service does not exist. In this case, it can be attempted to achieve a differentiation in the additional benefits of the product, that is, to attain a unique position in the consumer's realm of experience. This type of competitive advantage is reached through the establishment of additional and sustained emotional benefits. This includes the fact that these must be hard to imitate. Only then one can speak of competitive advantage through experience profiling. It is finally the higher social or psychological importance of the product that determines why it is preferred to other functionally similar products.

At the same time, it must not be forgotten that the existence of basic benefits is still a necessary prerequisite for market success. A beach destination such as Rimini can have its differentiation advantage in the area of the additional benefits but must also ensure that the basic benefit of a beach destination is still intact. If this is not the case, the destination suffers regardless of the competitive advantage that exists in the additional benefits (see also Example 8).

Because of the fundamental interchangeability of many destinations as regards basic benefits, this type of competitive advantage is of increasing significance. The efforts to attain a differentiation within the area of additional benefits can be observed, for example, in Spain – the traditional destination for beach holidays – where emotional dimensions are constantly emphasized within the strategic marketing measures. But even various African destinations try to connect emotional aspects to their beach holidays in order to make them more competitive (excursions to slavery documentation centres are one of many measures within the framework of the WTO's Slave Route project, which should establish competitive advantage in this product area; WTO, 1995).

A particular quirk of this competitive advantage is its imaginary emotional basis. This makes it especially susceptible to negative events because spoiled realms of experience cannot be reproduced by objective arguments. Moreover, the fundamentally long-term formation of these competitive advantages demands considerable temporal and financial resources. Both make it clear that the possibility of a negative event must be considered very promptly, that is, in the planning process of additional emotional benefits (see also Sections 3.1.2 and 4.1).

Diagram 13 depicts, in brief, the significance of a destination's basic and additional benefits, independent of the various competitive advantages.

	Basic benefits	Additional benefits
Differentiation advantage in basic benefits	Competitive advantage	Do not exist or are not decisive regarding competitiveness
Differentiation advantage in additional benefits	Essential prerequisite	Competitive advantage

Diagram 13 The significance of basic and additional benefits

2.2.3.4 Cost advantage

Cost advantage describes, besides the differentiation advantage, the second fundamental form of competitive advantage. With a cost leadership strategy, the organization offers a comparable standard product at a lower price than its competitors (Porter, 1998a). It is important that the product attributes are perceived by the tourists to be identical or equivalent to that of the competition.

Interchangeable beach destinations that develop in regions with favourable infrastructure and wage costs are an example of this type of competitive advantage. They conceal particular risks from the point of view of negative events. Their perceived interchangeability and concentration on price, on the other hand, means that only the price can be used as an instrument.

Price, indeed, proves to be an appropriate instrument for reducing increased risk perception but this behaviour leads to a fundamental problem with regard to cost advantage: it comes from the fact that, as a rule, the reserves to cut the price are lower than for a company with differentiation advantages. Whilst this will be dealt with later in the section on strategic crisis management (see Section 4.1.1), the signal effect due to price-cuts should first be mentioned as it makes the range for price-cuts known and will lead, in the future, to changed expectations.

2.2.3.5 The time dimension

On initial consideration, the temporal aspect is of significance within the context of the onset of a negative event and travel phases (see Section 2.1.2.5). Depending on the travel phase in which the customer is, a negative event has different consequences. The customer's situative involvement, which varies over the course of time, was fixed as the essential determinant for this difference.

The temporal aspect has further significance in the area of offer where it can be used to define competitors. In this sense, destinations are not static but dynamic products (Dolnicar and Mazanec, 1998, p. 57, suggest, therefore, the use of the term 'destination circles'). This can be traced back to the offer's natural components. This influence is illustrated, for example, in the competitive assessment of the Canary Islands. There, those responsible for tourism assumed, for a long time, that Morocco, Tunisia and Madeira are year round competitors for the European source market. Only later was it discovered that summer competitors are not the same as winter ones. Whilst the Greek Islands and Majorca should be seen as competitors in the summer, this changes to the Caribbean Islands in the winter (Gutiérrez and Bordas, 1993).

The circle of competitors can, therefore, differ depending on regular and recurring temporal intervals. In extreme cases, this can mean that there is, temporarily, no substitute destination due to the temporal factor.

Altogether, it remains to be recorded that knowledge of this temporal dimension should not be underestimated because it helps, in case of a negative event, to assess not only the effect on the destination but also on the competitor.

2.2.4 The image of a destination

The fact that the image a consumer has of a destination is dependent on factors that are of both the tourist and non-tourist sphere of influence makes the most comprehensive approach possible seem advisable in order to be able to assess the effect of negative events on the product.

Image describes the abstract mental copy that a person has of an object, in this case a destination (it is possible to distinguish four fundamentally significant types of image: product group image, brand image, company image and country, region or town image). Images are always useful when thus describe pictures or visual constructs that function comprehensively, demonstrate a high degree of complexity and, although stable and inflexible, can still be influenced (Mayerhofer, 1995).

Images are the result of a continuous process of opinion-forming, which takes place independently of concrete decision situations. They are composed of objective and subjective, right and sometimes also wrong ideas, attitudes and experiences. (The term image should be distinguished from the stereotype related to people that is marked by value assessments. Furthermore, it should be distinguished from prejudice, which is taken from the external social environment and, as such, less open to influence; Trommsdorff, 1975).

Trommsdorff (1990, p. 121) describes image as 'a multi-dimensional construct made up of denotative and connotative product characteristics . . ., which simultaneously reflect the structure of a one-dimensional attitude phenomenon'. If the attitude towards characteristic was illustrated on a good–bad continuum, 'the image has characteristics on several dimensions, namely the subjective impressions of the product's individual (non-material) characteristics'. (The number of attempts to define the terms attitude and image are ample and can be explained by the fact that they describe hypothetical unobservable appearances which means that there can be no correct or incorrect definition.)

Scientific analysis spent a long time on the question as to whether image should only incorporate connotative, that is, non-objective items, or also denotative, that is, objective, criteria. Most recent practical use proved that a division is inadvisable (Mazanec, 1979, believed in this separation and only wanted to use attitude measuring to include denotative items and image measuring to include connotative items).

Schrattenecker's (1984) attempt, which tried to explain the destination assessment process using partial models, also confirmed this. (With partial models, a central construct that is expanded by further constructs is the focus of consideration. In contrast to total models, the opportunity for empirical examination exists. Total models attempt to explain the entire decision process to the consumer.) She used the attitude model and, if product knowledge was inadequate and subjective ideas dominated, the image model to analyse the objective characteristics of the country. (Moreover, she used the risk model to measure negative events that have to do with the consumption of the holiday and the dissonance model to explain experiences of conflict after a holiday.) However, Schrattenecker (1984, p. 230) had to admit that clearly assigning tourists to one of the various partial models is extremely difficult due to the degree of complexity of the decision object 'holiday'.

This difficulty has already been observed many times and led to considerable problems when measuring image (Mayerhofer, 1995). It is made even more difficult by the great significance of emotional values, above all, in tourism. The positioning of products through their emotional experience values, the use of pictures to convey these values but also the knowledge that not only linguistic but also pictorial information processing exist, allows a call for action to be recognized (Kroeber-Riel, 1993b).

One result was the introduction of non-verbal image measurement (NVIM), through which pictorial images can be better grasped just as it is becoming easier to understand emotional mood factors (an overview of the advantages of NVIM can be found in Mayerhofer, 1995). Problems that previously arose due to linguistic formulation by the interviewees of visual stimuli and their subsequent retranslation into pictures through market researchers were omitted (this also applies to the problem of translating word stimuli in international image elevation; nevertheless, the various meanings that pictures can have in different cultural circles should also be taken into account).

A further consequence was the introduction of the term 'realm of experience' as a description of a widely fanned-out image. First used by Fuchs (1993, p. 10), realm of experience is defined as:

> The total of all ideas and perceptions which a person or group of people connect to a particular object. It is based on cognitively recorded, learnt and examinable facts and the connection with subjective, emotionally loaded *interpretations* of certain characteristics of the object in question.

This then agrees with the idea that subjective and objective assessments almost always flow together in product assessment and cannot be considered without one another. Further, realms of experience concern a construct that should be more widely understood than image. Where the former only incorporates denotative and connotative word stimuli in its measurements, non-verbal stimuli are also included, which allow the pictures to be understood (the consumer's realm of ideas is described as the most comprehensive even if the pictures can, in the widest sense, be seen to be smell, taste, hearing or other stimuli; Kroeber-Riel, 1993a; Mayerhofer, 1995).

The construct realm of experience can be used, therefore, to record more extensively how a consumer or tourist experiences an 'object, brand name, company or county, town or region' (Mayerhofer, 1995, p. 103). In the rest of this book, the terms image and realm of experience will be used synonymously; however, it is expressly indicated that the term image is meant in its wider form to include connotative and denotative characteristics.

2.2.4.1 Country image

A general image of a country is built automatically and independently of whether the country comes into question as a holiday destination.

(Of interest in the following is the external image of a destination. Self-image, that is, the way the inhabitants of a destination view that destination, is of no significance for tourism itself.) This image is a result of general information that the consumer constantly takes in. It is the constant news stream of political, economic and social events as well as the impressions that have been gained about the country's products. The result is a non-tourism specific country image. The term country image used in the following can be synonymous with destination image. As a rule, however, this image is closely related to political or geographical borders with which the country's characteristic details are particularly emphasized (Meyer, 1981; Fakeye and Crompton, 1991).

According to Mayerhofer (1995, p. 142), country image particularly influences the following areas:

- population characteristics,
- countryside,
- cultural aspects,
- landmarks,
- food and beverages,
- famous personalities,
- the country's competence as product and service manufacturer (made-in-image),
- representative products of the country

This influence is not one-sided. As the country's image is influenced by these factors, it also reflects back on these (Kulhavy, 1981; Mayerhofer, 1995). There is also a constant relationship of change between country image and its influential factors (see Example 10).

Country image is also formed dependent on the respective political system and the relationship with other nations. In that sense, a national component of the consumers has to be taken into account for the country's image assessment, similar to the cultural differences of risk assessment previously discussed (see Section 2.1.2.3.1.3). For example, American tourists class Iraq, Somalia, Libya, the Lebanon and Syria as risky destinations due to lasting political tension, prefer products from 'free' countries to those from 'unfree' countries (Lebrenz, 1996; Sönmez and Graefe, 1998a) or judge products from more developed countries to be of higher quality (Lebrenz, 1996).

Example 10 Swissair: the End of a national symbol

The example of Swissair demonstrates the correlation between the country's image and the factors influencing it and shows the importance of a negative image transfer.

Up to now it was thought that mainly products and companies could use the positive sides of a country-of-origin image. Airlines are a prominent case for those who use and stress the image of a country.

The bankruptcy of Swissair is an example that this positive image transfer can easily fall back negatively on a country's image. As many airlines do, Swissair used and promoted the country's traditions on board, painted on the aircrafts the national colours and used the national flag on the tailfin. It was widely perceived as an ambassador for such Swiss values as reliability, quality, solidity, security and openness to the world.

Source: Unique (Flughafen Zürich AG).

The white cross on the tailfin was a symbol of Swiss values carried around the globe.

But the highly ambitious expansion plans in an always more complex and competitive environment led finally in 2001 to the closing of the company. What was once useful turned to be a handicap of enormous consequences for the country as a whole, for tourism and for other sectors that profited from the classical Swiss values.

An editorial in the newspaper *Le Temps* concluded: 'The white cross on red on the planes carried our reputation around the globe: it stood for quality and discipline. Since yesterday that's history. Worthless!' The broadsheet *Neue Zürcher Zeitung* (NZZ) pointed even clearer: 'The pictures screened around the world of confiscated planes and planes grounded due to lack of fuel; the reports of stranded passengers ... will not only inflict massive damage on Swissair's image but on the whole of Switzerland.'

Source: *Le Temps*, 3 October 2001

NZZ, 3 October 2001

The non-tourism-specific image has a considerable influence on whether a destination comes into question for holidays or not (Meyer, 1981; Schweiger, 1992; Gutiérrez and Bordas, 1993; Kotler, Haider and Rein, 1993). This is in accordance with the fact that the decision as to whether a destination is one of the considered alternatives is taken very early and mostly without aid of from, for example, travel agents.

2.2.4.2 Regional image

From the point of view of negative events, the regional image is of great significance in the sense of an area that covers several states. It can be consciously constructed and used in order to market a region as a tourism destination. This approach is often used if the individual image is not perceived by the market (the WTO's Silk Route and Slave Route projects are examples of this).

But even an unconsciously constructed, potentially undesired regional image can emerge and has no specific tourism background. Such an image of a region is based on information that is constantly taken in – above all, by news coverage. Examples of regional images are offered by Uzbekistan and Kazakhstan whose country images are normally not individually experienced by consumers. This is different, on the other hand, for countries such as the United States or Japan, which are attributed an independent country image by European tourists.

Within these areas, which are perceived to be regionally connected, negative events have an effect on all countries independent of whether they have actually been affected. This case has already been observed many times. For example, India and the Maldives suffered from the terrorist events in Sri Lanka and the putsch in Uganda affected East African tourism as a whole (Buckley and Klemm, 1993; Hall, 1994; Mansfeld, 1995).

Mansfeld (1995) submits a more extensive analysis: he believes that the negative regional image of the Middle East can be traced back to the continuous Arabic–Israeli conflict. A result of his analyses of the most important conflicts from 1967 to 1992 was the proof that these respective negative events caused a general negative trend in the region. At the same time, is was possible to observe different effects on the countries analysed, which correlated with the extent of their involvement in the conflict (see Diagram 14).

If we speak of the degree of actual involvement, it should be noted that it depends on the degree of involvement perceived or understood by the tourist. For most events, this is strongly influenced by news reports in the consumer's country and in line with predominant public opinion.

Another result of Mansfeld's (1995) investigation was the observation that Turkey, Greece and Cyprus, which also belong to a region, were only affected by the events when these became international crises and

Event	Israel (%)	Egypt (%)	Jordan (%)	Syria (%)
The six-day war, 1967	−7.0 (1)	−45.0 (2)	−52.0 (5)	−17.4 (2)
The Yom Kippur war, 1973	−14.8 (3)	−1.1 (1)	+5.3	−31.6 (1)
The Lebanon war, 1982	−13.0	+3.4	+29.5	−24.1 (2)
International terror, 1986	−17.0 (1)	−13.6 (1)	+2.6	+5.0
Intifada, 1988	−15.0 (1)	+3.8	+26.0	+4.6
Iraqi threats, 1990	−5.0 (2)	+3.8	+16.2	+5.8
Gulf war, 1991	−17.0 (1)	−15.0 (1)	−15.4 (1)	+8.8
Al Asqa Intifada, 2000	−54.4	−45.6	+16.3	+12.4

Note: The numbers in brackets stand for the number of negative trend years that followed the event.
Source: Based on information from Mansfeld (1995) and WTO data.

Diagram 14 Relative change in international arrivals in the Middle East, 1967–2001

caused general problems such as an increase in transport costs. Otherwise, these countries have been spared by the effects. Sometimes they even profited by being substitutes. This development is explained by the relatively well-developed country images of Turkey, Greece and Cyprus, which made the countries immune to the spill-over effects.

In brief, it can be concluded that countries or regions that incorporate several states can be doubly affected by negative events:

- First, the country is directly affected by the negative event. This refers both to involvement in the conflict as well as the location of the event.
- Second, because the country is affected by spill-over effects of the negative event.

In the second case, the surprise effect is unequally greater. This can frequently be traced back to the fact that those responsible in tourism were not aware that their country was perceived by tourists in the same image sphere as the affected destination. This effect that self-image differs from the external image can always be observed when the analysis of tourists' image is carried out unsatisfactorily or from the perspective of the destination's manager.

2.2.4.3 Destination image

The image of a destination is vital for the customer's product choice. The customer decides what is understood as a destination, that is, whether it is a resort or even a region. This means, in addition to the finding made already that a geographic area can host several destinations, that a geographical area can have several different competitive advantages at its disposal.

This also shows that, even under normal circumstances, a differentiated analysis of important customer segments should be aimed at. Provided that overlapping and contact points exist due to the 'scenery effect', the most consistent strategy possible should be aimed at. (The scenery effect describes the circumstance that other target groups in the same geographical location considerably influence destination perception and product assessment. This effect will be considered later in more detail; see also Section 6.4.1).

This aspect is also of significance within the context of negative events because, different customer segments related to these destinations normally react differently. Influenced is this reaction by the strength of the respective competitive advantage as well as the different acceptance thresholds.

This can be also seen in Israel where violent and terrorist acts over the course of 1996 caused a decline in international tourist arrivals. The effects were more extreme in the area of normal package holidays than in the segments of round tours, pilgrimages and cultural trips where there were hardly any cancellations (Priel and Peymani, 1996). Competitive advantages embodied in basic benefits, as with cultural trips or pilgrimages, prove to be more resistant when the security situation worsens. Other areas such as beach holidays, where Israel has no recognizable competitive advantage, react more delicately to the same events.

This already indicates that there are strategic possibilities to manage a crisis. This will be discussed in detail later (see Section 4.2). It is important, however, to first examine three essential variables that influence the imagination, assessment and effect of negative events of the destination image.

2.2.4.3.1 The experience dimension

The tourist's experience of a destination has – as has already been illustrated – influence on the purchase risks associated with product choice (see also Section 2.1.2). This diminishes if the destination is repeatedly chosen. However, experience also influences the susceptibility of the destination image towards negative events.

The increasingly more important emotional product differentiation must first be learned by the consumer in order to be effective. This can occur in the form of symbolic experience or direct learning. If the product differentiation is learned by direct experience, that is, by having been on holiday, it is clear and free of contradiction to the actual experience of the product. The customer is in this case aware of the emotional product advantages and can better assess whether the negative event had an effect on such components.

However, if the product differentiation is a result of symbolic experience, that is, learned through advertising and other influential components, it can come to differences between the attraction and experienced image (Fakeye and Crompton, 1991; Ahmed, 1996). Handling and correcting these differences must be the constant aim of destination marketing since also under normal circumstances differences can lead to dissatisfaction. Especially for the case of symbolic experience, it can be expected that potential tourists reject a destination more quickly due to a lack of understanding of the effect on the realm of experience, which remains still unknown.

This assumption is in accordance with attitude research according to which only attitudes gained by direct experience are relevant for tourist behavioural prognosis (Kroeber-Riel, 1992; Frömbling, 1993) (see Example 11).

Example 11 Terrorism as a tourism mood killer?

The Basque separatist group, ETA, has been targeting Spain's lucrative tourism industry since the 1980s. But rather than killing tourists, ETA aimed at hurting as much as possible the Spanish economy with a dependency of some 12 per cent of its GDP on tourism. The activities were mainly committed along the Costa Dorada around the places of Cambrills and Salou and in southern Spain. No tourists were killed in any of those attacks. The most serious tourist-related attack was in 1996, when an ETA bomb exploded at Reus airport in Tarragona, injuring thirty-five holidaymakers.

After a 14-month peace period since September 1998, ETA reinitiated in 1999 its terrorist campaign and warned foreign tourists in March 2001 explicitly not to spend their holidays in Spain as there could be 'unexpected consequences' of such a stay. Since then, several car bombs in Gerona, Valencia, Malaga, Tarragona and Madrid, with injury and deaths, have underlined the seriousness of this warning. Surprisingly, however, neither have the arrivals of foreign tourists to Spain been affected nor have tourists expressed interest in cancelling their holidays after such attacks. This is mainly to be explained through the direct experience that most of the visitors have made already in Spain, a classical destination with a high number of repeaters.

The same observation can be made in the case of Turkey, also a destination that has a strong interest in international tourism but has had to struggle in the past because of several terrorist attacks by the Kurdish PKK. Here, investigations of the German market research institute 'Studienkreis für Tourismus und Entwicklung' have shown that only 24 per cent of the German population feel subjectively secure after domestic conflicts in Turkey happened, whereas, on the contrary, 79 per cent of those who actually have been the year before in Turkey expressed they would not feel affected at all.

2.2.4.3.2 The geographical dimension

The consumer's background also has an influence on destination image. Depending on which regional sphere the tourist comes from, they link other experience dimensions with a destination. In contrast to the previously discussed influence of cultural and national components on risk assessment (see also Section 2.1.2.3.1.3), the geographical dimension has a much more concrete product reference (see Example 12).

Example 12 Geographical roots influence the tourists' perceptions

The image of a tourist destination consists of the sum of more or less individual and subjective ideas, impressions, beliefs and expectations that a potential tourist has accumulated over a specific period of time. Each of the segments has been shaped by various factors such as media, press, friends' and relatives's experiences, literature, etc. It is evident that each visitor has developed his or her very own image of one specific destination. However, it is possible to attach specific groups to specific types of images. Groups could be classified by age, type of holiday, travel experience, life-style and actual position within the life-cycle.

Ahmed investigated the significance of a tourist's geographical origin in the relation to its image of the US state of Utah as tourist destination. He could prove, based on more than 1900 questionnaires of residents of six different US regions, that the ideas of potential visitors to Utah were different depending on their respective geographical background.

Analysing Utah's total image and its five major constituents (outdoor recreation resources, outdoor recreation activities, culture, nightlife and liquor laws), he found significant differences of the perceived images: in respect to the total image as much as for the perception of culture, people from the 'Intermountain-West' (Arizona, Colorado, Idaho, Montana, Nevada and New Mexico) found Utah to be 'most impressive' whereas people from the Eastern States (Connecticut, Delaware, Washington DC, Kentucky, Maine, Maryland, Massachusetts, New Hampshire, New Jersey, New York, Ohio, Pennsylvania, Vermont, West Virginia) were 'least impressed'. Concerning the image of outdoor recreation resources, people from California where 'most impressed' whereas people from Washington and Oregon were 'least impressed'. Residents from the Midwest (Illinois, Indiana, Iowa, Kansas, Michigan, Minnesota, Missouri, Nebraska, North Dakota, South Dakota and Wisconsin) made up the group that was 'most impressed' of Utah's nightlife and 'most liberal' concerning the liquor laws.

Ahmed traced these different perceptions back to regionally differing moral concepts, tastes, behaviour and subcultures amongst others. He emphasized that the mere identification of the total image of a tourist destination is not sufficient for promotional success, as the total images might be negative whereas constitutional segments might be perceived positive or even outstanding.

Source: Ahmed, Z. (1996): The need for the identification of the constituents of a destination's tourist image: a promotional segmentation perspective. *Revue de Tourisme*, No. 2, pp. 44–57.

Within the context of this analysis, this means that regionally differing destination assessments are not influenced in the same way by negative events. This opens a further opportunity for crisis management. People from regional areas whose perceived images are less affected by a negative event could be preferred as a target group.

2.2.4.3.3 The image effect of security events

Even the security issue is important within the context of destination image. Whilst, in its first form – which has already been considered (see also Section 2.1.2.3.1.4) – it is responsible for the general security situation being classed as dangerous, security events can also destroy experience values of the destination image. Buckley and Klemm (1993, p. 193) describe, for example, the damage to experience values in Northern Ireland:

> A favourable image is an essential requirement of any tourist destination. The problem with any kind of civil unrest is that unfavourable images are beamed across the world so that even those who are not afraid of terrorism will be discouraged from taking holidays there. It is not so much that the area is dangerous; more that it does not look attractive.

If such an influence applies for a long time, it can be assumed that the security event not only influences the image but actually dominates it. Lennon (1999) illustrates this in the case of Belfast, which is still classed as a war zone.

Gartner and Shen (1992) could empirically prove that security events bring about a change in image dimension. By comparing the image of China both before and after the tragic events on Tiananmen Square, the authors surprisingly ascertained that this incident mainly affected the perception of natural attractions that became significantly worse when influenced by the violent clashes. Gartner and Shen (1992) correctly assumed, therefore, that these previously unperceived elements are also important for the tourism image under normal circumstances.

These comments illustrate that the effect of security events must been seen in a wider sense as it was previously the norm. Whilst, as a rule, the aspect of the increased insecurity has an immediate and short-term effect, the parallel observable influence on image also comes to fruition in the long term. In the most extreme cases, security events dominate the image so much that they are seen as independent from the actual threat. (A typical example of this is Vietnam. The destination's image is still marked by the Vietnam War regardless of the actual security situation. Instead of fighting against this image, the destination knowingly uses it as an attraction.)

2.2.5 Product responsibility

Changing market conditions and the demand-oriented understanding of the destination also influenced the reorientation of responsibility and realization of the various planning, design and coordination activities. If, due to the legal framework of an organization, it is clear within a company where the limits lie and what the management's responsibilities are, we meet a more difficult situation in tourism. Moreover, this is made more difficult by the small- and medium-sized business structure of European tourism.

Following the question of responsibility, three concepts can be distinguished: the tourism structure, the tourism organization and the tourist office (see Diagram 15).

Whilst the term tourism structure describes the organization and the workflow structure of a destination and the tourist office is responsible for operative daily business, the tourism organization is the bearer of the services to be provided for the destination. Special attention will be paid to the tourism organization as it is responsible for the overall planning and marketing as well as the representation of interests, whether governed by public or private law (at the same time, however, Bieger, 1996a, points out that the normative planning function remains unchanged in political institutions).

Problems appear even under normal circumstances. They are caused by restricted influence possibilities and the fact that decisions for

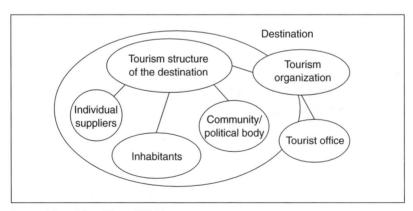

Source: Adapted from Bieger (1996a).

Diagram 15 The concept system of the tourism organization

something at the same time imply decisions against something, which, because of the larger number of participants, often leads to a compromise with the smallest common denominator. Thus, a responsibility problem arises. Therefore, Bieger (1996a) cites the minimum requirement that tourism organizations must be non-profit organizations to help reduce conflicts of interest. The result is that there are a number of interest groups who are interested in having product responsibility but do not want to share this. Then, there is the problem of statement, the answer to the question what product, respectively, destination image, should be build up and maintained. (Homogeneity of interests, the existence of centralized structures, the acceptance of leaders, etc., belong to those factors that exert influence over the problems.)

Even if it is implied that these problems are solved in times of a positive, market-creating marketing, particular difficulties arise in the case of negative events, which, in part, have their roots in the consequences of the decision and special responsibility.

If the problem of responsibility in crisis management is analysed, it can be realized that the legal responsibility is not necessarily identical to the responsibility for the destination. Comparing companies and destinations reveals a further interesting facet. Normally, it can assumed that the management of a company becomes active to ensure its continuing success or to lower the impacts and, in a worst case scenario, it can be made legally responsible. Destinations, on the other hand, only consider the problem of responsibility in times of crisis and disregard preventive possibilities. Whilst, normally, there are a number of persons 'interested in power', under these circumstances, no one wants to take on the responsibility.

However, this is not sensible. Crisis management is a public good for a destination because the exclusivity principle cannot be used. Besides, the image, an important part of the confidence-building measures, for which normally the tourism organization is responsible, is strained. Therefore, in order to be prepared for negative events, the tourism organization must be aware of its responsibility and assign it from the beginning, particularly if it concerns a public–legal structure in which calm, careful and balancing actions dominate. This is even more important taking into account that correct and solving actions are seldom rewarded while actions that fail are almost always sanctioned. Consequentially, management responsibility is not as freely taken on in such situations especially if multiple responsibilities allow the decisions to be shifted to other institutions.

Moreover, there is also a statement problem in crisis management. The lack of understanding of marketing strategies even in normal circumstances, which applies for most destinations (Gutiérrez and Bordas, 1993), often leads to an ineffective cocktail of activities, which, normally, only has the aim of playing the events down. However, what is destroyed or impeded is exactly what is important in the long run: the organization's credibility.

It remains to be ascertained that the regulation of product responsibility is important for a destination. In a crisis situation, the destination image is placed under close scrutiny as the otherwise rather seldom observed statements and behaviours of the tourism organization are viably carried out directly in the public eye. This also can be seen as a chance for crisis management, which should be used with the right and proper preparation.

2.3 Competitors as spheres of activity

The competitors of a company or a destination can, in the case of a negative event, form an alternative for the affected as well as also being affected.

The aspect as to who should be considered a competitor has already been mentioned (for competitors, see Sections 2.2.1 and 2.2.3.5). It brings forward the question of the advantage that a competitor can gain from a situation of a negative event. Viewed in general, the disadvantageous development of a destination is an advantage for competing destinations. This applies all the more if it concerns negative events that are limited to a local area and do not influence the volume of tourists as a whole.

In the first case, when only one company or a particular destination but not the competitors are affected by negative events, the following reaction possibilities exist for competitors:

- First, they can refrain from every form of advantage taking.
- Second, they can use the event to their advantage in that they emphasize the defects of the competing product within the

framework of comparative advertising. This behaviour is clearly directed against the affected organization and contributes actively to the problem being publicized.
■ Third, competitors can confine themselves to indicating the non-existence of the defects in their own products. This type of reaction always comes into question if it is already well known that a negative event has occurred.

Up to now, the second and third reaction possibilities have barely been perceivable in tourism. One of the few exceptions was the reaction of the competitors of the Fijian Islands who reacted to the political instability of 1987 with advertisement comparing the safety of their own destination (Hall, 1994, p. 100):

Golden beaches, coconut palms and no coups!
War in the Solomons ended 1945. Why risk Fiji?

In the future, a more active form of reaction on the part of competitors will have to be reckoned with. Continuously growing pressure to compete as well as the legal expansion of advertising possibilities (comparative advertising), introduced in Europe by the EU in October 1997, are two essential influential factors. This applies, above all, to the third case in which the non-existence of the defect for the own product is indicated in a 'cautious manner' without directly mentioning the competitor (see Example 13).

Example 13 Think Swiss – Fly Thai

The following example illustrates the growing competition between companies. In October 2001, the Swiss airline company 'Swissair' went bankrupt (see also Example 10). This bankruptcy was unexpected and was followed by a very emotional discussion of managerial and ethical values in Switzerland. The Star Alliance member 'Thai Airways' used this moment and launched in early 2002 a Swiss-wide promotional campaign directed against the efforts to rebuild what became the successor airline 'Swiss'. The campaign, which included in its advertisements all graphical elements used before exclusively by 'Swissair' was widely recognized and accepted by the public. It also received mainly positive comments from the specialized travel press.

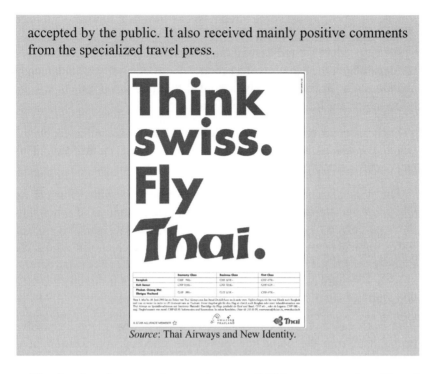

Source: Thai Airways and New Identity.

The legal and economic sanction possibilities open to the affected organization determine their opportunities to stop this advantage-taking. They can be classed as low. Seen from a legal point of view, there is no way of stopping such behaviour on an international level.

Even from an economic point of view, sanctions are of relatively little use due to the polypolitical market structure of destinations and businesses (this is different, e.g. for tour operators building an oligopoly in Europe).

Independently of the possibilities that the affected organization has, it is finally the consumer who decides about the success of the attempted advantage-taking. Only if he approves the competitor's behaviour and, therefore, buys their product, do these actions make sense. Fundamentally, it can be ascertained that the willingness of a customer to accept such rival behaviour rises with increased distance from the moment the negative event occurred. Behaviour initially interpreted as exploitive is then understood as informative and explanatory.

The acceptance of active advantage-taking is also influenced by the customer's will to sanction. Because of the stronger growing tendency of sanctioning nowadays, some already speak of it as a fundamental need of our time (Dyllick, 1992; Drosdek, 1996). Moreover, the decision against a product is favoured by the interchangeability of products as a result of which the sanction of a product does not signify a fundamental abandonment. It remains to be assumed that this development will be more important for tourism in the future.

In the second case, several or all competitors are affected by the negative event as well as the originally considered organization. This can occur either directly or indirectly.

The generalization effect is responsible for the indirect effect by which an undifferentiated transfer of attitudes is applied to other similarly perceived objects (Jungermann and Slovic, 1993a). This occurs, for example, because products belong to the same categories, the same branches or to the existence of a 'meta attribute' such as the same nationality. In comparison to those directly affected, those indirectly affected will find out about this normally only at a later stage.

In both cases, rival behaviour is fundamentally oriented to solve problems. From the point of view of the affected organization, it is advantageous that mutual efforts are undertaken to counter the event and its effects. Associations to which the affected organization belongs also have an important function. As representatives of common interests, they are in a position to be objectively active towards the political sphere and social pressure groups (see Example 14).

Example 14 WTO's Tourism Recovery Committee

As a consequence of the attacks of September 11 on the United States of America, a worldwide necessity of communication and coordination was advocated by WTO's 14th General Assembly and led to the establishment of a Crisis Committee (later renamed 'Tourism Recovery Committee'). This Committee was the first of its kind to deal on an intergovernmental and worldwide level with the issue of crisis management in tourism. It is comprised of representatives from most of the affected countries (twenty-one), representatives of each of the subsectors of the tourism industry that represent the industries' experience and needs (fifteen) and leading experts on the subject.

Members of the Tourism Recovery Committee at
the Madrid meeting

The Committee met for the first time in London on the occasion of the World Travel Market (11 November 2001) and discussed the initial report on the consequences, which had been prepared by the WTO Secretariat. The members of the Committee presented the experience of their countries and companies in facing the actual crisis as well as their first solutions, both strategic and operational, of how to handle this situation. This first full meeting of the Committee was followed by two regional meetings for the Mediterranean countries where tourism plays a very important role (in Madrid, Spain, on 30 January 2002 and in Tunis, Tunisia, on 1 March 2002). Two other full meetings followed (in Berlin on 15 March 2002 and in London on 12 November 2002), especially in view of increased terrorism actions against the tourism sector (Djerba, Tunisia; Bali, Indonesia and Mombassa, Kenya).

All meetings were based on the mutual interest to recover as soon as possible from the initial crisis and to discuss issues of importance to all members. The Committee discussed especially the following issues:

- monitoring the evolving situation and its impacts on tourism;
- strengthening WTO's activities in the areas of security and tourism image building;

- supporting WTO members, providing them with regular information and recommendations on how to handle the situation;
- ensuring the coordination and consistency of the messages communicated regarding the evolving state of the tourism industry.

In addition, the Committee used whenever possible, either through its Chairman or another representative, the chance of communicating the messages of all countries concerned in a single voice.

2.4 The state as a sphere of activity

Companies or organizations are limited in their freedom of action by the intervention of the state. Regarding its tasks and functions in most West European countries, this covers a development from liberal constitutional state to the welfare state of the present (state describes all horizontal administrative bodies, namely legislative, judicial and executive). The state perceives increased tasks whose common characteristic is providing a service for society, such as environmental protection, the promotion of specific economical areas and catastrophe precautions. This is accompanied by an increased interlocking of the public and private spheres, which then leads to a restriction on private autonomy. Seen as a whole, legal regulations are influencing more and more the different areas of life (Dyllick, 1992).

This tendency has to be classed generally as inopportune for the organization affected by a negative event. This is particularly the case, if it comes to regulations through laws or decrees that are cost-effective for the affected organization or limit their freedom of action.

Following the question on which factors lead to these cost-effective decisions or decisions that curb the freedom of action, phase models can be used to illustrate the political decision process. According to Dyllick's (1992) three-phase model, the first phase describes the articulation of the problem in which a great number of problems compete for the attention of political instances and public opinion.

Regarding perception and assessment, the same criteria apply for political decision makers as were mentioned in the consumer sphere of activity. Moreover, it is confirmed that political representatives behave like rational vote maximizers (Bieger, 1996a). As a result, their preferred interest applies to that which promises them more votes, leads to more fame or helps them to get increased support from important groups. Already today, it can be observed that, in this phase, influences take on unconventional forms and the significance of stakeholder and interest groups increases (see Example 15).

Example 15 The Aviation and Transportation Security Act

Since the terrorist attacks of September 11 in the United States, the issue of transport security – and, in particular, increased air transport security – has moved to the top of the agenda of the US Government. The governments recognized that in the current situation this critical issue cannot be handled anymore by airlines and airport operators alone.

How fast such a process of market articulation, policy formulation and implementation can be is illustrated by the Aviation and Transportation Security Act (ATSA), which President Bush signed into law on 19 November 2001, just 10 weeks after the attacks showed the vulnerability and failing of the actual system. Among other things, the ATSA established a new Transportation Security Administration (TSA) within the Department of Transportation. The main objective of the Act was to enhance the national airport security services, which are now under federal management and control. In particular, the screening of individuals and property is now operated by the TSA and companies under contract with TSA. The new law requires additionally the qualification, training and testing of all employees as much as the presence of uniformed Federal law enforcement officers at all commercial airports. In detail, the Federal Government is now in charge of the following actions:

1. supervision of the passenger and baggage security at 420 commercial passenger airports within the USA;
2. performance of intensive background checks, training and testing of screeners and security personnel;
3. purchasing and maintaining all screening equipment;

4. oversee patrolling of secure areas and monitoring of the quality of the airport's access control;
5. cooperating with other law enforcement authorities at the federal, state and local levels as well as being a key facilitator of coordination regarding homeland security.

In the phase of policy formulation, the concrete and already prioritized problems are combined with programmes and aims. Because it has already been indicated that experts and laymen scarcely agree on the ways and forms of assessing risks (see also Section 2.1.2.3.1.3), it is significant which way of risk assessment decision makers should follow. In this phase, an important role falls on the lobbies and pressure groups, who are heard as experts and affected people, who, through self-obligation, can influence further legislative activities.

In the phase of policy implementation, programmes, respectively, laws, are issued, monitored and, if necessary, sanctioned as offences. It is only with this implementation that the actual effect of a political decision can be judged.

State regulations should not only, however, be viewed as cost-effective but also as a measure to ensure a sustainable tourism development. For environmental problems that are not necessarily caused by tourism, state intervention is sometimes the only opportunity to prevent negative events. The careless contact and misuse of resources in the form of water contamination or air pollution frequently appears as a causal area of tourism crises (see Example 16).

Example 16 Erika and Prestige

The legally complicated issue of international cargo transported by seaways illustrates that only the state or, like in the following cases, the international community is able to prevent effectively negative events of enormous consequences for nature and tourism.

On Wednesday, 13 November 2002, in stormy weather conditions, a serious accident occurred with the oil tanker 'PRESTIGE', which was sailing off the West Coast of Galicia (Spain). It was reported that the ship, with 77 000 tonnes of heavy fuel on board, was in danger of sinking because of a large crack in the starboard side of the hull. Upon request of the owner and his insurer, the Dutch salvage company 'SMIT' took control of the vessel. The ship was towed to sea, and while the discussions were on-going on where it could find a safe haven to transfer its cargo to another ship, the situation deteriorated on board.

On Tuesday morning, 19 November, the ship structure collapsed and the tanker broke into two some 100 miles off the Spanish and Portuguese coast. The dangerous cargo was spilled into the sea and caused enormous pollution off the Galicia coast, a very important fishing area and zone of tourism.

A similar accident happened less than 3 years ago, when the oil tanker 'ERIKA', which carried 35 000 tonnes of this persistent and difficult to clean oil, polluted the coast of France. Both oil tankers were old single-hull tankers that offer little safety in case of an accident.

As measures by single countries are of no major impact in the case of maritime safety, the European Union took the initiative and adopted a set of measures that will ban effectively these substandard ships from Europe's waters in the near future. These initiatives, which have no doubt financial implications for the parties affected, will benefit not only the environment but also the tourism sector, both of which were strongly affected by both events.

For the sake of completeness, the other side of the welfare state that helps businesses affected by negative events must be cited. This side appears if the state compensates damages or losses caused by the incident in order to ensure, for example, the further existence of a company or the whole branch.

However, the state as a sphere of activity reacts more slowly than the other spheres. Whilst the latter forget negative events over the course of time and, therefore, do not have any effect, political decisions that lead to laws or other political norms have from then on a quasi-everlasting effect. This is cost-effective both for the organization directly affected and the rivals included in the legal decisions. Practice shows, however, that in every case it is possible to influence the reaction of the state and, therefore, the consequences through exemplary behaviour. This option is recommended not only for the case the organization has a legal responsibility but also for the case that the organization is just attributed this responsibility.

2.5 Other spheres of activity

Capital investors, employees and suppliers of the company or destination belong to the other elements of the institutional environment. (Suppliers are only mentioned to complete the picture. They should not be considered as the observations made within the area of the tourism product as a sphere of activity can be also transferred onto the components of the service bundle.)

Financial resources are of great importance above all in tourism infrastructure projects. (Above all, hotels prove themselves to be particularly investment intensive. This is intensified by the high proportion of foreign investment.) As long as the real estate, which serves, as a rule, to secure liabilities, is not affected by the negative event, it is of interest for the capital investor even if the effects can be controlled in other activity spheres and have no long-term consequences. This applies in the same sense for other business activities where it concerns relations with external capital investors (illiquidity, excessive debts, etc., are intentionally not dealt within this book). Thus, the handling of capital investors is of an indirect nature and concentrates on the efforts undertaken in other areas.

From the personnel point of view, it has to be considered that tourism companies have a strong interest in the temporary employment of personnel (for further personnel aspects, see also Section 6.3.2). This is because seasonal fluctuations in demand, which scarcely allow year-round employment, are responsible for this. Furthermore, the tourists' individual needs or national habits contribute to the employment of foreign personnel such as bakers, chefs and tour guides. On this temporary staff, especially if it is foreign, negative events will always have an effect if their personal safety is threatened.

Altogether it remains to be ascertained that these spheres of activity are of subordinate importance in the area of crisis management (this does not apply for the personnel aspect to be considered in Section 6.3.2).

2.6 Summarized evaluation and ranking of activity spheres

An essential characteristic of crisis situations is the limitation on the resources available to the affected organization. At the same time, this means that the affected spheres have to be weighed and prioritized based on their importance. For most organizations, this importance is derived from the influence that the respective areas exert over business success.

Seen from a general point of view, the consequence for the different spheres vary according to the respective branches. For production companies, for example, they will basically increase costs, as the effects will be primarily legal norms and less from the sales market.

In tourism, it should be assumed that the consumer, that is, the sales market, occupies first place in the activity spheres. In the majority of cases, the events unleash a sales rather than cost-sided effect. The consequence of the effect is essentially determined by the market constellation in which the affected unit or units are located. From this point of view, competitors are also important.

The social environment of the affected organization, which can be more widely viewed than the amount of actual or potential customers, is also important in tourism. At present, interest groups and stakeholders are of little importance but the generally high interest that is shown towards tourism contributes to the fact that themes with negative events are quickly disseminated and paid great attention.

Moreover, this influences the state sphere of activity that should be ranked after the social environment sphere. Its mobilization is essentially dependent on public opinion on which the affected organization should already have concentrated. The potential for catastrophe of the event has an accelerated effect on the inclusion of the state. If it is great, it can induce the state institutions taking on a leading role. In this case, the affected organization unexpectedly and very quickly takes on a defensive position.

Findings made within the various spheres of activity form, like knowledge of the general order – this can, of course, change due to events and other influences – the basis of preventive measures as well as helping to contribute to the overall optimization of the company's actions in coping with crises.

3

Methods of analysis and prognosis

As has already been illustrated, preventive and coping crisis management must be distinguished within crisis management (see also Section 1.2). The aim of preventive crisis management is taking precautions and to avoid crises. In addition, areas of the organization must be identified that are especially threatened by negative events or are of such significance that they must not be exposed to threat at all. This interior-oriented identification and evaluation of possible problematic areas within crisis precautions is followed by strategic and operative measures with which the organization protects itself from the environment. Only then and on basis of these findings is the environment of the company to be looked at by early warning systems in order to indicate possible changes and allow a prompt reaction on the part of the organization (also, internal areas of the company can be the causes of crises but should not be considered further as they are subject of normal management).

The sequence of identification and early warning systems is not a hard rule as the results of early warning can lead to a complete change in the previously defined areas at threat. Nevertheless, the consideration in this sequence corresponds to practical actions.

3.1 Identification of important areas and events

Every business has a number of critical or important areas that are responsible for its success. In first place are the company's competitive advantages. There are also other areas that turn out to be important once the negative event happened. Whilst the definition and maintenance of competitive advantage is already the task of normal business management, competitively irrelevant areas must also be examined in the present identification process in order to promptly recognize their unknown influential effect on the organization in unfavourable circumstances. This examination should, as far as possible, include a future perspective.

If this perspective is extended to the fact that, from the point of view of negative events, a number of incidents are known through the occurrence of which crises in tourism were unleashed, the situation in Diagram 16 arises.

1   The first quadrant describes the situation in which an already known negative event occurs and effects an area classed as important. Because both areas are known, a more comprehensive analysis is at this point unnecessary.
2   The second quadrant refers to the circumstance that an area classed as important is affected by a negative event previously unknown

		Events	
		Known	Unknown
Areas	Known as important	1	2
	Unknown as important	3	4

Diagram 16 Situation matrix

in its effect or appearance. The surprise is caused by the event or the form of the event.

3 If the event is known in its threat potential, but it affects an area classed as unimportant, it is the third situation.

4 The constellation classed as the most problematic for crisis management describes the fourth case. An unknown negative event affects an area, the importance of which is unknown. Therefore, almost every piece of information is seen to be relevant because a differentiation according to its importance appears to be impossible.

Apart from the simultaneous increase of knowledge about the importance of certain areas, the ideal is to strive for the reduction of unknown events. The latter is, however, scarcely feasible due to the sheer number of negative events. For this reason, the identification of tourism product areas classed as important is the main practical aim of crisis precautions. It is only with this knowledge that effective preventive measures can be taken and, on the other hand, early warning can be made possible.

In the following, selected analysis and prognosis techniques should be judged on their ability to identify important areas and events for crisis management. The prognosis techniques already considered at that point serve under these circumstances to identify important areas if the event is known or, vice versa, the identification of important events if the area is known. At the same time, they are of use in the fourth case when especially the scenario analyses is used to identify weak signals (the consideration of the fourth case in which the importance of neither the area nor the event is known takes place in Section 3.2.2).

3.1.1 Selected methods to assess important areas and events

3.1.1.1 Cross-impact and vulnerability analysis

The cross-impact analysis is a quantitative method of analysis from which correlation between factors is determined and illustrated. The aim is to be able to assess the strength and succession of these correlations. Among the number of forms that the cross-impact analysis has experienced over the course of time, it is at this point the ability of this analysis instrument to evaluate the effect of possible events on important areas within an organization or its strategies that is of interest (see Diagram 17).

Environment	SBF 1	SBF 2	SBF 3	SBF 4	Effect	
					+	–
1. Economy as a whole						
Gross National Product	–3	–2	0	+1	+1	–5
Interest	–3	–3	–3	–2	0	–11
2. Political-legal environment						
Environmental protection	–1	+2	0	+1	+3	–1
Subsidies	0	+1	+1	0	+2	0
3. Technology						
New product technology	+2	+2	+3	–1	+7	–1
New process technology	–1	0	0	+1	+1	–1
4. Demography/culture						
Population development	–1	+1	0	0	+1	–1
Attitude towards consumption	+2	+2	–1	0	+4	–1
Effect +	+4	+8	+4	+3		
Effect –	–9	–5	–4	–3		

Legend: SBF = strategic business field

The expected effects can be marked on a scale from –3 to +3.
Example: Environmental development … depicts a threat/opportunity of SBF … .

Threat   Opportunity

–3   –2   –1   0   +1   +2   +3

Source: Adapted from Köhler and Böhler (1984).

Diagram 17 Cross-impact analysis

For this, possible environmental developments are placed on the rows of a matrix and the pursued or planned strategies of the important areas are placed in the columns. Subsequently, experts assess the effect of environmental developments on the areas or strategies in that they enter the assessment value of a given scale into the matrix. The positive assessment values of a scale describe opportunities arising from environmental developments, while the negative ones describe threats.

To finally evaluate the effects of events, positive and negative assessments are added up separately in each row. The value acquired by this process makes noticeable which of the various environmental events should be seen as a particular threat (high negative value) or opportunity (high positive value). The equally carried out additions across the columns allow the assessment of the important areas or their strategies across all general conditions.

The results of cross-impact analysis can be improved by the vulnerability analysis that allows the information to be extended to the event's probability of occurrence. This value raised by questioning experts is applied to the relevant scenarios and their effects acquired by the use of cross-impact analysis. By illustrating by this way the urgency of the reaction, the necessity of adjustment is indicated as well as information is generated about the importance of the events to be observed.

It can be concluded that the cross-impact analysis is generally a suitable instrument with which important areas of the organization, respectively, events, can be identified. It is however, problematic that the selection of events and areas for the evaluation is already a pre-selection. In addition, it should be borne in mind that the use of this generated information is strongly determined by the corresponding qualification of the experts.

3.1.1.2 Interaction matrix

Similar to the cross-impact analysis, the interaction matrix relates the selected areas with one another in order to identify dominant and critical cycles. Therefore, it is valued how strong the causes, which are entered in the rows, are influencing the effects, which are entered in the columns, using an assessment range of 0 (no) to 3 (strong influence) (see Diagram 18).

Active (AS) and passive sums (PS) arise from addition by row or column. Finally, the product P (AS*PS) and the quotient Q (AS/PS) are calculated and an active, passive, critical and inert value is defined.

These elements help to answer various questions.

With the active value, the highest Q figure, the element is defined which influences other areas the most but is least influenced by other areas. Thus, this variable has the greatest leverage at its disposal. Vice versa, the lowest Q figure, which is exposed to the strongest influences of the other areas but itself has the weakest influence.

The critical value, the highest P figure, indicates the area with the highest level of dependency. This exerts great influence over other areas but, at the same time, is most strongly influenced by these. Thus, chain

Active relationship To ↑ → From	1. Mot. individual traffic	2. Pedestrians	3. Traffic infrastructure	4. Tour. attractivity	5. Countryside	6. Air/noise	7. Trade/business	Active sum (AS)	Quotient (AS/PS)
1. Mot. individual traffic	–	3	2	3	1	3	2	14	1.4
2. Pedestrians	1	–	1	1	1	0	2	6	0.5
3. Traffic infrastructure	3	2	–	3	3	2	3	16	2.3
4. Tour. attractivity	2	1	0	–	1	1	3	8	0.5
5. Countryside	1	3	2	3	–	1	1	11	1.2
6. Air/noise	1	3	0	3	2	–	1	10	1.1
7. Trade/business	2	1	2	2	1	2	–	10	0.8
Passive sum (PS)	10	13	7	15	9	9	12		
Product (AS*PS)	140	78	112	120	99	90	120		

Source: Adapted from Müller and Flügel (1999).

Diagram 18 Interaction matrix

reactions are a consequence of changes to this value. This is different for the inert element, which records little influence both on and from other areas.

The interaction matrix is an instrument with which areas and events can be comprehensively and systematically examined with regard to their dependability. Particular strength lies in complexity reduction and extensive analysis possibilities. However, the expert experience that is also necessary in this case influences the value of results and is disadvantageous when the events and mechanisms are unknown.

3.1.1.3 The Delphi method

The Delphi method is a qualitative prognosis method, which aims at making relevant and uncertain events more precise. It is attempted by repeated expert surveys under step-by-step publication of the results of each round to acquire information and, in particular, to evaluate the value of extreme judgements. Anonymity amongst the participants should counteract the pressure to conform, which is otherwise expected. At the same time, however, this causes an increased risk of isolated individual prognoses. In order to avoid this, the participants are given after each round statistically prepared information on the results of the previous round.

From a general point of view, the Delphi model is suitable for the prognosis of the importance of individual areas or events. The lack of a pressure to conform is of advantage as is the possibility of allowing newly acquired information to be included in the survey.

The fact that the required anonymity only allows an indirect learning process between participants should be noted as a disadvantage. Furthermore, the Delphi method is only of limited use for complex processes. The obligation to justify extreme judgements also contributes to avoid these in view of a lack of will or ability to explain. Not to be neglected is the amount of time involved, which can be up to 6 months and, thus, is not applicable for the assessment of many events. Finally, it is important to recall that the quality of the respective moderators determines also the quality of the prognosis result.

3.1.1.4 Scenario analysis

With scenario analysis, a technology is available for the analysis of the environment as well as for the estimation of the consequences of certain strategies pursued by the organization (Kahn and Wiener, 1967). In contrast to most quantitative and qualitative prognosis methods, the scenario analysis is not based on the premise of time stability. That way, problems that have become visible through the use of traditional prognosis technologies and became especially clear in the context of the 1973 oil crisis can be mainly avoided (Kreikebaum, 1993).

Global and firm-specific scenarios are distinguished according to the considered area. Whilst the former considers general environmental scenarios, the firm-specific scenarios, which are of special interest for our analysis, explore concrete business conditions.

In contrast to quantitative trend extrapolation techniques, several possible, plausible and consistent future pictures are developed but, at the same time, illustrate the development paths that lead to these events. Therefore, a number of other prognosis techniques such as creative technologies are used secondarily. This allows both quantitative and qualitative information to be processed. In order to reduce the efforts, the number of scenarios to be drawn up is normally restricted to two or three. They should include both of the extreme future situations and, if necessary, continue to depict the current situation. Typically, the process has a seven to eight step approach and includes analysis techniques such as the cross-impact and vulnerability analysis.

The quality of the results produced by the scenario technique is influenced, to a great extent, by the qualification of experts who are responsible for the content. The same applies for the selection of the extreme and trend scenarios. Depending on the complexity and dynamics of the environmental situation, which is especially high in an international context, the problem is intensified by the non-consideration of influential factors.

The greatest advantage lies in the hypothetical description of future pictures, which, although not exact, are, however, logical. Through this, possible interactions in the various situations with their consequences are made clear independent of the probability.

3.1.1.5 Comparative assessment of analysis methods

The selected analysis techniques previously considered are all in a position to provide a specific contribution to the definition of critical areas and important events.

Whilst the cross-impact analysis and the interaction matrix have their strengths in the cross-sectional analysis, the Delphi method and scenario analysis prove to be helpful in the assessment of future important areas and events. All methods have individual strengths and weaknesses.

What they have in common, however, is that they all depend on the experience of experts. Therefore, the presence of correspondingly qualified personnel is a necessary prerequisite without which these methods can produce no helpful results.

Also critical is the fact that one relies on the experience of those who assess. This applies especially if new developments and unknown events must be evaluated. Then, the analogy conclusion based on experience has a negative impact as it does not consider unknown influences.

Also taking into account that the assessment takes place from the view of the experts and the affected organization instead of from the consumer's perspective, who's reaction is the focus of the assessment gives rise to criticism.

Of heaviest weight, however, is the fact that the methods produce no deep understanding of the respective mechanisms. The classification of an area or event by experts as critical does not explain why this is so and what specifically can be done.

Therefore, it seems useful to take Pohl's (1977) recommendation into account to concentrate on the identities of social, organizational structures in crisis management. By identities of individuals or organizations, Pohl (1977) understands a class of values, the injury of which unleashes an unavoidable and extraordinarily urgent reaction. Transferred to crisis management in tourism, this means that the organization has to identify the defining and essential criteria of the product from the consumer's standpoint and to protect them.

Nevertheless, the identification of these factors is generally not the task of preventive crisis management. Knowledge of the product positioning and the factors that influence this belong to the area of normal business management. However, in tourism, especially at the level of the destinations, there are still considerable deficits.

Finally, the analysis of relationships and beneficial circumstances between these factors and events should be viewed as the task of preventive crisis management. This is carried out with the aim of identifying important areas and events.

Therefore, the use of image transfer knowledge suggests itself to improve the analysis possibilities, which, moreover, offer the advantage of considering the aspect of increasingly important experience values.

3.1.2 New opportunities using image transfer

The concept of image transfer, is based on the assumption that associations related to the brand or product influence consumer behaviour. Thus, it is normally attempted to transfer associations already connected to a brand or a product, and which influence the consumers' behaviour positively (positive image components) onto another product. This image transfer includes associations that must be perceived with the product but must not necessarily be marked by this.

Image transfers are also taking place when negative events occur. The predominant number of negative events, if they do not result in direct, lengthy and objective destruction of the product, are only so effective because similar to a positive image transfer, they construct certain negative values or destroy image dimensions positively connected with the tourism product. Both forms of image transfer are based on the same mechanism, the only difference is that reverse effects occur. Romeo (1991), who examined the retransfer of negative information to family brands, also confirms this. He found this to be aided by the same factors that otherwise influenced positive image transfer.

3.1.2.1 Influential factors

The circumstances that favour or impede image transfer can be divided into four influential areas (Mayerhofer, 1995, p.124):

- image concepts,
- type of product and event,
- businesses and
- consumers.

In the discussion about the consumer and product spheres of activity, the last two circumstances have already been explored in depth (see Section 2.1 and 2.2). Therefore, image concepts and types of products and events are made the focal point of further considerations.

3.1.2.1.1 Image concepts

To explain the influences of image concept, Park, Lawson and Milberg (1989) distinguish functional, symbolic and usage situation-based brand concepts. Whilst functional brand concepts are based on sharing the similar physical characteristics or performing similar functions, usage situation-based brand concepts are based on sharing the same usage context, for example, camping equipment. In both cases, the consumer's image is marked by certain individual product characteristics. On the other hand, symbolic brand concepts are characterized by an abstract and holistic image. The authors trace this back to different memory structures that are the basis of these concepts.

In addition, Park, Lawson and Milberg (1989) could ascertain that the products of functional and usage situation-based concepts are perceived as similar and matching even in the absence of a brand concept. This can be traced back to the same characteristics and situations of use which form their basis. (Hartman, Price and Duncan, 1990 also come to the conclusion that the differentiation between functional and symbolic image is of considerable significance for image transfer. Hätty, 1989, who saw transfer potential in product-oriented images only if the physical product showed great similarities, came to similar conclusions. Emotional value added concepts, on the other hand, had the greatest transfer potential.) On the other hand, similarity is not seen in products with symbolic concepts under the same circumstances. Here, only a present brand name increased the perception of the product as fitting. Their similarity assessment remains, however, unchanged (Park, Lawson and Milberg, 1989).

This different transfer potential is also of interest from the point of view of negative events. They make public a fundamentally different endangered position of products with functional and usage situation-based image concepts in comparison with symbolic concepts. The initially attested low scope for image transfer for functional and usage situation-based image concepts also limits the amount of possible negative events. They can, above all, be found where a use or function reference to the product exists. At the same time, these findings make the essentially higher susceptibility to symbolic concepts clear.

3.1.2.1.2 Types of product and event

The second group of influential factors deal with the type of product and event and the relationship between the two. If the type of product is considered, the effect of image transfer is considerably influenced by the possibility to asses the product. Experience goods that are only examinable by utilization are far more suitable for image transfer than search goods with which a previous assessment is fundamentally feasible (for further influences such as age of the product, brand strengths, etc., see Chakravarti, MacInnis and Nakamoto, 1990; Smith and Park, 1992). Applied to crisis management in tourism, this means that the tourism product as experience goods is generally more susceptible to image transfer in the aftermath of a negative event.

The event, on the other hand, is assessed differently depending on how well it is remembered. An easy to remember, typical event has a clear, limited effect. Knowledge of risk research also confirms this. On the other hand, it was ascertained that incidents that cannot easily be integrated into the explanation pattern have consequences that are more difficult to estimate and cause fundamentally greater uncertainty on the part of consumers (see also Section 2.1.2.3.1.2).

The variable essential in explaining transfer possibilities, which is now an indication of transfer probability, forms the relationship or proximity of product and event. The constructs: similarity and fit are used to better analyse this.

The similarity, relevant in this case only from the consumers' perception, refers in the case of a positive image transfer to how similar product attributes, the satisfaction of needs or the use are. It was fundamentally confirmed that the possibilities of image transfer are greater the more similar two products are (Boush and Loken, 1991; Muthukrishnan and Weitz, 1991; Smith and Park, 1992). This must be transferred to the situation of a negative event as it does not concern two products but a negative event that is similar to the product benefits, its satisfaction of needs or its use. Experts perceive both superficial and more deep-seated similarities better than laymen but they assign them low significance if they are only superficial (Muthukrishnan and Weitz, 1991). This supports the previously mentioned supposition that a high personal and product-specific involvement on the part of tourists encourages a fundamentally more extensive and thorough assessment of the incident (see also Section 2.1.2.2).

In practice, the construct is of great significance for analysing the effects. If we take a look at use relationship, it explains why events have a different meaning in destinations than those that befall the tourist in his hometown. A company transport bus accident in the tourist's hometown, for example, has a different effect to a bus accident at a holiday location because the event is seen now in connection with the tourism product.

For this reason, strategies that ignore such circumstances can already be classed as unsuitable. Nevertheless, it is still quite common to compare the destination's low criminality rate in comparison with the home country of tourists, which have been victims.

The second construct, 'Fit', describes how far the product and event fit together and are perceived as matching by the consumer. Obvious matches, coming from basic benefits and competitive advantages, are distinguished from not so obvious matches. As obvious associations increase the image transfer possibility, negative events are more damaging if specific tourism associations accompany it or if the area affected by the incident is associated with tourism in general. In addition, the finding that, with the decrease of product or function-specific relation, transfer possibility increases (Chakravarti, MacInnis and Nakamoto, 1990) can be confirmed also for tourism where events perceived not limited to certain areas are quickly transferred to entire regions.

3.1.2.2 Similarity measurement

Various systems exist for the measurement of proximity between product and event, which is referred to as similarity and includes now the associations of the previously described 'fit' (for a discussion of the various image transfer models, see, e.g. Hätty, 1989; Meffert and Heinemann, 1990; Mayerhofer, 1995).

Mayerhofer's (1995) system for similarity measurement of image transfer in the wider sense makes use of the concept 'realm of experience'. This offers the possibility to use the extensive portrayal of the consumer's complex images by registering mutually objective and subjective assessment components (see Section 2.2.4). Problems that previously arose from a separated assessment can, therefore, be excluded to a great extent. Above all, the inclusion of pictures in image registration makes the recording of difficult to describe feelings easier (for the registration of feelings using pictures, see Weinberg and Konert, 1985). This is of advantage, on the one hand, not only for the subjectively assessed product in tourism but also for negative events. Those are, if not experienced directly, mainly communicated through pictures.

Furthermore, the registration of similarities is improved by its indirect measurement. Both the limited preliminary selection of product characteristics, which leads to problems, above all, with symbolic concepts and related associations and the potential danger that too much is expected of the test people is excluded (Mayerhofer, 1995).

In the first stage of measuring similarities, relevant realms of experience are raised using picture and word stimuli; this is carried out separately for brands, product groups and regions (also important in the selection of pictorial material is a comprehensive portrayal of all relevant assessment dimensions through pictorial motives). Using these three areas is also recommendable for tourism (Mayerhofer, 1995, names this inclusion of regions and countries as image transfer in the wider sense). As has already been discussed in the section about country image, in most cases, country image is greatly dependent on products and vice versa.

In the next stage, registered assessment values are transformed into multidimensional realms of experience with the help of correspondence analysis. (The aim of correspondence analysis is to portray the connection between assessment objects and the assigned stimuli in a multidimensional manner. The advantage of correspondence analysis over other procedures results from the combined portrayal of assessment objects and criteria; Mayerhofer, 1995; Backhaus et al., 1996.) In a first analysis between brand and product group image, it can be ascertained whether brand images have an independent realm of experience. This is the case if they are located correspondingly far from the positioning of the product group image.

The position within the realm of experience finally allows the assessment as to what extent it concerns similar realms of experience as well as the identification of the main dimensions responsible for this positioning. The further away an assessment object is from the focal point of the illustration, the more distinctive is the corresponding image. On the other hand, no distinctive realm of experience can be assigned to an assessment object located nearer to the focal point of the illustration.

This is made clearer by Diagram 19. The positioning of the assessment objects: **BRANDS**, PRODUCT LINES and **REGIONS** in the two most essential dimensions (the horizontal axis portrays the first, the vertical axis the second dimension) gives a first impression of their spatial proximity to one another and to the assessment criteria used. (These two dimensions explain 57 per cent of total variance in the case examined. Altogether, thirty-three dimensions contribute to the explanation of the total variance; Mayerhofer, 1995.) On the one hand, this makes the multilayered effect of the image clear, on the other, influential relationships become visible (see also the explanations in Section 2.2.4). Realms of experience are recognizable in the concrete examples of the destinations Vienna or Salzburg, which are characterized by terms such as exclusivity, noticeable promotion and enjoyment and by pictures that show a theatre box and a couple embracing each other (for other realms of experience of this portrayal, see Mayerhofer, 1995). These realms of experience also have relationships with the product groups sparkling wine, chocolate and crystal, and with the brands Darbo, Riedel and Römerquelle.

These results are improved by similarity quantification and spatial proximity to the assessment objects (furthermore, Mayerhofer, 1995, suggests the use of 'data doubling' to make the otherwise unknown

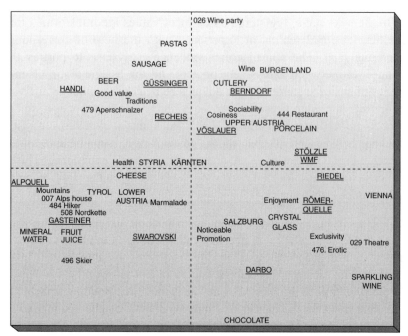

Source: Adapted from Mayerhofer (1995).

Diagram 19 Realms of experience

strengths of the profiles visible in correspondence analysis). This is especially of interest in the identification of the transfer axis. The position data acquired in correspondence analysis is further examined in a cluster analysis. Both the graphic presentation within the dendrogram and the matrix of squared Euclid dissimilarity coefficients indicate clearly the image defining dimensions, the position with regard to other products and brands as well as association with the country image.

3.1.2.3 Summarized assessment of image transfer possibilities

The use of image transfer knowledge and the possibilities of measuring the spatial proximity are also of interest within the context of negative events.

Understanding the image concepts makes the fundamental estimation of potential threat as a result of negative events easier due to the different transfer potential. This helps also to limit and prioritize the analysis and protection of important areas and the events that might affect them.

Furthermore, it offers the visual portrayal of the differences by means of the correspondence analysis and the following measurement of the similarity the possibility to not only analyse comprehensively the products in their realms of experience and to their competitors but also to indicate the important areas that influence this perception.

Negative influences coming from these products, respectively, the identified image factors, should be classed as particularly critical in the same way as interference on these areas themselves. The transfer possibilities and probabilities of a negative event can be classed as greater the closer they are to the realm of experience of the respective tourism product.

To conclude, it can be said that the use of image transfer offers new opportunities to identify relations and mechanisms between the negative events and the tourism products. Especially interesting is the fact that this instrument hardly requires the assessment of experts and complies fully with the need to use the consumer's perspective. This is particularly helpful in the analysis of new events (see Example 17).

Example 17 Not involved, but suddenly affected

How important the understanding of such negative image transfers has already become, but especially how surprisingly they affect third parties, illustrates the airplane accident of the charter company BIRGENAIR in 1996.

A charter plane with 164 German tourists on board crashed into the sea shortly after departure from the Dominican Republic. The investigations demonstrated later on that the pilots, who were of Turkish origin, had to be held responsible for the accident. Also the owner of BIRGENAIR, which was a typical low-cost carrier used until then by tour operators, was of Turkish origin as well as the CEO of the tour operator who organized the tour. Not only did all the companies involved in the accident suffer in the aftermath from the absence of tourists, but surprisingly for most, also tourism to Turkey in general, to the Dominican Republic and nearly all business handled by all foreign charter companies. This happened although there were no objective reasons.

3.2 Systems and methods of early warning

Apart from the analysis of potential events and important areas, preventive crisis management must identify latent events of importance in good time. This is achieved by generating information early on emerging developments in the organization's environment, that is, to enable the analysis of effects on the organization. Three generations of such information systems are used to achieve these aims.

With early warning systems of the first generation, shortfalls and the exceedance of threshold values should be determined and warnings generated. These systems concentrate on result- and liquidity-oriented indicators already existing. Through an extrapolation based on past data, the expected actual situation should be checked against determined targets. This procedure enables the introduction of certain countermeasures and planning corrections, but is not suitable for identifying latent crises, which means the company can only react to them. In this sense, first-generation early warning systems show shortcomings that considerably limit the scope for action of preventive crisis management. In spite of the disadvantages, these systems are still used as short-term information systems.

Systems of the second generation are based on the conviction that organization-internal and -external chance and risk areas can be covered by a series of indicators and, through observation and measurement of these, timely early warning information can be generated. As a consequence, efforts are concentrated on determining the relevant observation areas and on choosing suitable indicators. The latter must be sufficiently early in the cause and effect chain that the time interval allows a timely introduction of measures. Assuming stable environment conditions, these systems form a suitable basis for timely crisis management.

Through the early warning systems of the third development level, a new generation of systems has emerged that are based on the finding that it is difficult to ascertain complex environmental developments using systems of the second generation (based on causal relationships). Their main focus are strategic surprises, that is, future significant differences in information that influence strategic planning. Strategic surprises are based primarily on discontinuities, which are difficult to predict, but that have the quality of announcing themselves through the so-called weak signals. Systems of the third generation, therefore, concentrate on the timely detection and evaluation of these weak signals.

If these systems are assessed comparatively, it becomes clear that the objective is always the same: to provide the organization with information about changes in the environment as early as possible and to help to estimate the consequences. Although it became clear that early warning systems of the first generation cannot provide any suitable support for preventive crisis management, there is no doubt that the second and third generations are capable of this. Their applicability to crisis management should be made clear with the help of the situation matrix in Diagram 20.

For situations within the first cell in Diagram 20, indicator-based early warning systems prove to be the most suitable tool. The choice of usable indicators is relatively easy to make, just as the timely indication of a negative event is also relatively certain.

For the cases in the second and third quadrants in Diagram 20, indicator-based systems are to be considered as partially suitable. In the case where the importance of the area is known, but it is not possible to put the threatening events in concrete terms, it depends above all on the type of area and the relevant environment whether a indicator-based solution is possible or whether third-generation systems must be used.

The situation is similar with known events, which as a rule can be detected by indicators. The special challenge in this case lies much more in the correct interpretation of the possible consequences. Therefore, the use of exclusively indicator-based methods would be insufficient here.

		Events	
		Known	Unknown
Areas	Known to be important	Second-generation systems	Second- and third-generation systems
	Not known to be important	Second- and third-generation systems	Third-generation systems

Diagram 20 Suitability of early warning systems in the situation matrix

For the fourth quadrant in Diagram 20, due to the high number of unknown components, only third-generation systems can be used.

This emphasizes the fact that both indicator-based systems and early warning achieved by the identification of weak signals offer a suitable preparation for promising preventive crisis management.

3.2.1 Indicator-based early warning

Indicator-based early warning systems use measurable indicators through which observable change should give timely hints about events that can otherwise only be detected at a later stage. The construction of those systems is carried out in a step-by-step approach (see Diagram 21).

3.2.1.1 Determination of observation areas

Out of the huge array of possible areas for observation, those particularly important or critical for the specific aims and markets of the organization have to be selected. The determination of these areas has already been covered extensively, as has the fact that these observation areas can be both within and outside the organization (see also Section 3.1).

3.2.1.2 Determination of early warning indicators

In order to ensure that they have good early warning qualities, it is necessary to choose indicators that will point, in good time, to essential changes in the environment. In addition, they should allow clear statements to be made regarding the consequences the organization has to expect with the exceedance of the tolerance value, as well as remaining important over a longer period of time. In addition, when choosing the indicators, it must also be considered whether future regular data collection is economically justifiable.

Various methods are suggested for choosing early warning indicators:

- Pümpin (1980) suggests the identification of suitable indicator cause and effect chains. By looking at the factors that precede a negative event, it is possible to work backwards systematically to the future indicators. An additional analysis at each choice stage by means of the cross-impact analysis is to be recommended so that only the most important preceding factors are included.

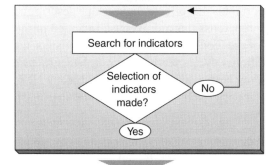

1. Determination of observation areas for the identification of threats and opportunities

2. Determination of early warning indicators for each observation area

Search for indicators

Selection of indicators made?

No

Yes

3. Determination of target value and tolerance for each indicator

4. Determination of tasks of the information processing office(s)
   – Receive and check warning signals
   – Process
   – Forward early warning information

5. Arrangement of information channels

Source: Adapted from Hahn (1979).

Diagram 21 Development stages of an indicator-based early warning system

The complexity of crisis situations and the multitude of possible dependencies mean that an exclusively causal determination of the indicators is only to be recommended to a limited extent.

■ Another method is deduced from feedback diagrams. This, based on Gomez's (1981) system-theoretical approach, sees the symptoms as part of a complex system determined by diverse influences. To identify the causes of a particular problem situation, this is set first of all in relation to the essential influential factors and then the type of relationship is put in concrete terms (in addition to positive and negative relationships, other important-seeming aspects can be considered such as strength, long-term nature or cause area of the influence) (see Diagram 22).

What is important is that effect relationships describe a cycle situation through which repercussions are likewise included in the analysis. The improvement of the feedback structure in further steps through the integration of additional cycles leads to a complete structure model of the problem situation. Not only is the relevant subject well structured but it is also easy to see if certain factors have a stabilizing or strengthening effect on the system as a whole.

For the final determination of indicators, the various identified, influential variables of the feedback model are examined and evaluated in the previously described interaction matrix (Diagram 18). The variables

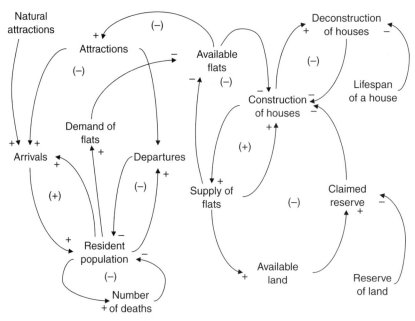

Source: Adapted from Gomez, 1981; Copyright by Paul Haupt Berne.

Diagram 22 Structure of a feedback model for analysing population growth in a holiday area

identified as active and critical are especially suitable as early warning indicators.

3.2.1.3 Indicators for specific areas

3.2.1.3.1 Indicators for the political environment

Many crises in international tourism are caused by negative events that have their origin in the political environment of the destination. Traditionally, these risks are especially important in foreign trade where they – described as country risks – have already often been the subject of examinations.

Below, two important information services that process information from the political environment and, as a result, make indicators available will be covered.

3.2.1.3.1.1 Business Environment Risk Index

The Business Environment Risk Index (BERI) is one of the best-known indices in foreign trade. It is based on a multidimensional concept and it predicts and evaluates business climate and political stability in 130 states. (There are single- and multi-dimensional point-evaluation systems. In the former, the evaluation only concerns a single criterion, whereas multidimensional methods cover individual components that are normally judged by country-specific panels of experts, evaluated according to the gravity of the problem and summarized into a total value.) Three times a year, the qualitative and quantitative data upon which it is based are raised, evaluated and finally aggregated to an overall assessment.

The BERI comprises three components: the Operations Risk Index (ORI), the Political Risk Index (PRI) and the Remittance and Repatriation Factor (R Factor).

The ORI serves to evaluate business climate and concentrates on fifteen factors that impede the realization of profit abroad, that is, it indicates the investment climate. The index is based on the evaluation of over 100 experts from banks, industrial companies and government offices, whereby at any given time five to ten experts, with comprehensive lists, assess a country they know well according to set criteria. The scoring of the factors evaluated ranges from 0 (unacceptable conditions) to 4 (very favourable conditions). The ORI for each country is made up of the sum of the arithmetic mean of the criteria evaluated by the experts (with the total point score for the ORI, PRI and the R factor, there are four classes of risk: 100–70 points = low risk, 69–55 points = moderate risk, 54–40 points = high risk, 39–0 point(s) = unacceptable risk).

The PRI serves to assess political stability in a country. It covers ten criteria; eight describe the causes of instability and two describe symptoms. Political scientists and sociologists are predominantly enlisted as experts for the evaluation, whilst business people are consciously avoided. In this case, the possible scores range from 0 (extraordinary problems) to 7 (no problems). A further thirty points can be allocated to criteria of particular importance (the division of the risk classes is identical to that of the ORI).

The R Factor covers a country's ability and obligation to pay and evaluates the possibilities of converting capital and profits into other currencies in order to transfer them (the relevant regulations of the country, which could trigger a transfer risk, are evaluated to the same extent as the balance of payments, monetary reserves and foreign debts). In contrast to the other subindices, the R factor is based on predominantly quantitative data.

The overall result of the BERI is the classification of a country into one of the following categories:

1 Business transactions not recommended. Advise against all business relationships.
2 Suitable for trade only. The situation in the country allows no investment. Only short-term transactions without movement of capital are recommended.
3 Suitable for profit-independent payments only. Realization of profit via the transfer of know-how or licences only is to be recommended.
4 Suitable for investment; investment of capital recommended. Problems in relation to conversion of currency or transfer of dividends are not expected.

The BERI has come in for criticism because it has been noted that certain quantitative statements, for example, from international organizations such as the World Bank, in spite of all efforts, are only internationally comparable to a limited extent (it has been criticized that some criteria have been assessed using an interval scale when they are only ordinal; different criteria are strongly correlated and the weighting of the criteria is firmly laid down; Meyer, 1987). In this respect, this criticism is to be seen in relative terms, as it refers to the absolute comparability of countries with each other and much less to the relative change of a particular country. It is the latter that is principally interested in early warning, because the BERI should be used for the identification of deviations over the course of time.

For this reason, and because it is published at short regular intervals, the BERI constitutes a completely sensible instrument for the judgement of political risks to tourism.

3.2.1.3.1.2 Travel advice

Travel advice from the Foreign Offices of the most important tourism source markets should be seen as a specific information system for tourism. The information generated by them is aimed, in the first instance, at tourists and only secondly at tourism organizations (see Diagram 23).

In the United States, information for tourists about other countries is made available through the US Department of State's Consular Information Program (see http://travel.state.gov). Basically, Consular Information Sheets are available for each country. They are a regular and

US	Consular information		Public announcement		Travel warning
UK	Country advice				
	Advice against travel unless on essential business			Advice against travel in any case	
DE	Country and travel advice				
	Security advice			Travel warning	
AT	Good security standard	Risk of security			Travel warning
		Alleviated risk of security	High risk of security	Very high risk of security	
FR	Advices for travellers				
	Advice against travel unless on essential business			Advice against travel in any case	

Diagram 23 The system of travel advice in major source markets

129

comprehensive description of essential topics to do with the country in question, that is, political instability, criminality, terrorism, medical care, etc. In this case too, the information is placed in the public domain and tourists are expected to make up their own minds [see http://travel.state.gov/travel_warnings.html (19 December 2002)]:

> Consular Information Sheets do not generally include advice, but present information in a factual manner so the traveller can make his or her own decisions concerning travel to a particular country.

Travel Warnings and Public Announcements complement Consular Information Sheets. If, on the basis of the information available, the State Department judges travel to a specific country as too risky for Americans, travel warnings are published, which advise against travel to this country in general.

Public announcements are dependent on events and are given when a significant threat to the security of American travellers is triggered by unforeseeable events.

The Travel Advice Unit of the Foreign & Commonwealth Office in Great Britain provides two kinds of information regarding tourism. A lot of important but rather general information for the most significant travel destinations is made available through consular information material.

In comparison, travel advice notices are given with the following objective:

> ... to help British travellers avoid trouble, especially threats to their personal safety arising from political unrest, lawlessness, violence, natural disasters, epidemics, anti-British demonstrations and aircraft safety.

There are two classifications of travel warnings: they advise British citizens either against '... all travel ...' or '... unless on essential business ...'. In both cases, the general situation is described and the warning justified.

The German Foreign Office assesses the situation with the help of more than 200 consular representatives for all the countries of the world.

Travel advice from the Foreign Office consists of a classification and a description of the situation together with appropriate recommendations. In politically sensitive areas, the information must be authorized by the appropriate permanent secretary. The evaluation process, which was initially carried out on a 3-month cycle, has since switched to a 12-month cycle that is only broken when there is an event worth reporting on.

The classification of travel advice can lead to security advice or a travel warning. As a rule, the latter is only used when the country in question has lost monopoly of the use of power. The Foreign Office stresses explicitly that the information is only provided to help travellers assess the situation; it should not take away their personal decision. In particular, responsibility is not accepted for any legal consequences relating to the travel advice.

In comparison to the information that goes into the BERI, information from Foreign Offices has different advantages. First, with its direct relationship to tourism, it is much more in tune with the needs of travellers. In addition, the Foreign Office takes all national components, that is, the country of origin of the tourists, into account and bases its judgement on these points. In terms of the issue of terrorist threat analysed earlier, this interpretation is particularly valuable if the terrorist activities are aimed at the tourists' country of origin and therefore, contain a national component (see also Section 2.1.2.3.1.4). Furthermore, the countries mentioned have a network of consular representatives that no other organization or company can provide (see Example 18).

Example 18 The Bali attacks in the Travel Advisories

On 12 October 2002, a bomb attack in Bali's popular Kuta Beach area killed 182 people (among them: 56 Australians, 17 British, 12 Indonesians, 6 Germans, 6 Americans, 5 Swedish, 2 French) and injured hundreds of others, nearly all of them foreigners. The following charts show how these attacks were seen and classified as dangerous by the respective ministries in major source markets.

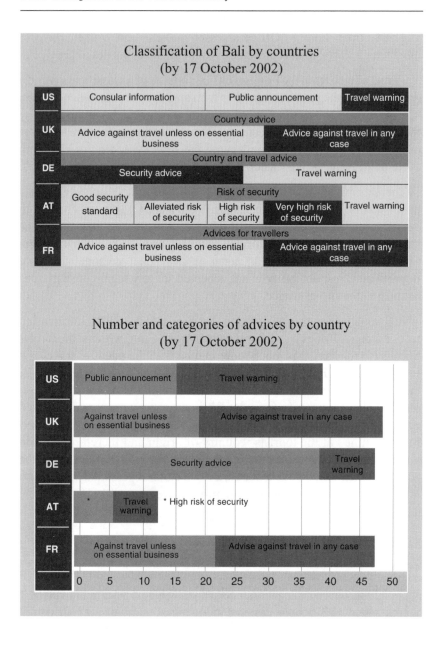

The down side is that the assessments, despite the breadth and relevance of the information provided, are subject to political and geographical restrictions. Since the economic consequences of a warning can be considerable, there is no doubt that the assessment is subject to political control. This can lead to two types of bias (Sharpley and Sharpley, 1995):

1 in order to punish the actions of a country, tourists are so influenced by a comparatively over-negative representation that they stay away from the destination;
2 on the other hand, so as not to endanger good relations with the country in question, comparatively positive classifications are given despite an unfavourable security situation.

Both situations are disadvantageous and undesirable because they do not convey the objective facts correctly. (This is particularly significant if, because of the given warning level, there is a higher signal effect, which may also bring legal consequences with it. In other words, the text version does indeed describe the circumstances but the classification of the report is too high.) However, a multitude of countries have committed themselves to conveying this information objectively, like, for example, the Member states of the WTO who adopted the Hague Declaration on Tourism, the Manila Declaration on World Tourism and the Global Code of Ethics for Tourism (see Example 19).

Example 19 Travel advice in the Global Code of Ethics for Tourism

The Member States of the World Tourism Organization adopted the Global Code of Ethics for Tourism in 1999, during their General Assembly in Santiago, Chile. The Code was later on also adopted by the General Assembly of the United Nations. The important role of governments when in comes to travel advices in times of crises and the necessity that the media reports as objectively as possible are pointed out in paragraphs 4 and 5 of Article 7:

  5. Governments have the right – and the duty – especially in a crisis, to inform their nationals of the difficult circumstances, or even the dangers they may encounter during their travels abroad; it is their responsibility however to issue such information without prejudicing in an unjustified or exaggerated

manner the tourism industry of the host countries and the interests of their own operators; the contents of travel advisories should therefore be discussed beforehand with the authorities of the host countries and the professionals concerned; recommendations formulated should be strictly proportionate to the gravity of the situations encountered and confined to the geographical areas where the insecurity has arisen; such advisories should be qualified or cancelled as soon as a return to normality permits.

6. The press, and particularly the specialized travel press and the other media, including modern means of electronic communication, should issue honest and balanced information on events and situations that could influence the flow of tourists; they should also provide accurate and reliable information to the consumers of tourism services; the new communication and electronic commerce technologies should also be developed and used for this purpose; as is the case for the media, they should not in any way promote sex tourism.

A further point that must not be neglected is that the tourism destination cannot be comprehensively judged from the capital of each country, where the diplomatic representatives are based. This geographic restriction can, however, be remedied by the supplementary information provided by a company's own network of representatives, tour guides and incoming agencies.

Taken as a whole, travel advice is a suitable indicator of political risk. On the plus side, in particular, are international comparability and the economic and comprehensive collection of information. Since it is possible to compare travel advice from different Foreign Offices, political influences can be balanced out to a certain extent. The public's ever greater heeding of travel advice also means that travel advice is an indicator of public opinion and customer reaction.

3.2.1.3.2 Ecological indicators

Ecological risks are often the cause of crises in tourism. For the most part, these events were foreseeable. Despite frequently complex scientific contexts, causal dependencies are known that allow measurable indicators to be deduced, which point to the approaching changes in good time. (Natural catastrophes, such as cyclones, storm tides, floods and earthquakes, are different and their predictability, i.e. early warning instruments, cannot be covered here. See instead, e.g. WTO, 1998b.)

Possible uses of ecological indicators include giving advice on the dangers of water pollution or the threat of an avalanche in a winter sport area (WTO, 1996c, 1998b). Triggered warning announcements mean that countermeasures, or at least precautions, can be taken, which protect tourists against the danger.

Therefore, it must also be emphasized that in most cases ecological risks are very easily observed by indicators (an overview of further indicators can be found in WTO, 1996b). The important thing here is a timely analysis of noteworthy events and areas.

It must, however, be noted that some ecological risks, those caused by human beings, for example, a ship disaster, are not foreseeable either by means of indicator-based systems or third-generation systems. However, since the consequences in this case are easy to judge, the direct observation of the events is less important than the perception of this area as critical and the introduction of appropriate planning measures in the form of contingency plans (see also Section 5.2).

3.2.1.4 Collecting and analysing information

Once the indicators have been chosen, regular collection and analysis of data must be guaranteed.

Basically, there are two possible ways of collecting the data: first, the data can be obtained from someone else. This is particularly suitable when the data an already collected for other purposes. Since this form of data collection is, in principle, better than personal collection, the only thing left to check is whether the collection intervals meet the needs of early warning systems.

If is not possible to get someone else to collect the data or if the collection intervals are too far apart, personal collection of the data is the only option available. This is more expensive and is caused by the initial establishment and acquisition of the necessary procedures, staff training, and maintaining the equipment in the future (WTO, 1996b). In addition, the data collectors need to have the necessary abilities in order to ensure the validity and reliability of the data.

Regardless of the form of data collection, target values and tolerance thresholds for each indicator must still be assigned before the first collection of data. Measurements can then move within these limits without a warning being triggered (Hahn, 1979; Krystek, 1987; WTO, 1996b,c). If these limits are exceeded, the reports are forwarded to the appropriate management level in a manner agreed beforehand.

It is to be recommended that warnings be classified in terms of exceedance level so that management can interpret the forwarded warning announcements more quickly. Both the target and tolerance values and the classification of the warning announcement must be decided upon when the indicator is chosen.

3.2.1.5 Interim conclusion

Finally, it remains to be emphasized that indicator-based early warnings represent a completely suitable possibility for identifying negative events in good time.

The most essential requirements for the success of such systems lie in the choice of suitable indicators. This presupposes though that either the important events are already known or at least the important areas of the organization have been identified. Most suitable are indicators for those cases when both the event and the important area are known, whereby the prospect of success increases in direct proportion to the causal relationship between indicator and event.

The advantage of indicator-based early warnings is that they are comparatively easy to handle and are suitable for a large amount of the problems of crisis management in tourism, which have their origin in the political or ecological sphere. Since the metrological recording of ecological indicators can often be automated, it is possible to have permanently reliable and, as a rule, cost-effective data collection.

The standard solutions available for the political environment, such as the BERI or travel advice, offer a good basis for early warning. Whilst the particular advantages of the BERI come in useful above all for travel companies who invest abroad, travel advice offers a cost-effective alternative or supplement.

In addition, it becomes at this point already clear that the choice and observation of indicators depend above all on the size of the organization, its financial capabilities and the threat potential.

3.2.2 Early identification of weak signals

An essential prerequisite for the use of indicator-based systems is the presence of causal relationships between the observed indicators and the events. If this causal logic is not present, systems of the second generation normally fail. As a consequence, the events are classified as surprising and unpredictable. This situation appears increasingly more often in an environment that is becoming ever more complex and turbulent and it hinders the initiation of countermeasures.

Most of these surprises can be traced back to the so-called discontinuities. These are changes of direction, that is, new phenomena, for which there is no experience available. This hinders their detection and assessment considerably, but does not make it impossible. The suddenness of discontinuities affects rather less their occurrence and rather more their perception and assessment.

In principle, it is assumed that discontinuities are embedded in a longer-term development process and that they are influenced by human actions and interests. This is what the early identification systems of the third generation are based on.

In this context, Ansoff's (1981) concept of weak signals is of central importance. The aim was to show that even at a very early stage there is an opportunity for the management of a company to be proactive. It is, therefore, necessary to interpret and handle information in good time in an ongoing process of reality construction regarding peculiarity and effect. For the introduction of successful reaction strategies, it is imperative not to wait until the information has been well defined and its meaning assessed beyond all doubt. By that time, the affected organization is usually left with limited possibilities for reaction.

Ansoff (1981) clarifies this surprise problem for the organization by differentiating between available and used information, which he presents in three levels:

- The first information level concerns all of the information available – the 'general knowledge' – in the environment of the organization.
- The second level refers to the information available within the organization. This can be identical to the first level in terms of quantity, but differs qualitatively as a rule, because the organization does not pay attention to part of the information. The difference between this information and that of the first level comes from the abstractness, uncertainty and the lack of context of the received information, which does not permit a logically consistent assessment of the information. Consequently, the reaction gap is a result of the fact that information is processed but not correctly classified as relevant to the organization.
- The third level describes information that is finally only used by company management. Despite its availability, information may still be discarded as too abstract, without correlation to the experiences and without relevance for the type of problem in question. This difference between available and used information can be called decision gap.

According to Ansoff (1981), it must be a consistent aim of management to analyse and reduce both types of information gaps. The concept of weak signals, however, focuses specifically on the deficiencies from the first to second information levels, that is, on the increase of information from the corporate environment of importance for the organization.

There has been fundamental criticism of the concept, however. This focuses predominantly on the practical realization of the recognition of weak signals. On the one hand, the knowledge from problem-solving psychology is cited, according to which weak signals cannot be recognized due to the reduction strategies that a person uses because of his limited capacity to process information (Konrad, 1991). On the other hand, the concept is criticised in relation to knowledge from perception psychology that a person basically observes only those stimuli whose content and relevance he can judge (Konrad, 1991).

Both criticisms are justified in terms of normal human behaviour. However, the systems evaluated in the following text try exactly to overcome these human deficiencies. This means that even ways of think-ing and interpretations, which seemed irrelevant and deviant at the time of the analysis, should be paid consistent and systematic attention (this is in accordance with the aim of creativity techniques, that is, to develop new ideas, thoughts and solutions to problems, in order to overcome thought barriers for unstructured information).

3.2.2.1 Selected methods of early warning

3.2.2.1.1 Discontinuities survey

In a discontinuities survey, experts are questioned on the probability of occurrence and effects of particular events by means of a questionnaire. The aim is the assessment and classification of these incidents as threats or opportunities for the company.

Whilst the probability of occurrence is collected as a percentage, the experts class the effect using an interval scale from -4 for very unfavourable to $+4$ for very favourable. The two assessments must be carried out independently of each other.

Following the survey, the results are presented two-dimensionally and calculated '95 per cent probability ellipses and rectangles' are added. In this way, possible 'runaway' opinions can be identified. It is these opinions that are of particular interest. Through ensuing examinations, it is attempted to discover whether these deviations from the majority of the estimates should be put down to a consciously made new interpretation of the circumstances – a possible weak signal – or to another source of error, such as lack of understanding or expert knowledge. To do this, the motives of the outsiders must be examined more closely through individual deep analysis.

A further result of this analysis is the interpretation of the spread of the presented opinions. If this is high, this means that the opinions vary greatly and that there is great uncertainty about the possible effect of the events. In this case too, deep analyses must be used for further clarification.

The particular value of the discontinuities survey lies in conveying this outsider information, which does not sink without trace in a condensed value.

This system does, however, have some weak points. First, a minimum of twenty to thirty qualified experts is required. There is the selection of events through the pre-formulation of questions, which makes the quality of the results dependent upon the selection of events included. In addition, it should be noted that the separation of outsiders' opinion is practically impossible if the spread of the statements is high overall.

3.2.2.1.2 Portfolio analysis

In practice, portfolio analysis had already been well disseminated when it was further developed for analysing weak signals. All variations of this analysis were based on the system-theoretical finding that the development of an organization is dependent on the particular interrelation of different internal factors with the corporate environment. Further development took place under the conviction that no new subsystems needed to be introduced in order to locate weak signals.

The general aim of portfolio analysis is to assess, in a comparable way, the delimited 'strategic business units' of a company in various situations with regard to their opportunities and threats. The expert assessments are finally portrayed in a portfolio matrix. However, since an accurate determination of the position requires a consensus from the participants in the assessment process, the uncertainties and dissenting opinions are normally lost.

At this point, further development begins. In place of an exactly accurate determination, the deviations in the assessment are consciously emphasized, by carrying out an area positioning. In this way, the assessment discrepancies are no longer hidden from the management, which can process them further in a much more targeted way.

The size of the relevant blurred areas allows conclusions to be drawn about the degree of uncertainty in the estimations. These blurred areas can be interpreted as weak signals. To analyse them more closely, however, management must discuss the causes of the dissenting assessments. Only this deep analysis can provide information about what is causing the weak signals, how they are to be assessed and what effects are to be expected (see Diagram 24).

In contrast to discontinuities surveys, portfolio analysis has the advantage that it avoids the necessary pre-selection of events. In this way, an

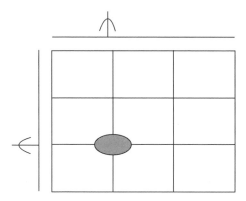

Source: Adapted from Kirsch and Trux (1979).

Diagram 24 Area positioning in the portfolio analysis

early restriction on the alternatives considered is prevented. In addition, a probability assessment, which is quite problematic, in particular with regard to events that are dependent on many influences, is spared. However, the high distribution of the portfolio analysis in practice and, therefore, the available knowledge, is useful.

In this case too, one disadvantage that stands out is the need for appropriately qualified experts. This problem is reduced at least in the case of already practised portfolio analyses. Nevertheless, deep analyses are still necessary and these require a thorough knowledge of the company on the part of the interviewer.

3.2.2.1.3 Structural trend lines

The development of structural trend lines as an instrument for early detection of weak signals goes back to diffusion theory and paradigm change findings (Krampe and Müller, 1981). Thus, new findings and models of behaviour spread in a kind of infection process, at the beginning of which there is an innovator or an event, and at the end, a widespread impact. The decisive point is the assumption, upon which the considerations are based, that distribution processes follow a specific pattern, which is shown as diffusion function or structural trend lines. In these patterns, which are not universally applicable but rather area-specific, the starting point for the formation of entrepreneurial early warnings can be seen.

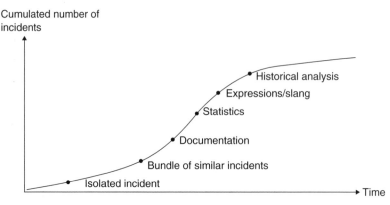

Source: Adapted from Krampe and Müller (1981).

Diagram 25 Structural trend lines for triggering events

Through the observation and analysis of the important observation spheres of the company, representative distribution functions are developed. In the beginning, when there is still little experience available, they can be improvized. Diagram 25 shows a visualized trend line for the effect of accidents, in this case, tanker accidents.

Using the forerunner of events and developments of interest discovered in this way, an observation system can be installed, which recognizes, earlier than before, similar events or developments or those from the same area of origin. The aim is to detect the change in the phase from isolated to cumulated incidents. Due to the purely qualitative nature of the information at this stage, this is not easy, but a later identification would barely still permit promising measures.

An example from social political legislation makes this point clear. Normally, the Scandinavian countries play a leading role in social welfare legislation. They, and in particular Sweden, therefore, come in the first position on structural trend lines for this area. If draft bills are introduced in these countries, this gives the first signal for similar processes at a later date in other countries. It should be noted, however, that in tourism, this national leading role – in particular, in terms of consumer protection – is attributed to Germany.

In summary, structural trend lines help to identify in good time a multitude of events in the environment, through the observation of forerunners. The quality and reliability of this system depends to a large extent on the adjustment of the trend lines to the specific peculiarities of the organization. This, in turn, is time consuming and the ongoing observation of the changes requires experienced and trained personnel.

3.2.2.1.4 Interim conclusion

All of the methods mentioned above try, through systematic procedures, to identify weak signals, which, due to typical human behaviour, cannot otherwise be determined. Overcoming these normal human reduction techniques automatically means that their use, especially when operated continually, quickly becomes complex.

For these methods too, experts and their experience represent a critical variable. This disadvantage is most easily avoided by the portfolio analysis, which has been highly disseminated as a planning instrument. A presentation of the Delphi method and scenario analysis, which can both be used in the early detection of weak signals, has been passed over because these assessments have unchanged validity (see Sections 3.1.1.3 and 3.1.1.4).

All methods were developed for the strategic planning of the organization. This considerably limits their usability for processes with shorter development cycles. In particular, quick changes in the social environment, which are shown to be responsible for many crises in tourism, can only be recorded with difficulty. This is surely the reason why, in practice, such early warning processes are only used to a limited extent.

3.2.2.2 New developments for early warning systems

3.2.2.2.1 Computer-supported early warning systems

In continuation of the manual analytical methods, there have been attempts at automating early warnings. The aim of these processes is to transfer the complex observations and evaluations, which go hand in hand with constant and comprehensive early warning systems, onto computers.

The various developments were strongly characterized by the performance capabilities of the appropriate available computer systems. One of the newer developments is the WARNPLAN system, put forward by Schulten (1995). First of all, freely chosen observation areas are defined and entered into the system. These should cover all essential internal and external threat and opportunity areas of the organization. Finally, the observation areas are transferred into an interaction matrix in which the relevant influence effects are assessed by the user with values between 0 (no effect) and 3 (strong effect). Whilst the qualities of the interaction matrix have already been covered, its strength at this point lies, above all, in the classifying and clarifying function of effect interrelation.

Between two and ten representative indicators are chosen to register the various influence factors of the observation areas. In addition, the organization is split into up to twenty strategic business areas. The system then automatically produces indicator matrixes for each of the observation areas. In addition to its strengths, the direction, that is, classification as threat or opportunity, is assessed. As a result, strategic business areas that appear either as promising or threatened are identified.

In principle, the system provides automatic support in the identification of critical areas and events, whereby weak signals can only be detected to a limited extent. It is not, therefore, a system that guarantees automatic early warning (Meffert, 1994). The advantage that this system can only be served by one person is, at the same time, a disadvantage as the comparable collection of information from several people is not possible that way.

Kelders (1996) has put forward an approach to early warnings that is based on the analysis of a large amount of external text sources. The collection component imports the information from the environment and converts it into, and saves it in, a machine-readable and machine-processable format. The data collection can handle both scanned text documents and online information from news agencies. The comprehension component transfers the information into a processable format that enables the system to understand the semantic content of the piece of news. From the total amount collected, the filter component filters out all information relevant to the user's 'interest profile'. The interest profile is defined to correspond with the user's area of responsibility and should guarantee the supply of all information relevant to this area. For the practical implementation of the comprehension and filter components, the programme TOPIC is used, which examines texts more by content and less by words. Documents classed as relevant to the user are automatically forwarded by the forwarding component.

In summary, this means that the system described makes it possible to organize the flow and saving of information. In this way, the information overload can be combated by the filtering and targeted forwarding of information. Thus, the system gets closer to the aim of generating decision-triggering impulses.

One criticism that needs to be noted is that developments in as yet un-modelled areas cannot be identified and assessed. What is more, the limitation to text information from selected sources has a negative effect on the findings obtained.

3.2.2.2.2 Early warning opportunities by defining the contextual conditions of matters of social concern

The social environment of a company is, to a considerable extent, responsible for determining which events trigger a crisis at the affected organization. This influence is strengthened by the fact that companies ever more frequently have to justify themselves concerning social problems and this means that they themselves become a topic of debate.

In order to have a better understanding of the underlying processes and to develop helpful courses of action for the affected companies, models that analyse matters of social concern are produced. They do not really focus on the prediction of events, but rather on classifying whether or not these events pose a threat to the organization.

The various scientific approaches that deal with matters of social concern are all part of a development process that is split into phases (an overview of the various lifecycle models of matters of social concern in literature can be found in Dyllick, 1992). In these phases, an examination is carried out to determine which influence factors are beneficial or harmful to development. The development of a matter of social concern will be described using Dyllick's (1992) five-phase lifecycle concept.

Triggered by an event that is in discrepancy to predominant expectations, a matter of social concern (need for action) is established in the latency phase. It is generally assumed that social matters of concern exist when '... there is a difference between the expectations about the state of reality and the perceived reality of a social area, which is considered to be intolerable' (Dyllick, 1992, p. 241). In the following emergence phase, the events occur increasingly often whilst, because of this, scientific discussion certainly increases. This discussion remains limited to experts. Only in the upturn phase is the matter taken up by interest groups (which have now become stakeholders) and brought to the attention of the public. These groups pursue the goal of achieving public awareness of the matter and influencing public opinion. In this phase, politicians join in with the opinion-forming process and the mass media also becomes active. Apart from setting the exact aim, the discussion revolves around the 'politically valid version of the matter'. In the maturing phase, the political/normative regulation of the matter is pursued, whereby expert opinion is once again at the fore. At the same time, media interest diminishes and public awareness stagnates. Finally, in the downturn phase, the completion of the regulations clearly moves back to the fore and public interest decreases.

The lifecycle model is, in this form, predominantly a tool for determining the current status of a matter of social concern and estimating its dynamics. The state of development, that is, the phase in which a matter is, can only be determined by indirect criteria such as the type and size of the participating groups, the social or political status of these groups or the dissemination and frequency of media reports that influence the degree of public awareness. Whether and how the organization should react is derived from these findings. It is generally true that the more important and urgent the matter, the higher the degree of public awareness reached.

It is clear that, with this procedure, the focus is on the analysis of contextual conditions and not on the prediction of events. The basic conviction is that a current event cannot be considered in isolation from its background variables when attempting to estimate its possibility for development. The basic contextual conditions, which result from a combination of social value position, public sensitivity and the agenda of relevant stakeholders, are to be considered much more.

In this context, Mathes, Gärtner and Czaplicki (1991) speak of the terms of reference according to which an event is classified. In concrete terms, they recommend that general coverage for all important company areas be analysed using quantitative content analysis in order to define these terms of reference. In this way, by means of separate encoding, news items, reports and commentaries are evaluated as to whether they contain positive or negative assessments, whether positive or negative characteristics or consequences are attributed to them, whether the events can be influenced by people and whether the experts are credible or not. Surveys, scenario techniques or regular contact with and observation of the interest groups are also suitable methods for determining the terms of reference.

Action taken at the pit accident in Borken (Germany) provides practical confirmation of this because it was proved that the classification of the accidents and risks as unavoidable and acceptable could be put down to the positive terms of reference for coal as a source of energy. The otherwise normal demands, that is, to improve security or even to abandon coal mining, were omitted (Mathes, Gärtner and Czaplicki, 1991).

Its significance is also highlighted by the events relating to the sinking of the Brent Spar oil-loading rig. Although Shell worked at that time with various early warning systems, none, however, indicated the upcoming conflict with Greenpeace nor could generate a warning. Even the additional analyses that were undertaken at a later stage would have changed this assessment.

This can be explained, above all, by the fact that it concerned an action planned by humans as a surprise, which, similar to terrorist action, can only be identified with difficulty, but which can be predicted as theoretically possible. By the cessation of the events in their terms of reference, however, whereby the North Sea – as a polluted area – has already often been the subject of environmental–political discussions, another conclusion would have been reached after the onset of the action. The so-called terms of reference were clearly recognizable and classified as negative; consequently, the later effects of the events were foreseeable. Herein lies a particular problem for most organizations, because it is difficult for people who are directly involved to recognize such slowly developing terms of reference and to assess them correctly.

It remains to be emphasized that an analysis of contextual conditions differs from the previous models because its approach is geared towards observed events. This procedure is of high practical relevance because, for many crises, it is less about the timely perception of events as unfavourable incidents, but rather about the correct estimation of further effect developments.

3.2.3 Summarized evaluation of possibilities for early warning

A prerequisite for successful crisis management is the timely recognition of negative events. This requires a systematically operated and well-functioning early warning system.

The analysis of various early warning possibilities reveals that both indicator-based systems and those based on weak signals are appropriate (Krystek and Müller-Stewens, 1992, point out that certain environment events are, therefore, only interpreted as weak signals, because no indicators have been determined for this early warning area).

The particular advantage of indicator-based systems is that they are simple to maintain. In addition, they offer the possibility, to a certain extent, of determining measurements by machine. This form of early warning seems suitable for the area of ecological risks. For the social and political environment, the usability of indicators is determined by the time horizon of the early warning. If this is more towards the short term – which is true for tour operators without direct investment in foreign countries – indicators offer completely useable early warning information.

The observation of weak signals is particularly important for the social environment. It is to be noted that, for destinations and international tour operators, these are in the source market of the tourists. The low use of third-generation systems is basically due to the high amount of time required and their complex handling. Furthermore, classic methods have been shown to be deficient in evaluating rapid changes in the social environment.

The automation of early warning and the inclusion of qualitative information in the assessment and evaluation process is a sensible and important step but, as yet, there are no satisfactory solutions to the problems involved. Machine comprehension of language nuances and uses has not yet reached a level that can guarantee reliability. Also, the important analysis of foreign language texts for international tourism is not practicable.

There is also the fact that none of the systems mentioned is suitable for processing and evaluating both quantitative and qualitative information at the same time. This does not mean, however, that the paths taken are not the right ones. It is the only way of collecting and processing a large quantity of information without limiting it beforehand. Moreover, typical human deficiencies in the perceiving of information, which actually hinder the detection of weak signals, are almost completely eliminated. Developments in artificial intelligence and in the portrayal of knowledge and machine comprehension of relevant scientific areas will lead to further advances in the future, which will make the most sensible use of these systems possible. However, these can only be but a supplement to human assessment.

The use of findings made in the framework of the lifecycle model of matters of social concern seems interesting in practice. Apart from the determination of the development process stage, analysis of the terms of reference allows statements about future development to be made. This offers – also totally in accordance with Ansoff's demand for graded reaction – the best possibility for avoiding crises.

4

Strategic measures of crisis management

All those responsible for the success and failure of organizations have to tackle with the different aspects of their corporate strategy if they want to achieve lasting success in the market. This includes timely analysis of the possible consequences that negative events have on these strategies.

The aim of generic strategy is to lay the foundations for the long-term success of an organization. Competitive advantage, which must be considered from the customer's point of view, embody a meaningful customer benefit, which ensures that the company, or product, permanently and clearly distinguishes itself from its competitors. Competitive advantages have, in order to be strategically significant, to fulfil three basic requirements:

- they must provide an important performance feature for the customer;
- actually be perceived by the customer; and
- be sustainable, that is, difficult for competitors to imitate.

In their basic form, there are two types of competitive advantage: cost advantage and differentiation advantage. Whilst the former achieves advantage by charging a lower price in comparison with the competition, for products with the equivalent benefits, differentiation advantage requires the company to create a unique benefit that justifies a higher price in the eyes of the consumer (Porter, 1998a).

Based upon the competitive advantages, cost advantage and differentiation advantage, and taking into account the scope of activities, three generic strategies can be distinguished: cost leadership, differentiation and focus strategy. (Porter, 1998a, points out that a company can use strategies of cost leadership and differentiation at the same time completely successfully, if it is in a position to keep the different company units strictly separate. The essential criterion for this separation is the consumer's perception.) The last strategy uses elements of cost advantage and differentiation but is geared towards particular market niches (Porter, 1998a).

4.1.1 Cost leadership

With a cost leadership strategy, the company offers a comparable standard product at a lower price than its competitors. It is important that the product attributes are perceived by the customers to be identical or equivalent to that of the competition.

The basis of this strategy is the company's ability to produce at a lower cost than its competitors. The causes of this are diverse and can be based on the learning curve effect, particular preference conditions or technology exclusive to the firm. When following this strategy, the company must be aware that there can only be one cost leader in the sector, unless a focus strategy is followed for a certain segment of the market.

As a consequence of the necessary comparability of the products comes interchangeability. This possibility for substitution could be a considerable problem if there is a negative event. If one of the basic product characteristics is harmed by the negative event, the basis for cost advantage – comparability – is lost. Substitution products would be bought in place of the affected product. The same effect occurs when personal safety is threatened by a negative event (see Section 2.1.2.3.1.4). In this case, the perception of risk increases and the tourism product in question is – after the exceedance of a certain threshold value – no longer seen as comparable (for threshold values, see also Section 2.1.2.3.2).

Since in both cases the necessary requirement of the comparable standard product is no longer fulfilled, the effect of cost advantage is lost. The only way to keep up this strategy in the long term and to make the product still saleable is with a price policy. This instrument can balance out the higher sensitivity by lowering the price. The leeway is, however, restricted because of the given cost structure. The consequences of lowering the price are short- and medium-term collapses in profit (there are also further consequences that limit the use of price instruments; see a discussion on this in Section 6.4).

The long-term problem lies in sustaining the cost advantage, since this is based as a rule on higher relative market shares. A change can cause a vicious circle effect: diminishing market shares, and disappearance of cost advantage, leading, in turn, to a limitation of the price policy. This effect can finally lead to the stage when a cost leadership strategy is no longer sustainable and must be changed completely.

The great susceptibility and limited possibilities for action in the framework of coping crisis management illustrate how important crisis precautions are in this case. They must be used to prevent the onset of such events, or to bring them to an end in good time.

4.1.2 Differentiation

With a differentiation strategy, the company's aim is to differentiate itself from its competitors through the characteristics of the product in such a way that it allows the firm to charge a premium price for it. Differentiation strategies are very important in tourism because the majority of products are interchangeable and there is little room for improvement in terms of objective differences (see also Sections 1.3.2 and 2.2.3). In contrast to a cost leadership strategy, several companies in the same sector can successfully follow a differentiation strategy.

The differentiation can be achieved both by material and immaterial changes to the product. It should result in a concentration on the immaterial differentiation – the 'signal criteria' – that are very important for tourism's end consumer market. The aspect of material differentiation – 'benefit criteria' – that occupies an important position in the business travel market shall not be considered here. The decisive thing is that as many customers of the sector as possible perceive the differentiation as unique and important. Only then is it possible for the organization to achieve long-term above-average profits that exceed the additional expenditure on differentiation.

The exact immaterial differentiation is carried out by developing and implementing an experience value strategy (Weinberg and Konert, 1985; Kroeber-Riel, 1992, 1993a). This strategy gives the product an image profile that has unique, distinctive and sustainable advantages over competing products. A clear dividing line has to be drawn between this strategy, which normally goes along with a 'Total Quality Management' strategy, and active publicity, which, in contrast to the experience value strategy, does not build 'company-specific preferences' (Konert, 1986; Kroeber-Riel, 1992).

To be relevant, experience value strategies must take the values, lifestyle and experiences of the target group into consideration. (According to Kroeber-Riel, 1993a, it must be checked whether the experience profile: has psychological relevance, is not in conflict with the company philosophy, appeals long-term to the target group and therefore keeps up with lifestyle trends, makes an effective positioning possible in comparison to the competition and is able to be introduced not only through advertising, but extensively.) Since image profiles can only be generated and established through ongoing and long-term conditioning, experience value strategies must not only be valid in the long term, but also developed with an eye to the future. This means that the development must be accompanied by a serious discussion of future social trends.

A point not considered until now is the demand for consistency and freedom from contradiction of experience-oriented positioning, also from the point of view of future negative events. Even at the conception and assessment of possible experience profiles, it is important to think about certain events that are more likely or more threatening than others.

This can make a considerable contribution to preventive crisis management. This can be clarified with an example: in image studies, Sweden as a destination is characterized, above all, by factors such as clean, easily accessible countryside and nature that is not overcrowded. It was this image that made Sweden particularly susceptible to the nuclear catastrophe of Chernobyl because exactly these dimensions were affected by the catastrophe (Hultkrantz and Olsson, 1995).

A further point to consider is based on the finding that destinations are strongly influenced by typical clichés and overgeneralizations (see also Section 2.2.4.1). This must likewise be considered while developing conceptually the image profile. The spillover effects of a regional image let even destinations that have not been affected by events suffer indirectly from it (see the example in Section 2.2.4.2). Indeed, in a normal situation, independent positioning goes hand-in-hand with increased expenditure; however, this effort pays off through a certain crisis resistance (in the practical implementation, the image dimensions, which are responsible for the whole region's image in the source markets, must be included, analysed and finally changed in such a way that an independent sustained positioning is achieved) (see Example 20).

This means that experience value strategies and experience profiles should be designed from the start in such a way that they can only be spoilt with difficulty by potential events. Even if crisis circumstances as a consequence of negative events cannot be totally excluded, there is the possibility of ruling out certain susceptible concepts in good time.

It remains to be emphasized that it is, above all the long-termness that demands a cautious and considered planning of the experience value strategy also from the point of view of negative events. Investment in the development of immaterial differentiation is considerable and the company only makes a return on its investment in the medium or long term, in the form of higher profits. Developed experience value strategies and built-up image profiles are not really changeable in the short term, likewise destroyed and influenced image profiles mean the loss of considerable investment. For the tourism market, in which the number of products with interchangeable benefits is increasing, and which is, therefore, more and more dependent upon immaterial differentiation, this kind of prevention is becoming ever more important.

Example 20 Egypt and its beach destinations

Although while developing the product of beach holidays as a new product area, Egypt did not explicitly consider it under the aspect of strategic crisis management. The later consequences proved that these decisions had positive results seeing it from the point of view of strategic crisis management.

The various terrorist attacks of 1992/1993 led to a negative overall image of Egypt. However, consumers in the various source markets did not perceive the beach destinations 'Sinai' and 'Red Sea' related to this image. This strategically unplanned separation into two products, independent of each other as far as image was concerned, was quickly recognized and used by the destination and tour operators alike.

Since then, the destinations on the Sinai and the Red Sea have been offered without making reference to Egypt. All textual and pictorial information was removed from advertising to prevent a connection between Egypt and the beach destinations.

4.1.3 Focus strategy

The focus strategy concentrates on a narrow segment and within that segment attempts to achieve either a cost advantage or differentiation. While the basis for the first strategy variation is different cost behaviour, the latter requires the existence of special customer needs. When there is sufficient structural attraction of the segment within the sector, several companies can, like with the differentiation strategy, follow a concentration strategy, as long as their target segments are different.

Typical for tour operators is concentration on segments of the supply market – destinations – or on segments of the sales market. From the point of view of a destination, the concentration strategy refers to the choice of certain customer segments.

Since concentration strategies go back to cost and differentiation advantages, observations made above are valid here too. However, in this case there is also the fact that a concentration on a particular segment

155

follows. Dependence on the choice of this segment limits the leeway for action considerably as is shown by the example of the German tour operator 'OFT Reisen'. The tour operator concentrated on study trips to Egypt. Therefore, there was considerable dependency on the development of this customer segment and of the destination. As a consequence of the attacks in 1997, participant numbers fell from over 30 000 to just 10 000 customers per annum. In the same period, turnover fell from 31.6 to 10.6 million Euro, contributing to a change of emphasis to other customer segments (FVW, 1996, 1997, 1998; Lettl-Schröder, 1998a). Pure beach holidaymakers, whose share rose from 20 to 82 per cent, replaced the normal 80 per cent share of student tourists (Dörr, 1999). As a consequence of these developments, the tour operator had to give up some of its independence.

In spite of the risk that goes with a focus strategy in terms of negative events, this strategy is becoming ever more important as an answer to the individualization of consumption. In order to introduce measures in the framework of crisis management, it is recommendable to use the international dimensions of these developments. Since this fragmentation of segments also happens internationally, there are intercultural target groups, which show similar needs structures and can be appealed to in the same way. If it is considered that negative events are also judged differently due to national and cultural differences, it makes it clear that there are reaction possibilities. These require an appropriate international capability for action, which, if it is not yet given, can be a preventive crisis management measure.

Finally, it must be emphasized that especially for this strategy variation, the extent of the precautions must increase as smaller the market basis is. If this is not done in an area as sensitive as tourism, unforeseeable negative events lead with greater probability to an abandonment of business activity.

4.2 Strategic actions as preventive crisis management measures

Besides the adaptation of generic strategies, four different strategic actions can be considered. They do not exclude, but rather clarify the different directions of possible measures. Since the actual success is basically strongly determined by the type of event and specific situation, the following discussions can contribute to a choice decision, but they are not universally valid. The four variations are:

- diversification,
- transfer,
- insurance and
- self-bearing.

4.2.1 Diversification

Diversification is understood to be the preventive measures that serve the distribution of company activities with the aim of scattering and keeping the consequences of negative events low. Through the distribution of activities on several profit sources, a balance is created that can compensate for the harming of one source. The strength of the counterbalance is determined, above all, by its perceived complementarity to the event in terms of crisis susceptibility.

For the horizontal diversification, that is, changing the sales programme through products that are complementary to the organization's existing activities, the viewpoint of the tourists must be taken into consideration for this balance assessment. What has been considered a balance from a risk-political viewpoint is determined by the event, or rather by how the event is perceived (see Section 2.1.2). If it has a regional reference, another destination creates the balance, if it has a functional reference, then the balance is achieved by a type of product. If the negative event shows a reference typical to the company, switching to another company is suggested. The diversification means, in this extreme case, the buy out or new formation of the company.

Vertical diversification, which refers to the preceding or succeeding stages in the organization's production process, is recommendable when dependencies on external suppliers, which are of existential importance in a crisis, come to light. Through vertical diversification, self-sufficiency (autarky) is achieved, which helps in the avoidance of crises. The completed relationships must not lead to a complete takeover of the other company. They can also be carried out in the form of strategic alliances. Through this interconnection, economic dependencies are achieved which serve the same purpose.

The downside of a diversification strategy from a risk viewpoint is that the company's resources are not used efficiently in a normal situation.

In addition, there is a danger that a distinctive personal image achieved through specialization will be watered down. Above all, it is important to note that diversification, particularly when it should create a balance as horizontal diversification, is a dynamic, never-ending process. This is to be carried out in close coordination with early warning systems (see Example 21).

Example 21 The case of Gambia

Gambia is a country of 1.2 million inhabitants in West Africa. As a former British colony, the country became an independent State within the Commonwealth in 1995. Gambia's economy is poor and depends almost entirely on the cultivation and exportation of groundnuts in the form of nuts, oil and cattle cake.

Tourism has rapidly grown and reached in 1994 more than 78 000 international tourist arrivals, thus becoming an important foreign currency earner. However, the distribution of this tourism proved to be quite uneven.

From the beginning, Gambia depended heavily on tourists from the UK. At this time, more than 60 per cent of all charter flights were originated in the UK and resulted into 52 000 out of the 78 000 arrivals the country had in 1994.

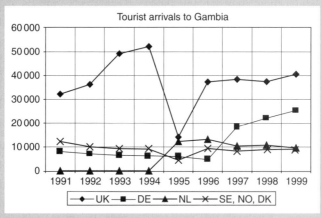

This special dependency proved to be fatal for the economy. In November 1994, the Travel Advise Unit of the British Foreign and Commonwealth Office issued the third travel advice within half a year concerning Gambia. Due to a military coup 5 months earlier, the political situation was considered unstable and travellers were recommended to postpone their travel plans, if possible.

In consequence, all British tour operators except one, cancelled immediately their operations and ceased the entire scheduled winter programmes. The Scandinavian operators followed quickly and left. Finally, only the Dutch and German tour operators continued to act normally. The number of British tourists dropped by 73 per cent to 14 000.

This loss had an enormous impact not only on the tourism-related sectors but on the entire Gambian economy. According to Sharply and Sharply, more than 1000 jobs disappeared in the hotel industry and at least eight hotels had to be closed. People indirectly dependent on tourism such as taxi drivers and souvenir sellers also lost their primary source of income. The sudden drop in revenue from tourism-related sources such as sales tax, airport departure tax and import duties led to a serious lack of foreign currency. In addition, with the abandonment of charter flights, who used to serve as freight carriers, products could no longer be taken out of the country and another 1000 jobs were lost in the country's largest horticulture business. Besides this, other sectors such as agriculture and brewing also suffered severe economic declines.

These heavy aftermaths of the issued travel advice can mainly be traced back to the particularly strong focus of Gambia's tourism industry on the British market and its dependency on a few tour operators. While in times of tourism growth this strategy is highly successful, in times of crises the problems rise disproportionately and can create a very serious situation. To prevent this, a further diversification on markets and products is recommended. As the case of Gambia showed, the arrivals of German and Dutch tourists remained stable during this travel warning, but nevertheless their share was too small to compensate the withdrawal of the British visitors.

Source: Sharpley, R. and Sharpley, J. (1995): Travel advice – security or politics? In *Security and Risks in Travel and Tourism, Proceedings of the International Conference at Mid Sweden University*, pp. 168–182.

WTO: Yearbook of Tourism Statistics (various years).

4.2.2 Transfer

The activities of transfer aim at, even before the onset of a negative event, transferring the consequences onto another economic subject. This basically requires that there is an object as target for the complete or partial unloading of the risk. This object can, on the one hand, be part of one's own group of companies, by which the risk is transferred through a spin-off. On the other hand, the consequences can also be externalized, by transferring them onto an economically and legally independent object.

4.2.2.1 Spin-off

The aim of the spin-off of certain identified risk areas in one's own company is to transfer the risk to a subsidiary company. If this activity has already been performed in the company, this happens in the form of legal independence. If the activity is new, a new establishment takes place. Spin-offs come particularly into question when activities are considered to be especially risky, but nevertheless important for one's own group of companies.

By maintaining the ownership function, the established company keeps essential company controlling functions over the spin-off. At the same time, the economic risk as a consequence of negative events is primarily limited to the assets of the spin-off (liability of the parent company, which results in financial penalties, control contracts, etc., will not be covered here).

Another advantage is that through the transfer of consequences a higher personal responsibility within the spin-off company is achieved. This is especially justified when the effects are influenced by the reaction of this area. Consequently, the spin-off offers the possibility for a more flexible crisis management determined by the area, from which the whole group can profit.

It is, however, not recommendable to use this strategy in order to get rid of easily solvable, generally known problem areas. In such a case, the measure can be identified and judged as a deliberate ploy and finally become the subject of social concern. As a result, the financial and legal consequences remain limited to the subsidiary, but damage to the image of the parent company cannot be ruled out.

4.2.2.2 Externalization

Through externalization, there is the possibility of transferring the consequences of the negative events onto an area that does not belong to the group, or rather, to the company's area of influence.

This can happen through measures of risk sharing and contractual risk limitation. Risk sharing includes the alternatives of splitting the risk or of risk alliance. In both cases, several companies share the financial consequences. While this sharing only concerns the negative deviation from aims for risk splitting, in a risk alliance, financial success is also shared.

In the framework of contractual risk limitation, attempts are made to transfer the consequences of a negative event silently onto the business partner using additional contract conditions or special contracts. While there are no explicit contractual references for silent transfer, the other two forms go into risks in detail.

Regarding the basic contractual rules for risk adoption in tourism, the different aspects of the effects of negative events need to be considered (see Chapter 2). Above all, it must be taken into consideration that, when it involves basic benefits that can be substituted, negative events cause customers to buy substitute products relatively quickly. Therefore, the use of non-binding agreements, that is, short-term terminable contracts is the goal. The possibly unfavourable contract conditions that result are preferable to a future, possible complete loss of revenue. The latter is to be suspected, since the interchangeability of the products leads to a 'ruled out – not put off' decision regarding concrete choice of product. (The tour operator 'Öger Tours' used this possibility in autumn 2002 in view of a possible war with Iraq. His contracts with service providers and hotels in Turkey did include a clause allowing him, in the case of war, to return capacities previously reserved.)

The consequences will be different for tourism products that form their competitive advantage on basic benefits and cannot, therefore, be substituted. Here, a higher risk threshold value can be observed as can the existence of a 'putting off' rather than 'ruling out' behavioural pattern. The latter ensures that the desire to travel will be made up at a more favourable time, which accounts for a quicker 'recovery possibility'. The higher risk threshold would also mean lower initial consequences. In this case, longer-term contracts are a possibility, which pay off above all when more favourable conditions about the contract period can be achieved.

To what extent it finally succeeds in transferring the risks onto a market partner is determined by general competition conditions; above all, the market power and negotiations strength of the company that is interested in externalization. In addition to the advantages of transferring the economics risks, it is also true in this case that by completely or partially adopting the risk, the market partner's interest and efforts strengthen the onset possibility and keeps the consequences of negative events low. In this respect, this action is especially justified and sensible when the contract partner has influence over the developments.

4.2.3 Insurance

Insurance against the possible consequences of a negative event is a special form of transferring risks. The basic consideration of insurance is the combination of risks, which threaten a single person or company, in a contractual solidarity committee, in which it is balanced.

With the completion of an insurance policy, the insurer is obliged to adopt the financial consequences of a particular risk. For this, the policyholder pays a regular premium. From the point of view of the policyholder, this means that a risk that is difficult to calculate and prevent can be transferred into firmly calculated costs. (A special form of cover can be observed repeatedly in practice, namely the intervention of the state. Destinations or large companies can almost always count on the fact that extensive damage or extraordinary events are blocked. This, which amounts to insurance for the organization, is difficult to comprehend; it is based on political considerations, the feeling of solidarity and also control interests. Even when they are not calculable in advance, they can still be worked out with a certain probability, which is determined by the profile of the organization or destination, the type of events and the political–economic situation.)

If the effect of a negative event can be borne by a solidarity committee, the risk concerned must meet various requirements:

- randomness of the onset and extent of the damage;
- measurability of the extent of the damage;

- sufficient number and independence of the damaging event, which guarantees that a risk balance within the group is possible;
- unambiguousness of the damage obligation.

This explains some limitations that restrain the usability of insurance as a strategic action. Above all, it is to be taken into consideration that the so-called speculative risks, which count as entrepreneurial risk, cannot be included in an insurance contract. The loss of a possible future market position is, therefore, not insurable. Furthermore, the fact that some negative events due to legal conditions or narrow distribution of the risk are not insurable must be taken into consideration (in Germany, e.g. it is prohibited to insure against kidnapping).

In addition, it should also be noted that through insurance neither probability of occurrence nor the magnitude of damage of a negative event is reduced and that the general insurance of all possible risks is contrary to the profitability goal of a company. In this respect, it is, above all, risks with low occurrence probabilities but serious consequences, that should be covered by insurance, as long as it is possible to insure against them.

4.2.4 Self-bearing

Despite all the precautions that the company can introduce there remains an area that – not in the end due to the novelty of the event – can only be borne by the company itself. On the part of the company, security measures can be made by forming liquid and non-liquid reserves. In both cases, it should be taken into consideration that it concerns purely passive measures that are besides cost-intensive.

Apart from this, active action is also possible in terms of an acceptance strategy (Dyllick, 1992). The aim of this strategy (which originates from the stakeholder management) is to have a good and anticipating look at possible events and the position of the organization in the social sphere. To do so, the environment of the organization is examined for potential events and themes of importance for the company (see Section 3.2.2.2.2).

Even before these matters are the topic of a debate, they are picked out as a central theme by the company and contact with the main stake-holders is sought. The significance and classification of and the solution possibilities for this event are discussed in form of a 'real dialogue', at which the differing viewpoints of the stakeholders are considered to be legitimate (Dyllick, 1992). This form of discussion of the possible negative events should finally increase the understanding and with it the acceptance within society. At the same time, it should be shown that for certain events only limited solution possibilities are known or in existence. But, nevertheless, the interested company underlines, like TUI did this for years with the environmental forum, its high interest in cooperating with stakeholders to improve the situation.

It should be also considered that it is not about a purely communicative concept. The acceptance strategy should be understood much more as a fully comprehensive management task, which goes far beyond the announcement of viewpoints. The approach is less aimed at eliminating information deficiencies, but rather at eliminating credibility deficiencies (this also makes it clear that this central task of the organization cannot be delegated to the powerless and ineffective public relations department; Dyllick, 1992; Becker, 1993). On the one hand, it is the task of the company to represent these events in the relevant contexts. On the other hand, the company must also be ready to actively put in its own resources in order to work out practical solutions.

In principle, this course of action is not without risk, because once initiated communication processes are no longer controllable by the company in their advanced stages. Nevertheless, the initiative function, with the contribution of functional solution approaches, contributes considerably to preventing a later emotionalization of the discussion and allowing the company to keep the initiative. In this way, a considerable contribution to the limitations of the effects of negative events is achieved, which is of advantage for both the company and the public.

4.3 Crisis handling strategies

A further area of strategic considerations concerns the determination of the basic courses of action for crisis handling. The aim of the crisis handling strategy is the influence of the developments of the effects caused by the negative event with the aim that a neutralization of the effect is achieved. At the same time, or as soon as possible, the crisis causing problems should be gradually eliminated. The target area of the strategy should be wide and include all spheres of activities (see Sections 2.6 and 6.2).

In literature, there are various approaches for handling strategies. A fundamental distinguishing feature is the form of coping behaviour, which has influence over the choice of instruments, problem solution orientation and the point of time when the activities start (an overview of the different strategies can be found in Holzmüller and Schuh, 1988; Dyllick, 1992; Meffert and Kirchgeorg, 1992; Hauser, 1994). The forms of a crisis handling strategy can lie between two extremes, offensive (oriented towards finding a solution) and defensive (oriented towards resistance).

4.3.1 Offensive handling strategy

The aim of an offensive handling strategy is the timely implementation of measures that eliminate and contain the causes and related effects of an identified problem area. This requires a functioning early warning system, which aids, even with vague and imprecise information circumstances, the implementation of reaction measures (see also Ansoff, 1981, who ascribed appropriate reaction strategies for the difference levels of uncertainty regarding the information circumstances). In addition, the organization must be prepared, voluntarily and independently, to admit to all spheres of activities, especially customers, stakeholders and the state, that something has not worked as expected.

A not necessarily occurring but often initial result of an offensive handling strategy is an immediate increase in public interest and media coverage. Since the affected company is right in the middle, the result is an unfavourable intensification of the crisis. This intensification is accompanied by a negative influence on the image, which the company must accept.

An offensive handling strategy does have some advantages: first, it should be noted that a negatively influenced image does not necessarily mean a loss of credibility (credibility is then important when the facts of the case are confusing and complex). The recipient of the information can then, because of the existing credibility, do without the complete information, that is, overcome uncertainty. Since credibility is the preliminary stage for trust (credibility stands for content-wise pure conveying of information, trust for agreement as regards content) continually credible company communication is of considerable importance in attaining trust in a crisis situation. These two areas, image and credibility, should be considered separately. The credibility of an offensively acting organization rises, or at least stays the same, in large parts of the public, among its customers and the media, especially because it acts. This is the basis for the future use of the marketing instrument, whose effectiveness is essentially influenced by credibility (see also Section 6.6.1.2). Second, it should be taken into consideration that, in spite of the short-term intensification of the crisis situation, the company still has strong communicative control, to a relatively large extent the facts provided by the company are used and speculation is mainly avoided. Third, this type of strategy contributes essentially to shortening a crisis since there is no staggered publishing of 'new revelations' that stimulate public interest.

In order to implement an offensive handling strategy in good time, the distinction of influences on the image and credibility loss, but also the future value of credibility, must be recognized. Only then is it possible to overcome resistance within the organization, which is based on the following consideration: 'why should an intensification of the crisis and a negative influence on the image be brought about by ourselves and consciously when it is possible that the incident will go unnoticed?'

The latest point at which an offensive crisis handling strategy must be introduced so that it receives an appropriately advantageous assessment is related to the 'voluntary nature of the decision'. The social environment will no longer adjudicate the benefits of this strategy to the organization once state institutions intervened.

An essential part of the offensive handling strategy is the effort to eliminate the causes of the problems. Despite huge efforts, there will remain always some problem areas for which this is not possible; for example, natural catastrophes. In such cases, a long-term organized offensive strategy can be used to accept and capitalize on the event. The aim is to change negatives into positives (see Example 22).

That this idea of capitalizing on an initial image problem is not so far-fetched is illustrated by the development and current importance of such destinations as Pompeii, Waterloo or Verdun, which are today places of contemporary history. In all cases, the negative events created a competitive advantage whose basic benefits were not interchangeable with another destination.

Example 22   Turning negative events into positive – the wildfires in Yellowstone and Glacier National Parks

In 1988, the most severe wildfires in the entire history of the Yellowstone Park broke out. A total of 50 fires started in the National Park together with 198 fires in the greater Yellowstone area. More than 25 000 fire fighters could not avoid the burning of more than 1.2 million acres and 36 per cent of the entire park's area. Hundreds of animals died, park facilities and infrastructure such as roads, campgrounds and cabins were destroyed.

As fire seasons and the peaks of visitor arrivals to National Parks coincide in the months of June, July and August, visitors suffer usually heavy restrictions such as closings of roads and campgrounds to avoid wildfires. These limitations and the intensive media coverage of the fire disasters have regularly led to a shortening of the tourism seasons.

Now, the affected National parks, such as the Yellowstone or Glacier National Parks, put heavy efforts into changing the visitors' awareness regarding fires. People mostly consider fire as a destructive and powerful force, an unpredictable enemy to plants, animals and men. For many, the aftermath of a fire is a blackened landscape that represents death and destruction. However, wildfires have occurred in the northern Rocky Mountains region at regular intervals since the last Ice-Age. Fires have shaped most of the natural beauty of landscapes, diversity of vegetation and wildlife. They are very important within a functioning, balanced ecosystem and have very positive impacts on the evolution and natural stimulation of plants and forests. Many plants and animals cannot even survive without the cycles of fire to which they are adapted. Fires break down organic matter into soil nutrients and rejuvenate soil with nitrogen from the ash, thus creating a new fertile seedbed for plants. With less competition and more sunlight, seedlings grow quickly and vegetation recovers fast.

The interpretation of the phenomenon and understanding of the impact and importance of fires within the ecosystem moved to the centre of the parks' objectives. The park managers succeeded, indeed, in turning the bad image of the destroyed landscape and fear of fires into a new attraction for visitors.

The Glacier National Park, for instance, has set up an exemplary educational programme for its visitors. It includes detailed exhibitions on the role of fire in the ecosystem in the Park's Visitor Centres, Road side exhibits in areas that have recently been burned and evening slide illustrated and non-illustrated talks at campground amphitheatres. Rangers discuss the impacts of fires on all hikes and offer special trails into burned areas so that tourists can see and get directly in touch with the aftermaths of a fire. In the event of a fire, special activities and information are set up. Various publications, which describe the pros and cons of fires in ecosystems are sold at the visitor centres. Television and radio spots inform and create awareness for this topic, even for people who are not visiting the park themselves.

These educational segments create not only a new consciousness, but also lead to the acceptance of further restrictions connected with fires. When in the year 2000 new heavy fires broke out, visitors could easily understand the managers' regulations and according to the Glacier National Park statistics, there was no real decline in numbers of visitors. Although some visitors cancelled their trip to the park due to the fires, others were encouraged to visit the affected area and were keen to learn about the fires.

Comprehensive surveys document generally consistent visitor-use patterns of the landscape before and after the fires of 1988 in the Yellowstone National Park. With a total of 2.7 million recreational visits to the Yellowstone Park and 1.6 million to the Glacier National Park in 2001, visitors provide an inevitable economic income to the communities, their businesses and their employees. Therefore, the Parks not only continue to work on shaping the new awareness of fire but are also interested in establishing a long-term relationship with their visitors, as the following slogan of the Glacier National Park proofs:

'Come along! There are many discoveries to be made in a post-fire area. And, come back again – next year, in five years, ten, in a different season – and witness the transitions, the increasing diversity.'

The explanatory brochure 'Wildland Fire in National Parks'

Source: US National Park Service.

It is very much the question of the time that determines the transition from voyeurism to contemporary history, from horror and shock to interest and culture. Titanic-trips or trips to the battlefields of Korea and Vietnam show that these time intervals are becoming ever shorter (see Example 23).

Example 23 The Southampton Titanic Walk

The sinking of the luxury cruise liner R.M.S. Titanic in 1912 can probably be considered as one of the earliest and best-known disasters in tourism. Only 3 days after leaving the port of Southampton for its maiden voyage, the liner struck an iceberg and sank in the freezing Atlantic. About 1500 persons lost their lives.

Until today this tragedy has not lost any of its mysticism and fascination. It has become a source for innumerable novels, stories and film versions. The success of the film Titanic produced in 1997 and starring Leonardo di Caprio and Kate Winslet shows the ongoing interest of the world in this accident. With more than 17 million spectators in Great Britain, 18 million in Germany and even about

104 million in the United States only during 1998, it became the most successful film in the entire history of cinema.

Southampton, a city in the South of England with some 211 000 residents, was the Titanic's port of departure. As the city lost more than 500 inhabitants, mostly crew members, it felt and continues to feel very strongly related to the disaster. Numerous memorials dedicated to those who perished were unveiled shortly after the incident throughout the city. But neither tourists nor tourism planers thought about converting the incident into a tourist attraction. The sorrow and shock as much as the close time relation of the disaster prevented all imaginations of this kind. In addition, tourism destinations and objectives differed very much from today.

Today, as tourists' habits and perspectives have changed, Southampton has discovered the benefits and the potential of this past tragedy and uses the advantages of its world-known fame successfully to attract more tourists to the city. The visitors are encouraged to experience the original setting and review the beginning of the famous story. Southampton's City Council designed the self-guided Titanic Walk, which leads visitors to all key memorials and landmarks related to the story of the doomed liner. During more than 1 hour of walking, tourists will pass more than ten points of interest, among them a first-class hotel, where some Titanic passengers spent their last night before boarding or the pub were many took their last beer before going on board.

The Titanic Walk

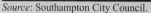

Source: Southampton City Council.

4.3.2 Defensive handling strategy

With a defensive handling strategy, it is attempted, despite the knowledge of the circumstances, not to act upon them, but to wait to react, in order to then bring the situation under control. The aim is to evade the crisis as far as possible and not to intensify the situation with one's own actions.

The activities of the affected organization are put off until the post-active point in the crisis (the post-active point is defined as the time when the actual event is no longer in conflict with the general, public interest; see Section 6.1.1). They can, for example, concern product modifications that eliminate the problems afterwards or leave the product as unrecognizable. Particularly important in this context is also lobbying, which helps, above all, to reduce the consequences in the political sphere. In an extreme case, the situation is resolved completely and comprehensively by quitting the market. Quitting the market is particularly to be recommended where business development was unsatisfactory, no kind of improvement could be counted on in the future or market position is too weak.

The essential advantage of a defensive handling strategy is that an intensification of the crisis by the company's own actions is avoided. On the downside, a defensive strategy can not only result in loss of image but also – in contrast to an offensive strategy – loss of credibility. The reason for this is that if a company reacts reluctantly and only when it is forced to do so, it is not believed that there is really an interest in finding a solution to the problem. In the end, the negative influence on the image and loss of credibility is determined, apart from by the peculiarities of the events, above all, by the behaviour of stakeholders. If they prove – more or less conclusive assumptions are sufficient – that despite knowledge of the circumstances and the possibility to act on them, that inaction prevailed, the damage will be considerable.

Furthermore, it is important to realize that by using a defensive handling strategy the company gives up its natural role as leading information provider (see also Section 6.6.1.2). In this way, the company loses a fundamental advantage and boosts the importance of other information sources. It should also not be neglected that the duration of the crisis will tend to be lengthened by this, namely when the successive leaking of new information continually ignites public attention.

171

In practice, the defensive handling strategy can be often observed. This is certainly also affected by the fact that offensive handling strategy and information providing come with unfamiliar attention in the initial period. In this respect, the behaviour is really a natural reflex reaction that values the initial negative influence on the image higher than the possibly not considered long-term loss of credibility. The frequency of its use does not, however, correspond with its success. Therefore, using a defensive handling strategy is only to be recommended in few cases. This is, for example, the case of situations in which there is conclusive proof that the negative event occurred, but it can neither be explained nor eliminated and the company is sure that criticism will be limited and will soon pass.

The greater scope with regard to handling and structuring but also the sensibleness of voluntarily taking on social responsibility means that an offensive handling strategy has a lot going for it. It not only promises bigger chances, but it is sooner paid off in the long-term (Berger, Gärtner and Mathes, 1989; Hauser, 1994; Wiedemann, 1994; WTO, 1998b). If the crisis is understood in such terms, it offers the chance to develop the organization further and ensures the influence in the various spheres of activities.

4.4 Summarized assessment of the strategic aspects of crisis management

The above discussions make it clear that a multitude of approaches exist through which decisive foundations for crisis management can be laid at a very early stage.

It is of particular importance that the organization is already in the initial phase of the strategic planning process aware of those negative events that threaten, diminish or destroy competitive advantages. This requires that positioning and competitive advantage are known at the same time. Considerable deficits are still predominant here, especially for destinations, and passive positioning can often be observed (for the passive positioning of destinations due to a lack of strategic planning, see Haedrich, 1998b). Finally, the knowledge obtained must be used in good time in order to guarantee that a competitive strategy followed in the long term is not made invalid by such influences (WTO, 1980, stressed that a one-third of all tourism plans never came to fruition; over 40 per cent of the plans drawn up were impossible to implement).

Moreover, strategic actions concerning the configuration of the company, the contractual relations to other companies and its own appearance can contribute to limiting, or rather easing, the effects of negative events. If the measures taken make also the causal areas of negative events at least jointly responsible in economic or legal terms, this will effectively limit the consequences of negative events.

In a complete assessment, it should be taken into consideration that strategic actions and strategic handling strategies embody the fundamental moral and ethical position of the organization. Since these are subject to particular attention in a crisis situation, their design should receive appropriate consideration. Independent of which position is finally chosen, the determination of the strategy should be seen important enough to be done at a calm moment and weighing-up all the possible consequences.

In particular, it should be checked that the crisis handling strategy, as only a temporary strategy variation, is reasonably compatible with long-term corporate strategy. Despite the necessity to realize short-term advantages within the framework of crisis handling, deviation must be kept as low as possible. A clear limit can finally be seen where the guiding function of the chosen competitive strategy is affected.

5

Crisis planning and organizational measures

Planning describes a structuring process that defines how the decision-makers want to see a future process developing. Planning is, therefore, the opposite of improvization, ad-hoc decisions that are dependent on chance.

The fundamental aim of corporate planning is to assure the existence of the business, which is constantly threatened by the uncertainty of future events, for as long as possible. This type of planning allows negative events to be taken into consideration as far as is possible and sensible. The result is a strategic configuration of the business that reduces proneness to crises. While this aspect has already been touched upon (see Section 4.1), the focus here is on the further possibilities of preventive crisis management. For this, a separate planning and implementation process, the so-called 'crisis planning', is used.

Since the number of conceivable negative events can be very large, there must be limitations put on the eventualities considered for crisis planning. Crisis planning should, therefore, concentrate on those events that are particularly destructive but rather unlikely and on those that are extremely time-critical.

The aim of crisis planning is to reduce the element of surprise and, through prepared measures, to gain a head-start in time. This early consideration of crises should also incorporate a fundamental review and evaluation of the chosen steps with regard to generic strategy and other possible consequences. (Above all, the interaction between liquidity, success and success factor must not be underestimated. Short-term liquidity measures must always take the long-term consequences for success factor into consideration.) Such a review is rarely possible in a situation of crisis, but is extremely important due to long-term influences.

Within this crisis planning and implementation process, there are three distinct stages: generic planning, contingency planning and preventive planning (WEU, 1995).

5.1 Generic planning

Generic planning lays the planning basis for possible situations. The aim of generic planning is to determine fundamental requirements and potentials. In addition, the ensuing planning stages should be simplified and speeded up.

In this sense, generic planning is rough contingency planning, in which the specific scenarios for the crisis situations remain purposely vague and determinants are consciously left unspecified (in many cases it is still impossible to predict the determinants, WEU, 1995). Questions related to the organizational structure of the company as well as to the workflow organization are as much the objects of the planning process as the results are influenced and determined by it (for further information on generic planning, see also Section 5.2).

5.1.1 Responsibility

A fundamental part of generic planning is determination of responsibility and authority. Subsystems for planning and future executive functions within crisis management are, as a rule, set up within the organization.

Since these subsystems plan, and in the case of crises, manage highly important processes, they are usually located at the highest management level or directly assigned to them. It is commonly agreed that a project organization faces best the challenges which are timely limited and irregular. In concrete realization, these are either organic subunit 'working groups' who have no authority to give instructions, or crisis committees, which are composed of representatives from several departments, but do not form a department on their own.

It is particularly advantageous to have a working group that should do the groundwork for management when it concerns the elaboration of different contingency-planning measures. By being assigned to top management and thus breaking free of the specific interests of different parts of the organization, distorted exertion of influence is avoided.

As from the moment of a negative event, if not before, the limited assertiveness will be problematic. A call is, therefore, often made to increase the authority of such working groups to allow them to impose their will. However, this makes a working group become more like a crisis committee.

In addition to members of management, a crisis committee is also made up of other relevant decision-makers such as a marketing manager, legal advisor, press officer, etc. The composition is easy to vary depending on the type of event. In this way, not only is the specialist knowledge of the members utilized, but it is also ensured that the decisions reached will be implemented by the persons responsible under normal circumstances. This form of functional similarity in cases of crisis and in normal situations has proved to be an important factor of successful crisis management (Höhn, 1974; Mileti and Sorensen, 1987).

To what extent the institutionalizing of a project group for crisis prevention will be carried out depends on the peculiarities of the organization, its size and threat probability. Normally, tour operators only set up small alarm units to which the initial coordination and informing of those responsible is transferred. The latter then decide on further measures. (The large tour operators maintain certain emergency services that are staffed 24 h a day, 7 days a week. Smaller operators have someone on call who must always be contactable.)

In spite of these variations in form, it must be noted that the clear assignment of responsibility is of the utmost importance. Based upon this, contingency planning then regulates the concrete steps and responsibility for each aspect. This should be arranged in greater detail the lesser the organizational and personal experience in dealing with such situations is (see Example 24).

Example 24 Years of experience – Lufthansa's crisis management

They can be called experienced or well prepared, but airlines have, like no other sector, done a lot already to prepare for the unlikely event of an airplane accident. The high emotional judgement, when it comes to flying, but also the companies' interest to demonstrate their promise of quality and service, even in those situations, were the major forces that lead to establish a well-thought crisis management concept and team.

In the case of the Star Alliance Partner Lufthansa, crisis management has played an important role for many years. Their case is thought to explain how such a system of strategic and functional responsibilities works.

Lufthansa defines the responsibilities and the organizational structure in its Emergency Response and Action Plan (ERAP), which is prepared and updated under the supervision of the Manager for Crisis Management Planning, a permanent position, which in the case of a crisis becomes Head of the Special Assistance Team Centre. Under his supervision, the different departments of importance in times of a crisis, for example, Medical Services, Communications, Personnel, Governmental Affairs and Security, etc., deliver their specific input to this ERAP.

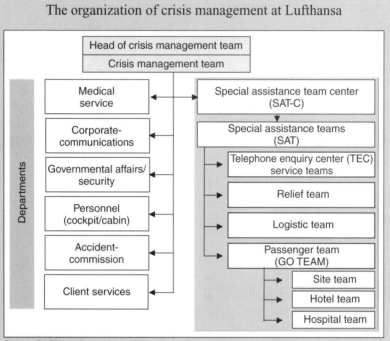

The organization of crisis management at Lufthansa

Source: Lufthansa.

In the event of a crisis, the so-called Crisis Management Team (CMT) is assembled. The Team is led by a high-ranking manager who represents as from then on the Board of Directors and is responsible for the overall Crisis Management of the company. He is assisted by the different departments participating in the ERAP, which send a previously designated representative to the Crisis Management Team's room, based at Frankfurt's Rhein-Main Airport. Special Advisors, who are selected according to the specific needs of the situation, join the Crisis Management Team. The main functions of the Crisis Management Team are the pooling of information, situation analysis and strategic decisions.

The Special Assistance Team Centre (SAT-C) supports the CMT (as a working group) and is assembled simultaneously in rooms prepared at Frankfurt's Rhein-Main Airport. The SAT-C manages and coordinates the different Special Assistance Teams.

Tasks and responsibilities of the Special Assistance Teams

Telephone Enquiry Center (TEC) Service Teams	True and complete information for the external enquiries ■ Handling of communication ■ Telephone service for families, friends, and relatives of the victims
Passenger Team (GO TEAM)	Caring for air passengers, relatives, persons at the sight, persons affected ■ Listen ■ Inform ■ Help
Relief Team	Support to the station concerned ■ Take over of routine activities ■ Maintenance of station service ■ Management of tasks assigned by the local head of station
Logistic Team	Handling of administrative tasks ■ Air tickets for relatives ■ Hotel reservations ■ Providing financial support ■ Answering further administrative problems

Source: Lufthansa.

Special Assistance Teams (SAT) are the operational arm within the company's crisis management and reflect the typical operations an airline is confronted within a crisis. These teams, which are available worldwide, are only activated in case of a crisis but they can easily be deployed to the place of emergency. The SAT members are volunteers and are recruited from different departments within the company, trained for their emergency function and activated on demand. The responsibilities of the Special Assistance Teams (SAT) are defined in a Special Assistance Team Centre (SAT-C) manual.

5.1.2 Access to expert knowledge

A further aspect of generic planning must deal with the fundamental willingness, whether, when and to what extent the company will fall back on external experts in a crisis. The basis of this consideration is the fact that handling a crises, on the one hand, is an exceptional situation, but, on the other hand, coping with it successfully requires experience and specialist knowledge. Although for the most part the latter is today available, getting access to this information is still very difficult. Accessing personalized knowledge in the form of experts is usually preferred.

Experts can either be part of the organization or brought in from outside. Reverting to external experts has the advantage that they only need to be around in an exceptional situation. The organization, therefore, only incurs costs for the duration of the possible service. In addition, due to their extensive personal experience of dealing with such situations, external experts have developed a capability to reduce complexity that enables them to come to decisions more quickly and with more certainty. There is also the fact that they are not directly affected by the events and as such they can work more rationally.

The use of external experts does, however, also bring disadvantages. Above all, this is true for those negative events that affect success factors or important areas of the business. In order to work effectively and to avoid long-term damage to the chosen competitive strategy, the not so obvious interrelations and facts must be known. External experts do not have such knowledge, as the specifications of the respective corporate culture are not fully known or, indeed, not known at all. In addition to this, it must not be forgotten that external experts are not immediately available. This poses a considerable risk, in particular, in the case of fast developing crises.

It is clear that, on the one hand, using external experts presents an opportunity, above all in special areas, to fall back on knowledge and crisis-specific experience. At the same time, giving external experts sole responsibility is risky and not sensible, when a successful crisis management should be guaranteed. For this reason, timely decisions need to be made as to which areas should be strengthened by external experts, should the need arise. This includes availability analyses, establishing contact, as well as preliminary negotiations about remuneration and performance. Considerations regarding a reinforced extension of computer-supported information systems seem sensible, since they can help to reduce complexity and pressure of time by preparing internal and external information suitable for the user.

5.1.3 Infrastructure

There is also a high infrastructural component involved here as a result of how unusual the circumstances considered here are. This covers special spatial requirements that come along with a crisis situation but also changed information technology needs.

First, the affected or responsible organization must consider the spatial requirements, which must satisfy two different needs. The respective decision-makers must be able to gather together in a suitable place, that is, a management centre, so that they can carry out discussions and take decisions. The demands differ from normal circumstances, in particular, in terms of the number of people involved and the necessity to work round-the-clock.

In addition, an information centre is required to deal with the multitude of outside contacts both with those affected and unaffected, for example, consumers or the media. The extent of this unit reaches an unusual size for the organization and is often underestimated. Like the management centre, the information centre must be prepared for a round-the-clock operation. This should reflect the necessary spatial requirements whilst at the same time making clear the number of staff required. The concepts used in practice are geared towards a kind of 'reserve concept', whereby employees and other special staff like psychologists, police officers, pastors, etc., are trained and prepared for their role and are only called into action at the time a negative event occurred.

Both infrastructural measures can also be implemented on an industry-wide level. A good example of this are the EPIC and the GAST crisis centres (see Example 25).

Example 25 GAST/EPIC Centre – example of an information and management centre

EPIC (Emergency Procedures Information Centre) in London Heathrow (GB) and GAST (Gemeinsame Auskunftsstelle – Common Information Centre) at Munich Airport (DE) represent the two best-equipped and most-experienced accident information and communication centres in Europe.

The EPIC at London's Heathrow airport was established in the 1970s and acts as a shared crisis centre for more than seventy different airlines. Its main function is the management of direct communications with the general public affected or unaffected by aircraft

---

accidents. Its acid test was the airplane accident of Lockerbie, when within 72 h some 100 000 telephone calls had to be handled.

GAST was established in 1995 at the initiative of the Munich Airport Authority, the Munich Airport Police and British Airways as a non-profit organization financed by German airports and various airlines. The main objective of GAST is, according to the EPIC-Model, the fast distribution of reliable information to the public. It serves as the central information point within a network, where passenger data from the appropriate institution (e.g. airline) and information of investigations by police, rescue teams, hospitals and the public are gathered and evaluated.

The GAST/EPIC centre

Source: GAST/EPIC.

GAST only works in case of a negative event, which must not necessarily be a civil aircraft accident, or necessarily be within the borders of Germany. In case of an emergency, GAST is able to operate within 10–15 minutes by calling upon more than 500 trained volunteers, who are recruited from the police and airlines staff. With their help and the latest technical equipment in an all-time ready prepared and secure office, GAST offers a 24-h telephone hotline as long as necessary and in up to twenty foreign languages.

Most recent examples of situations when GAST became active are:

■ train accident in Eschede, Germany (03 June 1998, 1000 calls);

- airplane accident of the Concorde in Paris, France (25 July 2000, 800 calls);
- fire of the Glacierexpress in Kaprun, Austria (11 November 2000, 2700 calls);
- air accident in überlingen German–Swiss border region (1 July 2002, 350 calls).

Management and information centres do not have to be attached to a certain place. Depending on the type of event or the development, it is sometimes advisable to be on the spot. In these cases, the British airline British Airways, for example, sets a 'Relief Aircraft' up, which is used to transport not only the necessary personnel, but also all kinds of infrastructure and communications resources.

IT requirements must also be taken into consideration (a quick supply of information is the prerequisite for a quick processing of information). These differ from those in normal situations in terms of obtaining and disseminating information. By obtaining information, a reliable and comprehensive picture of the situation must be drawn up quickly and presented to the decision-makers. The information channels should, therefore, establish as direct a connection as possible between the location of the events and the decision-makers. Both verbal and visual communication should be considered. Since the information exchanged is highly sensitive, the question of security must also be borne in mind.

The ability to disseminate information, not only outside but also within the company, demands further infrastructural measures (lack of knowledge is dangerous as it provides scope for incorrect information and thus loss of trust). The management and information centres must be constantly equipped with extensive information technology. Especially, for the information centre, the proportion of direct communication has to be taken into consideration. This means that the necessary number of communications equipment (telephones, etc.) is available and that the additional telephone lines can also be made available quickly. The increased importance of the Internet in the dissemination of information makes the necessity clear to provide direct Internet access in this area in order to provide information in as short a time as possible (see also Section 6.6.2.1.1).

5.2 Contingency planning

Generic planning is followed by the anticipative analyses of certain crisis scenarios. The aim is to work out and evaluate different options in order to keep them available as plans of action. This form of planning is also known as 'alternative planning' or 'emergency planning'.

In principle, contingency planning for anticipated events enables the company to get a considerable head-start that essentially helps them to be more sure about their decisions in complex situations and when under pressure. The planning process, especially its detailing, is limited by financial and human constraints as well as restrictions of imagination. It is, therefore, especially important to pay a lot of attention to the details when it concerns situations for which there is only a short reaction time available.

In standard situations, it is important to strive for a high level of detail. In this way, the focus is more on the reaction to the situation and less on the event. Furthermore, situations in which the strict following of certain steps are required, must be covered in detail in order to avert damage to the organization. In both cases, formulated planning modules are the result. They can be brought into use in a crisis situation and leave only the need to concentrate on minor adaptations (see Example 26).

If the modules from standard situations are not considered, planning must be interpreted again as situation bound, which requires adjustments over the course of time. Nevertheless, the ongoing planning updating must not lead into a permanent planning process that quickly exceeds the resources and can obstruct awareness of the essential. It is much more advisable to carry out a review at regular intervals. The assessment of the actual threat, which is a result from the real environment, determines the appropriate rhythm.

Example 26 A checklist for resort managers in the event of hurricanes, typhoons or tornados

Natural disasters like a tropical storm leave little or no time to prepare for the onset. The preparation of checklists is of major importance and should by no means be neglected by resorts in areas that are likely to be affected. The following example gives an idea of how a checklist can be prepared:

I. Activating the management team

Identify a person who will take on each of the following eight major responsibilities:

- Physical plant
- Emergency shelter coordination and supplies
- Communications
- Employee coordination
- Guest roster maintenance
- Evacuation coordination
- Travel assistance and transportation coordination
- Security coordination

II. Physical plant preparations

(a) Verify the status of:
  - ✓ Emergency communications equipment, including radios and mobile telephones
  - ✓ Fire protection systems
  - ✓ Lightning protection systems
  - ✓ Water-level monitoring systems
  - ✓ Overflow detection devices
  - ✓ Automatic shutoffs
  - ✓ Emergency power generation systems
  - ✓ Fuel supplies (top if possible)
  - ✓ Hazardous materials storage

(b) Define shutdown conditions

  - Determine who can order shutdown of major physical plant elements (including evacuation).
  - Determine how a partial shutdown would affect other facility operations.
  - Verify the length of time required for shutdown and restarting.
  - Specify the conditions that could necessitate a shutdown and provide this information to the decision-maker in

conjunction with information on what parts of the facility would be affected and the time needed to shut down and restart.
- Determine who would carry out shutdown procedures.
- Initiate shutdowns on command.

(c) Preserve vital records
- Secure vital records not needed during the emergency. Store computer tapes and disks in insulated and waterproof containers.
- Back up computer systems.
- Arrange for evacuation of records to back-up facilities.

(d) Secure outside facilities
- Move equipment to protected areas.
- Move furniture inside buildings.
- Remove banners, flags and vulnerable potted plants and artwork.
- Relocate livestock and move pets to indoor facilities.
- Secure materials to shutters or protect windows (2-cm marine plywood).

(e) Prepare shelter facilities (if appropriate)
- Clear and organize large interior rooms for:
  ✓ Guest and employee occupation
  ✓ Food, fuel and luggage storage
  ✓ Food distribution
  ✓ Sanitary needs (including infant changing and feeding)
  ✓ Communications
- Provide for emergency heat, lighting and cooking.

III. Emergency shelter coordination and supplies

- Determine for whom the facility will be used as an emergency shelter site (i.e. guests, employees, essential operational employees). Base action on the items below on this decision:
  - If the facility WILL NOT be a shelter, identify official shelters and evacuation sites and prepare directions to them.

- If the facility WILL provide shelter, verify the accessibility and adequate provision of fuel, food water, blankets, pillows and first aid supplies to the sheltered areas of the facility. Verify telephone and backup communication lines to civil authorities and emergency assistance.

IV. Communications

- Move communications equipment to the shelter space and test it to verify it works. This should include radios and, where possible, telephones and televisions. Battery operated radios and telephones should be included wherever possible.
- Distribute portable short-range two-way radios to managers, coordinators, critical facility locations and security staff.
- Establish back-up communications procedures that might include human messengers (runners).
- Coordinate with civil authorities regarding facility intentions and status.
- Establish a 'Message Board' for posting announcements on the status of the storm, warnings, evacuation notices, travel advisories and telephone numbers for assistance and emergencies.
- Copy and distribute checklists and advisory notices for tourists and guests.

V. Employee coordination

- Identify and notify critical employees needed at the facility for the preparation or maintenance and operation during the storm.
- Provide checklists and advisory notices to employees and their families.
- Determine the need for employee sheltering and inform shelter coordinators.

VI. Guest and employee roster

- Provide a log for guest and employee sign-in and sign-out.
- Prepare and maintain a roster of current employees and guests.

- Establish a file in which to maintain data provided by guests about their home addresses, emergency family contacts and travel plans.
- Upon evacuation, update the roster with information on departures and intended destinations.

VII. Evacuation coordination

- Determine evacuation conditions for the various categories of tourists, guests, non-critical employees and critical employees.
- Verify who makes the decision to evacuate the facility.
- Determine and post the evacuation routes and destination points.
- Establish notification procedures to announce an evacuation.
- Upon the decision to evacuate, contact civil authorities on facility intentions and evacuation progress.

VIII. Travel assistance and transport coordination

- Identify commercial and emergency travel coordinators for airline, train and bus lines.
- Announce the availability of emergency travel assistance.
- Contact tour directors and determine transport requirements and the availability of any additional seats, if they have their own transport. Post the availability of such opportunities.

IX. Security coordination

- Determine security requirements during emergency preparations, onset of the storm and immediately after the storm.
- Establish when security resources should be brought to the facility and when they should be deployed.
- Identify a coordination centre for security resources and supply it with appropriate emergency communications equipment.
- Coordinate with communications in the event of security problems and the need for civil assistance.

Source: WTO (1998b). *Handbook on Natural Disaster Reduction in Tourist Areas*.

Another thing that must not be underestimated is keeping contingency plans secret, because if they leak out then enormous negative publicity ensues. Indeed, in the aftermath of a negative event occurring, the public has always a strong interest to know whether such plans existed. They criticize the wrong planning or their non-availability. Nevertheless, so far, it has always been of disadvantage to the market success of the organization when details of these plans are made known beforehand. And, it is interesting to note that the probability of negative consequences increases as the probability of occurrence decreases.

Alternative planning results in plans of action, normally in the form of files, that have been drawn up for different situations according to a certain scheme (in spite of the advantages of computer-supported systems, printed crisis instructions dominate in practice). They contain all information required for the situation, both the master data (e.g. the infrastructure) and the progress data (e.g. the internal and external decision-makers) (see Example 27).

5.3 Preventive planning

When a negative event is looming on the horizon, that is, early information points to the increased likelihood of a negative event, then preventive planning is used. Depending on the urgency with which the task must be completed, that is, depending on the speed with which the crisis is developing, this can happen through the formulation of various option plans. These consider – in contrast to contingency planning – the immediate and probable negative event.

The aim of these option plans, drawn up in the framework of preventive planning, is the formulation and preparation of actual possible solutions for overcoming the developing crisis situation. As high a level of detail as possible should be striven for, through which the pros and cons of the various options are made apparent.

In addition, it must be checked that the data, which the current plans have been based upon, are still valid in order to increase the certainty of the planning and the success of future actions. This is to be done with current planning too, which is to be constantly updated on the basis of the constant monitoring of the threatening situation.

Example 27 The handbook of TUI

The Tour operator TUI prepared such a file for different situations and called it 'Service Handbook'. In this handbook, among other things, major negative events of importance for a tour operator are listed and detailed instructions are given for the travel guide of how to handle a situation, what to prioritize on first, what to be taken into consideration and whom to contact. It comprises some 200 pages and is at the disposal of all the 1500 travel guides. The preparation of this handbook is the responsibility of the department of Destination Support Services, which regularly updates it.

Source: TUI.

For all planning measures of preventive planning, the findings and results of previous planning steps, above all, the contingency planning, are used as a starting point. Even though this rarely results in the formulated contingency planning being used in its entirety, the likely use of at least parts of the contingency plan considerably shortens the preventive planning process.

5.4 Conclusion

The above discussion makes it clear that it is as important to think through crisis planning and organizational preparation in good time as it is to implement it in reality. With its conception and implementation, one of the essential factors for a successful crisis management is met (Mileti and Sorensen, 1987; Reilly, 1987). This is still true when the contingency plans prove finally to be unusable in a crisis situation. Particularly if the organization is inexperienced in dealing with crises, the previously completed planning analysis contributes to more prudent and assured actions. In addition, belief in invulnerability, which has proved again and again to be extremely harmful in a crisis, is also avoided (Reilly, 1987).

In all cases, it is essential to ensure that, once developed, crisis plans are actually translated into action and not ignored when a crisis occurs. In practice, this is seen happening over and over again (Grewe, 1970; Leimbacher, 1992; Hauser, 1994). This can be explained by the need to reduce complexity, whereby personal experience is preferred to other knowledge. This underlines the necessity, even at the planning stage, to include the later decision levels. A management that only concerns itself with crisis plans at the time of the crisis is likely to be inclined to reject them. Regular exercises would also help to ensure the acceptance and internalization of crisis plans. In this way, a feeling for crisis situations gradually develops and helps those responsible, through the experience they have collected, to respond more successfully in a crisis.

6

Crisis management instruments

The marketing instruments employed in crisis management require no change or innovation in themselves. The instruments and fundamental decisions still remain the same. Only the different framework caused by the negative event has to be taken into account.

The following considerations use the differentiation of instruments predominant in literature into the following levels:

- product policy,
- price policy,
- communication policy and
- distribution policy.

These instruments are not used separately but always combined. This is the reason why particular attention should be paid to this interaction. The effect of the instruments is determined by the selected competitive strategy, which, conversely, influences also the selection of the instruments in times of crisis.

Before an in-depth consideration of the different instruments takes place, a few important questions arise that need to be clarified before selecting instruments, determining the marketing mix and finally employing the instruments.

Under normal circumstances, the form in which the market is targeted has to be determined. In times of crisis, the question must be answered once again regarding the sphere of 'interested' people and of activity change. In addition, there is the timing aspect, that is, the temporal implementation of instruments, which includes not only their sequence and duration but also their relation to the event.

6.1 Timing aspects

The temporal dimension of the use of the instruments has an important function. Even under normal circumstances, the effect of the marketing instruments differs depending on the time factor. Therefore, to analyse and optimize the effect of the instruments, the time factor is looked at more closely from three perspectives: the suitable moment in which to employ instruments, duration and sequence.

6.1.1 Different points in time

The onset of a negative event strongly influences the different points in time when the marketing instruments are to be employed. This external influence is a very important difference compared to the normal situation, when time plays a far less important role.

In a first step, the crisis has to be identified. This is accompanied by the previously discussed problems of perception and assessment. From the point in time a negative event is noticed, the employment of each instrument has to be seen from a changed point of view, even if it only concerns the continuation of marketing decisions taken previously. From then on, all the organization's activities are interpreted and understood as the result of a conscious decision-making.

At the same time, however, it becomes clear that the point at which instruments are employed in crisis management is divided in at least two parts. A first pre-active point in time can be seen where decisions are taken about the interruption of the marketing measures that were initiated under normal circumstances. In the first place, this has to do with the assessment as to whether the use of instruments is still appropriate. Therefore, the important variables of the communication policy – such as advertising, type of exhibition participation – and also of the product policy – for example, the introduction of new products – have to be checked against the negative event for contradictions.

A second, active point in time comes when the instruments are selected and knowingly employed as the result of a negative event. The determination of this moment is particularly influenced by the chosen reaction strategy (see Section 4.3). In this active phase of the instrument's employment, market and environmental conditions change constantly and to a far greater extent than usual. For this reason, instruments should be put in place during a crisis, which constantly monitor such changes and indicate whether strategy changes and/or corrections might be necessary (see the explanations in Section 6.6.2.1.3).

A post-active point in time can also be observed where the event is no longer of general public interest. Nevertheless, the negative event is still present as long as it can be remembered. The employment of instruments in this phase can trigger undesired memories and, therefore, cause intensified negative effects such as contradictions. Also in this case, the chosen reaction strategy determines how seriously the problem will be dealt with or whether it is preferred that the events should be buried in oblivion.

The seasonal aspect of the affected product has the strongest influence on the time that lays between the negative event and the different points of time. The overall period of time available for the employment of the instruments has to be defined in relation to the traditional peaks of the product's demand curve. Within this time span, the individual points in time must be determined. It is absolutely possible that the post-active point in time must be placed in a phase in which irritation cannot be avoided, that is, the product presentation is in contradiction with the negative event. This instrument employment must consider this inconsistency and aim at minimizing it.

Another peculiarity of marketing in times of negative events is the micro-level of the point in time. This describes the determination of instrument employment within the course of the day. Changing consumer attentions and product-technical peculiarities of the mass media show, for instance, that this micro-level is more important

The moment
the negative event
is noticed
↓

Points	Normal circumstances	Pre-active point	Active point	Post-active point
Macro-level		Affected by the seasonal aspect		
Micro-level		Affected by changing consumer attentions within the day and product-technical peculiarities		

Diagram 26 Points in time

in times of negative events than under normal circumstances (see Diagram 26).

6.1.2 Duration

Besides the determination of the point in time of a particular marketing activity, the duration is another important influential factor for the marketing mix. Normally, the duration of the marketing activity is marked by the improvement of the actual situation and the achievement of new objectives, such as higher sales, etc. In a situation of crisis, the main aim is the regaining of the positions kept before the crisis.

Because the majority of marketing activities are related to cost, the available budget imposes an essential restriction when determining the duration of instrument employment. Due to the crisis situation, the determination of the marketing budget must take cost and profit into account from a changed point of view. In the present case, no additional profit is gained by the investment of a particular amount but a loss is avoided. This means that the estimation of future losses is an important criterion when determining the budget.

Therefore, it must be the uppermost aim of company management to analyse medium- and long-term consequences as quickly as possible. This should describe the loss that would be expected if counteractive instruments are not employed.

Furthermore, the time at which a negative event occurs has an influence on the determination of the overall duration of instrument employment (see Section 2.1.2.5). The duration is longer, the further away the onset of the negative event is from the normal booking time (see Section 2.1.2.5.1). As there is more time available, the emphasis of instrument employment can be placed on the post-active phase. Thus, potential consistency problems are avoided. Conversely, the duration of instrument employment decreases if the negative event occurs in temporal proximity to concrete travel decision and, therefore, demands a quick reaction.

6.1.3 Lead time

Almost all instruments have a certain lead time with regard to their planning and implementation. The reasons for this can be seen within the company or outside of it. An important exception is the media-oriented instrument that has only a short lead time and also considerable coverage. For this reason, the majority of crisis research has a media-oriented perspective.

The technical developments that took place in the meantime caused at least one further exception with similar or even higher qualities than the media-oriented instrument. The Internet is an instrument that not only has a comparably short lead time but also offers far more comprehensive and better possibilities for control (see Section 6.6.2.1.1). This new and extended possibility for action is used increasingly by companies in times of crisis.

6.2 Standardization and differentiation aspects

The decision whether to target a market in a standardized or differentiated form is taken by the company under normal circumstances in view of markets with their current and potential customers. Whilst a standardized approach targets all spheres of activity similarly, differentiation aims at the differences between segments. In times of a crisis this question has to be answered again. This comes because of the different reactions towards the negative event but also as the marketing activities will now be observed by a much larger audience.

Low costs are an argument in favour of standardization, even in times of crisis. Because instruments are used in the same way towards all spheres of activity, there are no additional planning or adjustment costs and quantity advantages can be obtained. There is also the fact that time advantage can be gained by a standardized use of instruments. Furthermore, the employment of instruments is less complicated because the segments must not be dealt with individually.

The non-optimal satisfaction of needs of the different spheres of activity is of disadvantage. This way, an important opportunity for crisis management, which is based on differing needs and reactions to a negative event, is wasted.

The necessity of differentiation first arises in the area of operative activity. Here, it is important to ensure the protection of the individuals' sphere. In concrete terms, this means that those directly affected by the negative event and their relatives, especially if so desired, are kept separate from the uninvolved. For this reason, British Airways, for example, makes the distinction between: those affected (uninjured), injured, collecting relatives and media representatives.

This operative aspect of differentiation follows a strategic one. With regard to the segments of the sales market, a revision of differentiation criteria appears to be appropriate. Depending on the type of event, segmenting characteristics used under normal circumstances should be extended to risk-relevant behavioural characteristics. Various individual factors with influence over different reactions have already been determined (see Section 2.1.2.3.1.3).

The cultural circle membership factor through which differing reactions to one and the same event can be explained is particularly noticeable (see Section 2.1.2.3.1.3). It suggests that segments should be targeted differently depending on their risk perception. This means that, in the initial phase, those markets should be concentrated that react less sensitively and have a more stable image of the service. In other segments, the employment of the marketing instruments should be planned and carried out with a medium- to long-term perspective. At the same time, other influential factors discussed previously, such as the dismay of a national group, can be useful differentiation characteristics.

Furthermore, travel decision phases were identified as important criteria. Within these periods of time, the tourist goes through various stages of involvement and, therefore, has different information needs. Consequently, it would seem to be sensible to differentiate the employment of the instruments over these phases. This poses a particular challenge as it must be ensured that no contradictions arise.

Apart from this segment differentiation aspect within the consumer sphere of activity, it should be assessed whether the remaining spheres of activity should be handled differently. In the first place, it must be ascertained what ranking the other spheres of activity should be granted and what their specific needs are. The resulting differentiation refers predominantly to the scope of information made available and less to the differentiation of the instruments themselves.

It generally applies both under normal circumstances and for crisis management that only as much differentiation as necessary but as much standardization as possible should be practised. This is not simply due to high costs that are the consequence of differentiation but also the risk of the different strategies interacting. The latter means that differentiation, especially when used in crisis management, must be carefully thought and applied. In practice, the use of personnel as an instrument, which offers certain differentiation possibilities, must be taken into account more often than in normal situations. It should also not be forgotten that differentiation takes more time, an essential influential factor for crisis management, to implement. Therefore, standardized behaviour is to be recommended at the start of a situation (see Example 28).

Example 28 Egypt's marketing plan

Egypt's marketing budget amounted to 586 000 USD in 1991, which, if converted, equals to 0.28 USD per international visitor. The Ministry of Tourism asked, even before the first negative events occurred, to increase this relatively low international marketing budget to at least 1–3 per cent of the tourism receipts generated.

The budget, which was step-by-step adjusted to 815 000 USD, was later extended to 21 million USD for 1994 and 1995 due to the events of 1992/93. It was to be distributed among the following source markets: USA, Great Britain, Germany, France, Italy and Japan.

In this way, there was no fundamental change in the selection of contending countries as these markets already existed in the selection in 1991, before the first negative events. There were changes, however, in the selection of Egypt's contending product areas. In 1994 and 1995, activities concentrated on the independently perceived beach destinations of the Sinai and the Red Sea. These alone received 25 million USD of the 42 million USD budget for advertising.

The distribution of financial resources was divided into the following:

Advertising campaigns in the general and specialist press of the six core markets	7 million USD
TV spots in the six core countries	22.4 million USD
Conventional advertising in the remaining source markets	2.6 million USD
Trade shows, conferences, Egyptian nights and receptions	3 million USD
Road shows	1.2 million USD

The increase in the budget was maintained the same way as with the concentration on electronic media. This end consumer advertising was to continue the newly trodden paths of advertising for the new beach resorts on the Red Sea. In addition, the diminished cultural tourism of Nile cruises was strongly encouraged once again. The tour operators welcomed this form of marketing which stimulated demand.

The period of time which went by until financial resources were made available and which, as a result, formed the starting point of a new marketing offensive, progressively decreased over the various events which shook the tourism industry in Egypt.

If the events of Luxor in 1997 are considered, estimations of the expected costs were made available in the shortest possible time.

The IWF estimated this at a maximum of 500–700 million USD, which proved to be extraordinarily precise. It can be assumed that, under these circumstances, the decision for an early post-active point of employment of the marketing instruments, scarcely three and a half months after the event, was encouraged. Without doubt, this was also influenced by the traditional purchasing period for trips to Egypt in its most important source markets, which begins in March and ends in May.

With its stronger orientation of the marketing activities since 1994 directly towards consumers, where Egypt itself saw its biggest mistake in the past, the most standardized market treatment was aimed for. A differentiation took place only between the European and the American market, on the one hand, and the Arab market, on the other.

Sources:

Sayed, M.K. (1997): The case of Egypt. In *Shining in the Media Spotlight* (WTO, ed.), pp. 21–25.

Wahab, S. (1995): Terrorism – A challenge to tourism. In *Security and Risks in Travel and Tourism, Proceedings of the International Conference at Mid Sweden University*, pp. 84–108.

WTO (1994e): *Budgets of National Tourism Administrations*.

Peymani, B. and Felger, S. (1997): Angst vor der großen Stornowelle. *FVW International*, No. 26, pp. 1 and 4.

WTO (1996a): *Budgets of National Tourism Administrations*.

6.3 Product policy

The task of the product policy as an instrument of crisis management is to form or adjust the product in line with the reaction strategy in order to alleviate the consequences of negative events. All spheres of activity of the negative event should be taken into account. Nevertheless, the consumer sphere of activity is generally paid more attention due to its function in ensuring the existence of the organization.

6.3.1 Product development

The first task of product development is the elimination of the event's negative effects on the services on offer. Against this background, measures of product development aim at re-establishing the original condition and benefits on offer. For a negative event that would endanger a tourist's personal safety, steps should be introduced that prevent or curb this threat. In the case of beach pollution, beach cleaning or the immediate readiness of alternatives, such as swimming pools, could be an action of product development. This cause/event-oriented behaviour must be introduced immediately because consumers follow them with increased interest in all the various travel phases. Tourists in the holiday phase take an immediate interest in the speed with which the measures are introduced.

In the active but mainly in the post-active phase of instrument employment, the question must be answered as to whether the product positioning can be maintained in spite of a negative event. If this is affirmed for the long term, various short-term product development measures can be taken to lessen the consequences.

One possibility is the temporary or lasting use of combined effects. By linking the negatively affected product with other important services, the product can be still sold. It is conceivable, for example, that the destination becomes the venue for music concerts or other events. This draws attention away from the affected product, which, as a result, is no longer the main object of purchase interest. Subsequently, the event takes on the travel trigger function. Furthermore, such events are suitable for imparting a certain communication content, assuming an appropriate selection. Because the realization of many events is accompanied by media reports, a bridge is formed between the event and the venue (see Section 6.6.2.4).

For example, WTO (1991a) recommended temporary product variations to countries affected by the Gulf War (if product variations are spoken of, it is implied that it has to do not with a new but with a changed product). The aim was, by means of temporary product changes, to reach segments of intra-regional and domestic tourism, which reacted less sensitively to the events. The success of short-term product variation depends above all on whether the segments approached have a comparable readiness to pay. If this is not the case, it does not only reduce profit but the 'scenery effect', with its long-term consequences, comes into place (see Section 6.4.1) (see Example 29).

Example 29 H.I.S. – a Japanese tour operator proves the unthinkable

Japanese tourists are normally known and aimed for because of their high spending habits. When it comes to negative events, however, tourists from Japan are classed as one of the most sensitive national segments. They disappear fast after a negative event has happened and it is taking every destination a long time to recover and re-convince Japanese tourists that their attractions are safe, back in place and intact. Japanese tourists usually start returning only when others have returned.

It is because of this that it is very important to realize that not every nature-given thing is insurmountable. H.I.S., a Japanese tour operator with headquarters in Tokyo and 171 offices nation-wide, faced the challenges after the attacks of September 11 in a way so far unknown. Rather than cancelling all its activities in the United States, H.I.S. launched shortly after the attacks a product that is best described as 'Solidarity Trips' and labelled it with the slogan: 'We love New York'. This new product was fully aimed at supporting the tourism industry in New York City by continuing the visits to the city rather than staying away. In addition, H.I.S. showed its solidarity with the families of the victims and conveyed to its clients that 5 per cent of all income generated by these Solidarity Trips would be donated to NYC ex-Mayor's Guiliani's Twin Towers Fund. With these Solidarity Trips, H.I.S. encouraged Japanese tourists to travel in times of fear and insecurity, like no other product had done before.

A total of 1600 bookings were generated during the promotional time of 2 October until 19 December 2001 and proved its success not only in commercial terms but also showed that tourism is a form of expressing emotions. These emotions do not necessarily have to have a pleasant origin, as it is very often assumed.

The H.I.S. press release

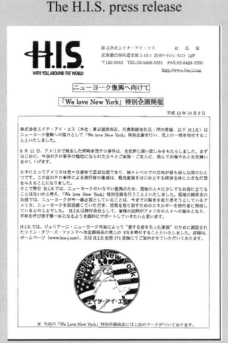

Source: H.I.S.

Translation:
The re-establishment of New York
Special project: 'We love New York'

The company H.I.S. (central office in Tokyo, Shibuya-ku, Executive Manager: Mr Hideo Sawada) will organize a special project 'We love New York' in order to collaborate in the re-establishment of New York City. Part of these benefits will be donated.

The terrorist attacks of September 11 plunged into grief the entire world. First of all we want to transmit our condolences to the families and friends of the victims of this act of terrorism.

The United States mean a lot to Japan and at an individual level it is one of the countries that developed the closest relationship with our country. The decrease of tourism after the terrorist attacks has damaged the economy, starting with the tourism sector.

Consequently, wishing a fast recovery for New York, H.I.S. has organized a special project called 'We love New York'. In its own view, the most important thing for New York is that people perceive that the city and the United States are trying to recover their brightness and to receive the energy of tourism to regain dynamism. This tour operator wishes that the visit of tourists will encourage citizens of the United States and wishes to go on and to give a complete support as a first step to peace.

H.I.S. will donate 5 per cent of the income of this project to the foundation 'Twin Towers Fund' created by the ex-mayor Giuliani for 'the families that have lost their loved ones'. Details can be consulted in our web page (www.his-j.com) and in our 171 national offices.

The products related to the project 'We love New York' are identified with this label.

Tour operators can, by means of a change to the contracted quantities, balance temporary fluctuation and shift the burden of the event. This opportunity is limited by contractual developments and economic relationships. The increasing vertical integration of services, such as flight or accommodation services, formerly contracted by the tour operator, has, from this point of view, a restrictive effect on action possibilities. At the same time, this makes the particular significance of preventive measures clear, which must be introduced to make these investments safe. Apart from the purely contractual perspective, the aspect of future cooperation must not be neglected because, in spite of short-term necessities, long-term success is decisive.

If, however, the analysis indicates that the product positioning can no longer be maintained, other steps must be initiated. Whilst a destination itself could initiate a difficult repositioning, in this case, the tour operator carries out an assortment adjustment, by which the affected product is removed from the programme on offer.

6.3.2 Personnel

The personnel of the affected organization are not only its 'ambassadors' under normal circumstances but also make an important contribution to success if a negative event occurs. This applies in two different ways: on the one hand, towards ones' own customers as the tourism product is marked, to a great extent, by the human contact between the provider and consumer of the service; and, on the other hand, towards the wider social environment for which personnel are an important contact point.

In both areas, personnel's statements and behaviour are paid particular attention after a negative event has occurred. Inconsistencies in official announcements are perceived immediately. Because it has to do with employees, their behaviour and comments are classed as being in accordance with the facts. For this reason, it is important to create and convey guidelines for these unusual situations. In this way, actions that do not conform to corporate goals, if not avoided, are at least less probable. An adequately developed corporate culture, which turns out to be the guidelines for behaviour in unpredictable situations, is also beneficial. It ensures that the organization's fundamental principles and values are internalized. A developed corporate culture thus fosters the conformity of the individual employee's reactions with the organization's reaction.

However, providing information for employees is also important. It must be ensured that they are constantly kept informed about important circumstances. This aspect is frequently neglected and information provision is carried out in a predominantly exterior-oriented manner. In this way, the company lessens its chances. Experience confirms that employees develop a high, as a rule, positive relationship to the company in times of crisis (Derieth, 1995). This predestines them for a credible multiplier function. However, switchboard employees and guards, who are paid great attention due to their exposed position and help to form first impressions, should not be disregarded.

One should also note that it is important to understand, above all, in a situation of crisis, the implications of one's own actions and to be able to estimate the effect on the system as a whole. This aspect of company-wide thinking and acting becomes more important, the greater the spatial distance is, since it can complicate the exchange of information and coordination. Companies such as McKinsey, which rate the understanding among their employees highly and have a number of branches around the globe, put on regular national sporting events, for example, to bring their employees together. This is especially often the case in tourism. Therefore, special training sessions, which impart this company-wide perspective, and the regular transfer of employees are possibilities to improve the situation.

In addition to these measures, which should not be understood as the exclusive task of crisis management but as part of normal management, exercises can also be used to prepare for crisis situations. This applies for all areas. Because the crisis is an exceptional situation, understanding and routine must be achieved for important sequences. The frequency and organization of the exercises should be planned depending on the function and responsibility of the relevant employees.

In brief, it remains to be ascertained that personnel are one of the most important instruments of crisis management. With it, the spheres of activity, can, like with no other instrument, be targeted in a differentiated, reliable and in a dialogue-oriented manner. Because they make an important contribution to the success of crisis management, training and practice measures should be correspondingly comprehensive. Limits on these preventive measures can be seen where precautions lead to an unfavourable behaviour (keeping crisis precautions secret should not be ignored; see also Section 5.2).

6.3.3 Guaranteed services

A particular characteristic of a crisis situation is that the consumer's ability to assess the tourism services on offer is decreased. This is even more relevant because the tourism product, as has repeatedly been illustrated, is a belief and trust product (see Section 2.2). Apart from the fundamental problems of assessing the service on offer, there is the difficulty of estimating the actual consequences of a negative event on the product. All consumers, regardless of their product experience, are affected by this restriction on assessment ability.

For this reason, measures must be taken that lessen the risk of a tourist making a mistake. The organization's commitment in the form of guaranteed services, for example, belongs to this category. In general, this is understood as promises and regulations that the supplier gives to a service and through which he assures the perfect condition of the goods on offer. Two messages are conveyed to the consumer by means of this method:

- first, the customer is assured that potential damage will, in part, be reimbursed;
- second, it is documented that the guarantee provider is convinced of the service he is offering.

For these reasons, the use of guaranteed services is, above all, suitable for consumers in the orientation and travel decision phases. Guarantees should be especially implemented more quickly for those products for which the competitive advantage does not come from their basic benefits. Due to the great number of choices available, a quick alternative reaction on the part of the consumer should be assumed.

The guaranteed service must not be recoverable or documented in order to be understood as such by the consumer. The principal reaction in the form of an offensive handling strategy or the long presence in difficult markets are already signals to the consumer. The final design of the guaranteed services and the strength of the obligation depend very much on the type of event as well as on the accompanying circumstances.

In comparison to most instruments, the guarantee has the advantage that it quickly makes an instrument available that can be traded with immediately after a negative event has occurred. Nevertheless, this should not tempt those responsible into implementing the instrument too early. Before its use, the company must be completely convinced of the quality of the guaranteed service. An assurance that cannot be fulfilled would not only trigger legal and economic consequences in the sense of paying the promised compensation but would also lead to a serious loss of reputation.

Example 30 The TUI statement of guarantee – customers' confidence in charter airlines

German tour operators used to have various charter airlines under contract and usually did not guarantee the employment of one specific airline for one specific flight or destination. This circumstance formed part of each contract between tour operator and client and was also published in the catalogues. The right to change airlines without the customers' approval and knowledge provided more flexibility to the tour operators. If for any sudden reason the planned aircraft could not be used for the flight, tour operators had the chance to employ another airline or aircraft and thus avoid the cancellation of the flight. Particularly in the case of long-haul flights, this procedure was the only practical alternative to fulfil one of the clients' primary demands, which was to get to the holiday destination on time.

However, this sub-chartering system was dramatically affected when in 1996 a charter flight crashed, off the coast of the Dominican Republic, leaving 189 persons (most of them German) dead. An Alas Nacionales Boeing 767, which was originally earmarked for the flight but was not ready for use, was replaced with a Birgenair Boeing 757, which crashed shortly after its departure. A very emotional discussion followed the accident. German tourists started feeling insecure towards charter airlines with rather unknown brand names and they tried to avoid using them.

The tour operator TUI recognized this problem immediately and issued only 2 days after the disaster a *Statement of Guarantee*, which was distributed to travel agencies. In this Statement, TUI listed all cooperating charter airlines and guaranteed to only use the listed companies, even in the necessary case of replacement. This quick reaction helped to regain some of the customers' confidence.

The TUI guarantee

Garantie-Erklärung

TUI garantiert den Einsatz *ausgewählter Fluggesellschaften*

Qualität auf hohem Niveau: Bei der Auswahl unserer Fluggesellschaften stellen wir hohe Ansprüche an Sicherheit und Wartung. So kommen nur die unten aufgeführten Fluggesellschaften zum Einsatz. Sollte aufgrund unvorhergesehener Gründe ein kurzfristiger Carrier-Wechsel notwendig sein, werden selbstverständlich nur Flugzeuge der aufgeführten Gesellschaften oder namhafte Linienflieger eingesetzt. Garantiert.

TOURISTIK UNION INTERNATIONAL

Karl Born
Vorstand Touristik Service
Spezial-Veranstalter

Norbert Munsch
Vorstand Vertrieb

Von TUI eingesetzte Fluggesellschaften, die auch in den Katalogen ausgeschrieben sind:
Aero Lloyd · Air Berlin · Air Europa · Austrian Air Transport · Britannia · Condor
Crossair · Deutsche BA · Eurowings · Futura · Germania · Hamburg Airlines
Hapag Lloyd · Lauda Air · LTU · Luxair · Martinair · Sobelair · Spanair · Sun Express
Transavia · Virgin Express · Viva Air

Carrier, mit denen TUI ausgewählte Zielgebiete anfliegt:
Air Malta · Air Transat · Air Via · Arkia · Croatia Airlines · Eurocypria · LOT
Nouvelair · Portugalia · Royal Air Maroc · Tunis Air

Zusätzlich werden weitere renommierte Linienfluggesellschaften eingesetzt.

Schöne Ferien!

Source: TUI

Translation:

TUI Statement of Guarantee

TUI guarantees the employment of selected airlines.

Quality on a high level: When selecting our airlines we put high demands on security standards and maintenance servicing. Therefore we employ only the above named airlines. If, because of any unforeseen reason, a short-term change of carrier is necessary, we guarantee that we will only select aircrafts of the listed airlines or of other renowned scheduled airlines.

TOURISTIK UNION INTERNATIONAL

Karl Born
Executive Board, Tourist Services
Special Tour operators

Nobert Munsch
Executive Board, Distribution

TUI employed airlines which are also named in the catalogues:

Aero Lloyd, Air Berlin, Air Europa, Austrian Airlines, Britannia, Condor, Cross Air, Deutsche BA, Eurowings, Futura, Germania, Hamburg Airlines, Hapag-Lloyd, Lauda Air, LTU, Luxair, Martinair, Sobelair, Spanair, Sun Express, Transavia, Virgen Express, Viva Air.

Airlines with which TUI operates for selected destinations:

Air Malta, Air Transat, Air Via, Arkia, Croatia Airlines, Eurocypria, LOT, Novelair, Portugalia, Royal Air Maroc, Tunis Air.

Other renowned scheduled airlines are also employed.

6.4 Price policy

The object of price policy is the fixing of sales prices. This includes price policy decisions in the narrower sense as well as condition policy measures. In this way, price structure and price progression policies can be distinguished.

6.4.1 Price structure policy

The task of the price structure policy is the establishment of price structures for product and company areas. This establishment has a strategic function and takes the circumstance into account that price essentially influences the product's position in the consumer's perceptions. Price structure policy decisions, therefore, are not taken lightly. Inasmuch, such decisions should initially be seen as given within the framework of crisis management.

Under normal marketing circumstances, all operative price–political measures must be set in motion in the spectrum claimed by price structure policies. Only in this way can repercussions and consumer irritations be avoided.

If the question is investigated in depth as to what the scope of price policies is, it can be established that pricing is a suitable instrument for reducing the consequences of increased risk awareness. In principle, it offers the opportunity to stimulate and keep demand constant. This is also confirmed by the concrete experiences of Sri Lanka and Egypt where an increase in holiday bookings was the result of price reductions (Stobbe, 1994). Provided that operative price decisions are taken within the given price structure policy spectrums, no problems arise. However, it remains questionable whether a temporary abandonment of this corridor is understood by consumers in the case of a negative event and has no long-term negative effect to bear on the product's position.

Experiences confirm that a temporary and limited break from the price structure policy framework is possible. For example, the sale of high-price prestige goods, which were damaged in an accident – if this has to do with damage to the packaging, not to the core product – does not noticeably disturb the product positioning. This is, on the one hand, influenced by the fact that the distribution channels separate customers of the 'defective' prestige product from regular customers. On the other hand, potentially inconsistent target groups cause no problems as, in most cases, consumption takes place privately and separately.

However, this is different in tourism. Whilst here the division of customers in the act of buying appears possible, problems arise, at the latest stage, in the act of consumption. Because the tourist is normally in contact with other tourists during the trip or at least perceives them, he assesses their simultaneous presence as consistent to his ideas and expectations. This interaction effect among tourists can be described as the 'scenery effect'. If the 'scenery' does not correspond to expectations, the guest's well-being is affected. This is even more so, the higher ranking the product positioning, that is, the social value, is (for social risk see Section 2.1.2.2).

However, the actual consequence occurs not in the affected well-being but in negative word-of-mouth propaganda. In extreme cases, this can even be media reports that describe the destination as being in decline. Therefore, in tourism – in contrast to the previously described case of damaged goods – a generally cautious handling of pricing instruments is advisable. From a strategic point of view, it is, therefore, to be recommended that a short-term profit loss is preferable to a foreseeable long-term disturbance or the destruction of the experience value strategy. This is even more important as tourism is becoming more and more dependent on experience values and a cheap image is difficult to correct at a later stage.

If, therefore, operative price policies that exceed the given spectrum are pursued, it must at least be ensured that conforming target groups are reached and inconsistencies are excluded.

6.4.2 Price progression policy

Price progression policies incorporate operative pricing decisions, which, under normal circumstances, should shift in the framework given by the price structure policy. The practical task of operative price establishment in crisis management is the minimization of the effect negative events have on demand. The relevant scope is, at least in the medium term, given by breakeven aspects. For a cost leadership strategy, this is lower than for a differentiation strategy. On the other hand, the necessity of consistency with the strategy places fewer restrictions on cost leadership than a differentiation strategy.

Regardless of the competitive strategy pursued, the affected organization is interested to keep financial costs as low as possible. In a first step, therefore, it should be attempted to vary those elements of the total price that attract more consumer attention. For the tourism area, it can be assumed that tax, airport taxes, safety fees, etc., are those elements of the total price considered less whereas flight tariffs and hotel accommodation are generally paid more attention.

All price changes are interpreted as a signal from the affected company not only by the customers but also by all the other spheres of activity. Depending on the event and the wider circumstances, the price change can be classed more or less as an admission of guilt. This unfavourable interpretation makes it clear that, in cases of doubt, pricing action must be accompanied by the use of other instruments.

6.4.2.1 Price discrimination

Price discrimination describes measures within price progression policies that require different prices for goods that are exactly the same. The established price differences are greater than the cost differences, provided that they even exist. The different possibilities for price discrimination are related to conditions that can be of a spatial, temporal or customer-oriented nature.

Price discrimination opportunities are fundamentally limited by the fact that customers served differently when the service was sold could meet each other again when they go on the holiday. Price and service comparisons are usually made then. If different prices for the same service become visible, this leads to a loss of trust in the service supplier and has dissatisfaction as a consequence (Frömbling, 1993). In spite of this limitation, the use of price discrimination is possible because holidays cannot always be compared with one another due to there being a number of different features.

From a temporal point of view, price discrimination can be considered in two parts. On the one hand, various prices can be demanded depending on the point in time at which the product is consumed. This form of price discrimination is extensively unproblematic because it is justified by varying demand and is excluded from tourists who were served differently meeting with one another at the destination. On the other hand, the price can differentiate depending on when the holiday is booked. Here, incentives are offered to encourage people to book early. Therefore, the late booking behaviour often observed in a crisis can, in part, be counteracted. However, insecurity regarding the estimated effect of a negative event still remains. For this reason, a combined use with instruments that reduce this insecurity is to be recommended. More problematic, however, is the fact that the simultaneous use of a service offered at different prices cannot be ensured. This must be considered in the practical application to rule out the consequences of a 'scenery effect'.

Spatial price discrimination offers products at different prices in geographically different markets. These variants are offered if the event is perceived differently by various source markets (see also Section 2.1.2.3.1.3). The linguistic barrier counteracts a direct price and service comparison. But even the frequent spatial separation of these customer groups in the destination allows this form of price discrimination to appear successful as long as behaviour between the groups is not perceived to be too contradictory and the 'sceneries' must no longer be consequently classed as consistent.

Customer-oriented price discrimination is geared to the different function and personal characteristics of the consumer. To a certain extent, this differentiation can also be classed as suitable. This applies, above all, if the criteria that form the basis of differentiation correspond to the importance of the sphere of activity. Familiarization trips, for example, which grant price advantages to travel agency employees, can be seen from this perspective. Towards those multipliers, such offers express the interest that the product service is evaluated. In addition, these price differences are understandable for non-affected customers because a relationship between the reason for price discrimination and the target group is discernible.

6.4.2.2 Special offers

Special offers describe lowering of the selling price for a short period of time. These actions refer to certain commodities for which demand must be increased. Special offers are very popular in tourism. They are used especially if the product no longer appears saleable and threatens to expire.

In crisis management, the negative event is the original cause of the special offer. Inasmuch, price admissions refer to difficulties arising when selling the services. Under these circumstances, the aim is to sell the available services before their expiry. An indication of the extent of the discount arises from opportunity costs. Above all, however, the discount is determined by the estimated elasticity of the demand as well as the time remaining before the service is expiring.

The frequent use of special offers has the negative consequence of getting the consumer used to them. This has already been empirically proved to be true for the case of irregular use (Meffert, 1993). It is even more critical if the consumer does not see a specific reason for these special offers. This suggests normally a careful use of special offers. However, this effect is less dramatic in the case of a negative event as the special offer is justified by the incident. In this way, the probability that future expectations of further 'regular' special offers will be encouraged is judged to be low.

In the last days before expiry special offers are frequently described as last minute offers. The advantage of last minute sales is the availability of a separate sales track, which has established itself in the past few years. The use of airport sales points, specialized travel agencies and the Internet appeals to a price-sensitive group of customers. For these customers, the need to travel and the price are at the fore, the concrete service offer is of less interest. Another advantage arises from the precision with which the segment can be targeted with these sales methods. This avoids costly coverage waste and also irritations in the customer segment. However, the impact of the 'scenery effect', which might occur while using the tourism product service, cannot be ruled out.

Therefore, special offers are also as instruments of crisis management an effective instrument for increasing sales. They are, above all, suitable for selling services shortly before their expiry. The reason for the special offer given by the negative event prevents people becoming accustomed to it. Limits on special offer policies can be seen where they would have a negative effect on product positioning.

6.4.3 Condition policy

As a subsection of price policy, condition policy describes a supplier's systematic behaviour towards his customers in all areas – apart from the previously described price area – which can be the object of contractual agreements about service remuneration. In concrete, this has to do with the formation of discounts, commissions and terms of payment. In light of the following considerations, these condition policy instruments can be used towards end consumers as well as service mediators.

6.4.3.1 Discounts and commissions

In a general sense, discounts are understood as reductions to the listed price, which, according to various criteria such as quantities, points in time and functions, can be aimed at retailer levels and, from a loyalty point of view, at consumers. Commissions are the remuneration to a middleman for transacting a piece of business or performing a service. Similar to discounts, commissions are calculated as percentages on the value of the service provided and graded according to comparable criteria. Commissions are useful if the final level of the sales organization achieves no ownership of the goods. This is regularly the case between travel agencies and tour operators (Regele and Schmücker, 1998).

Towards the group of travel mediators, the affected service provider has, by means of the temporary raising of commissions, the opportunity to give an additional incentive for sales efforts. This is advantageous from two points of view: on the one hand, through the creation of the set of commissions the concrete obstacles, which are the result of a negative event, can be dealt with. The payment of commissions, which compensate for the additional expense incurred to the travel mediator as a result of a negative event, means that an incentive to maintain sales efforts can be given. On the other hand, this price–political behaviour keeps the sales price stable for the end consumer. In this way, the previously described 'scenery effect' is avoided.

It can be assumed that these measures prove to be especially suitable in the post-active phase. They ensure, in a subtle way, that attention is paid to the product again but, at the same time, avoid the 'flogging' of the product.

Of the discount possibilities for end consumers, loyalty discount is, above all, of interest under these circumstances. These are understood as supplier discounts that are granted for the preferred purchase of their services. Loyalty discounts are often used even under normal circumstances and are expressed in airline bonus systems. The particular importance that these systems enjoy can be traced back to the fact that the attainment of bonus points is no longer tied exclusively to flights. In the meantime, bonus points can be attained by using a number of tourism and non-tourism services.

Advantageous in the use of bonus miles is the uncoupling of air miles from the price. On the one hand, this means that even if the same service is more expensive, a preference over competitor products is created due to air miles. On the other hand, even a service that is not as good as a competitor's but costs the same can be made marketable by air miles. Moreover, this effect is intensified by the fact that, in the majority of cases, the cost is not carried by the recipient of the air miles. In this – predominant in business trips – case, this air miles change is preferable to a price change. At the same time, however, it must be ensured that the incentive created in the sense of a bonus is effectively communicated to the consumer who takes the decision.

6.4.3.2 Cancellations and changes to bookings

The opportunity to change or cancel a holiday or tourism service booking is not a peculiarity of crisis management. Nevertheless, it cannot be denied that this instrument within the crisis management is of particular importance for customers.

The legal possibilities that exist for the tourist have already been considered in-depth, taking various contractual conditions into account (see also Section 2.1.2.4). What is interesting at this point is the aspect of instrument if this cannot be traced back to a legal obligation.

In practice, the active use of the booking change and cancellation apparatus can be increasingly observed. The reason for this is the tour operator or service supplier's wish to adhere to the agreed travel contract. However, considerations, the long-term aim of which is to become known as a preferred service provider in the future, are also useful. The possibilities on offer range from booking changes within a destination to being able to cancel the whole trip free of charge.

Two points are worth noting: first, the isolated behaviour of a tour operator has a considerable signal effect on the consumer's attitude towards the competitors. If a company begins to offer the opportunity to change or cancel bookings, this puts considerable pressure on its competitors. This is derived from the fact that, by granting this correction, this implies recognition of the influence the negative event has on the product.

Second, these measures are very costly and quickly lead to a change in the consumer's expectations. All in all, therefore, use of booking change and cancellation instruments should be well considered and an active use is advised against.

6.4.3.3 Terms of payment

The terms of payment mainly regulate consumer and travel mediator payment obligations. As far as the consumer is concerned, this has to do with deposits; for the tour operator, payment obligations towards its service providers. These can vary in their amount as well as their due date. From the point of view of crisis management, a change in terms of payment is only sometimes suitable. If the deposit due date or amount changes for the travel service booked, this compensates the consumer's risk sense only to a certain extent. The cost of the change does not justify its use, particularly as other instruments can achieve better effects.

The effect on travel mediators can be classed as similarly low where a change to terms of payment is hardly worth the special sales efforts. Here also, other instruments, such as commissions, achieve a better result. For this reason, the terms of payment instrument is of little importance for crisis management.

6.5 Distribution policy

The objects of distribution policy are agreements and regulations regarding the route a product takes to the customer. A significant peculiarity of tourism sales is that it has to do, not with the sales of a tangible product, but the sale of a service promise (Frömbling, 1993; Freyer, 1997; Regele and Schmücker, 1998). The customers themselves must travel to the location of the service provider to redeem them of this promise.

Seen from a general point of view, the tasks of distribution policy are of a more strategic nature, comparable to the determinations of price structure policy. Consequently, these decisions must be accepted as fundamentally fixed. Thus, in the following considerations, the effects these determinations have and the action scope allowed for distribution-political crisis management measures are of interest.

Decision level	Complexity	Information, advice, confirmation potential
High involvement Inexperienced in travel Much time Economical	Individual travel Many integral parts Long distance Expensive	Personal advice (High) and sales Moderated, empathy High competence
	Standardized package Holiday Mainly transport and Accommodation Medium distance	
Low involvement Experienced in travel Little time	Only transport or only Accommodation Relatively cheap	No advice Impersonal Immoderate Limited competence (Low)
Customer	Product	Distribution channel

Source: Adapted from Regele and Schmücker (1998).

Diagram 27 Influences on distribution methods

The determination whether the tourism product will be sold in a direct or indirect manner is one of these fundamental distribution-political decisions. Whilst direct sales take place between service providers and consumers without interposition from other trade levels, indirect sales choose intermediates. Which of the two forms is finally preferred is decided by the peculiarities of the customer and the product. In Diagram 27, they are placed in relation to one another.

The design of the distribution system, however, is not just the decision between direct or indirect distribution. It must also determine whether primary or secondary distribution organs, from within or outside the tourism sector, will take on sales tasks. Diagram 28 gives an overview of the sales forms available for distribution-political decisions.

6.5.1 Direct distribution

Direct sales are traditionally dominating in domestic tourism where the majority of bookings take place directly between consumers and service

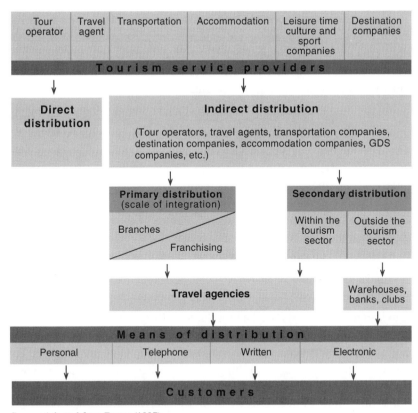

Source: Adapted from Freyer (1997).

Diagram 28 Tourism distribution channels

providers. An increased interest in direct sales on the part of the service provider can also be ascertained. This becomes possible because the tourist's travel experience is gradually increasing. Another favouring factor is that many tourism services are considered to be standard services and cause only a low object-specific involvement. Cost considerations are also part of this. The otherwise normal commission payment is omitted due to the omission of the travel agent. Moreover, direct customer contact is becoming more and more important for many service providers. This is the only way in which they can be in a position to generate relevant behaviour and customer data that is becoming more and more decisive in competitive markets.

One of the most important findings within the context of a negative event was that consumers had a suddenly increasing need for information. This is – as has already been illustrated – most suitably fulfilled by a differentiated statement (see also Section 6.2). The direct sales method must withstand these two requirements.

For the area of domestic tourism, the activities of direct sales are from the beginning accompanied by personal attendance. In this way, in the actual crisis phase, it is possible to immediately provide customers with information. Because this takes place directly and without third-party interposition, questions can be answered in a competent, differentiated and problem-oriented manner. As a result, the opportunity exists for the customer to paint a relatively precise picture of the circumstances and their consequences. Whether or not this is finally successful is decided by a number of other factors to which reputation belongs to a large extent (see also Section 6.6.1.2).

This is settled differently in the case of the increasing direct sales of standard tourism products. The fundamentally low need for information on the part of tourists as well as cost pressures cause that electronic distribution instruments are predominantly used. They are designed for a semi or fully automatic handling of sales. Therefore, it becomes clear that, within the framework of preventive crisis management, organizational precautions must be taken more into account as in the case of the less automated sales of domestic tourism. The aim of the actions must be the creation of flexibility potential that is normally swamped by the rationalization of sales channels but becomes necessary in order to be able to handle the increasingly individual information needs.

6.5.2 Indirect distribution

Retailers or wholesalers are used to sell services in indirect sales. If these intermediaries are legally and economically independent, this is known as 'secondary distribution'. If, on the other hand, it has to do with the company's own branches, this is described as 'primary distribution'. A number of other integration levels exist between these poles, which include cooperations and franchising, amongst others.

A fundamental advantage that indirect distribution has over direct distribution is already under normal circumstances a better opportunity to sell products that require an explanation. Travel agency employees can immediately respond to customer's questions and needs. This opportunity to inform and advise is also significant in times of crisis. The travel agency's concrete function changes depending on the travel phase in which the tourist is at that moment.

Customers, who have already taken a concrete travel decision, ask for specific information about the condition of the product. Here, the travel agency must be able to inform and act both in a competent and trustworthy manner. To do this, it requires appropriate information and support from the service provider. Practice has shown that this is a critical phase.

On the one hand, the information provided increases considerably and so does consequently the cost for the travel agency. The commission obtained by the sale is reduced by these additional advices and sales activities. This indicates the need for action and modification of the commission instrument. A service provider trying to maintain a booking can, therefore, introduce a special commission for bookings that are not cancelled and, at the same time, create an additional incentive for the travel agency.

On the other hand, many travel agencies are also interested to maintain the good relationship with their client. Consequently, loyalty to the service provider diminishes and often a tendency to give in instead of counteracting the customer's insecurity can be observed.

From these findings, it can be ascertained that the following are required for successful acting on the part of the travel agency:

1. *Interest*: this exists from a personal and economic point of view. The more strongly the sales are integrated with the service provider, the lower the necessity of creating separate economic incentives.
2. *Ability*: the service provider must provide the trade with appropriate information in order to be able to inform customers in a trustworthy manner.

However, if the customer is still in the orientation phase, there is a different problem. It has already been ascertained that destination images can be influenced before visiting a travel agency to such an extent that the product is not actively named anymore. From the point of view of the affected service provider, the opportunity of the sales talk must be used so that the ousted alternative is taken into consideration again. This requires in addition to the above-mentioned points:

3. *Quality*: there is no real negative effect on the product.
4. *Opportunity*: the customer's latent need can still be identified.

It is especially difficult to ensure the interest of travel agencies if sales are only integrated to a minimal degree. Specifically in this case, it is important that the service provider seeks contact with the customer and, in this way, exerts influence over the travel agency. The aim of this behaviour, also described as a pull strategy, can be the activation of consumers who are encouraged to search for more information. In addition, it can be attempted to convey the necessary information directly to the customer in order to maintain or re-establish the preference for the product. Which of the two objectives should be striven for in times of crisis depends on the event, the degree the product is affected and the cooperation with the travel agency. In the first case, it is above all important that travel agencies have the appropriate information at their disposal.

The push strategy suitably supports this objective. In this case, the travel agency is the target of the marketing efforts, for which reason this is also called trade marketing. Service providers use all marketing instruments, especially sales promotion and condition policy, to motivate the travel agency into greater sales efforts (see also the opportunities for higher commissions stated in Section 6.4.3.1 and the possibility of expedient holidays in Section 6.3.1).

As these comments make clear, indirect sales offer the opportunity to advise the customer extensively even when negative events occur. However, the solution of the travel agency information problem is important in the same way as incentives are in secondary distribution. Therefore, it is recommendable to use a mixture of push and pull strategies as well as to use in the post-active phase the opportunities trade marketing offers.

6.5.3 Sales in areas outside the tourism industry

Along with the previously discussed sales forms, distribution channels outside the tourism industry are increasingly gaining in significance. This is of interest also in crisis management from two points of view.

A frequent characteristic of tourism products offered by means of this sales method is the uniqueness of the product on offer. Church groups, banks and sports or automobile clubs temporarily include these holidays in their offers. In most cases, a repetition of the offer is not striven for and the scope of offers is possibly limited only to this product. Through the use of this sales method, service providers come into contact with groups of customers ready to go on holidays and who frequently have a preference for this sales channel. This preference has partly to do with the other people going on the trip. If the offer is not taken at this point in time, there is only a small chance of being able to undertake this trip again with the same group of people.

However, preference for this sales method can also be the result of great trust in the intermediary. Consequently, a reputation transfer can be used while selecting this distribution channel. If the service provider is successful in convincing the intermediary, who is foreign to the industry, of the good condition of the product, the intermediary functions as a guarantor for his clientele. As a result, the efforts can be minimized and price-political concessions can be made.

The particular value of this distribution channel for crisis management lies in the accessibility of consumers otherwise scarcely considered to be potential customers and in the trust that the supplier enjoys.

6.6 Communication policy

The principle task of communications policy is to convey information with the aim of influencing and guiding consumer behaviour, opinions and expectations. Traditional interpretations see consumers in the sales market as being the target audience of the communication policy. But even under normal circumstances, a larger communication sphere can be assumed, which incorporates at least part of the wider social environment and employees of the organization.

Whilst the consideration of the wider environment is under normal circumstances still a choice – the advantages of integrated communication have already been indicated (see also Section 2.1.1) – the inclusion of the wider environment as a communication sphere is inevitable when a negative event occurs.

6.6.1 Principle considerations

6.6.1.1 Types of communication and negative events

Within the context of negative events, two basic types of communication can be distinguished: risk communication and crisis communication. Risk communication pursues a long-term approach, the aim of which is the building of trust and understanding within the context of risks. At the same time, it can also aim at drawing attention to risks that would otherwise not be taken into consideration.

Crisis communication, on the other hand, begins suddenly. It describes the attempt, after a negative event has occurred, to minimize its consequences with the instruments of the communication policy and steer to such an extent that credibility is retained for product relaunch activities.

If the activity phases of both communication forms are considered, risk communication lies in the pre-event phase whilst crisis communication is only employed after the onset of the negative event, above all, in the active phase (see Diagram 29).

6.6.1.1.1 Risk communication

Because it takes place in the pre-event phase, risk communication has a preventive character. It is part of the considerations already dealt with which have to do with the strategic handling of negative events. It is used with the aim that the events will be avoided or their consequences will be lessened.

Risk communication, which aims to avoid negative events, is of use in tourism where the tourist himself or herself comes into question as the trigger of a negative event. On the one hand, careless tourists should be prevented from entering into risk by explaining risks and dangers. This way it can also be assumed that other potential tourists, who do

Pre-event phase	Pre-active phase	Active phase	Post-active phase
Risk communication	Crisis communication		

Diagram 29 Risk communication vs. crisis communication

not see the negative event as the result of careless behaviour, will not be scared off.

On the other hand, tourists should be encouraged to take on responsibility if it has to do with general risks, for example, such as criminal infringements. In this case, the aim of risk communication is to explain to tourists how to undertake precautionary measures. Because knowledge of general risks in the destination is low for most tourists, the responsibility of the destination's authorities and the service provider to undertake such a form of risk communication is generally pointed at (WTO, 1989, 1994c) (see Example 31).

Example 31 Preventive measures – the Bahia Tourist Protection Booklet

The Brazilian state of Bahia established back in 1991 the Tourist Protection Police Force (DELTUR), the first of such kind in Brazil to tackle the problem of crime against tourists. Besides its normal functions as a police force, DELTUR produces and widely distributes a booklet to all tourists visiting the State. In eight pages, this booklet provides the tourist with information of how to protect himself or herself, what to do and not to do in situations a tourist may typically be confronted with and the telephone numbers and addresses of those who can help him or her.

Source: DELTUR.

Another type of risk communication aims at changing the acceptance of risks. For this, the initiation of a risk dialogue between the organization and the public is recommended. The aim of this communication process is an increase in risk acceptance and a reduction of conflict potential.

This form of communication has only limited significance in tourism. At the same time, its fundamental approach has to be viewed critically. Luhmann (1991) for example, indicates that the declining acceptance of risk can be traced back to the loss of confidence. This can be balanced not by communication but only by authority. This authority, which should be understood as ability for the further explanations, aims to avoid additional communication in a time of information overload. Consequentially, it cannot be substituted by communication. Especially for tourism, it should not be disregarded that the discussion of risks, which have not yet occurred, leads to insecurity being heightened. This is a contrast to holiday trips that are intended for relaxation and the fulfilment of dreams.

6.6.1.1.2 Crisis communication

Crisis communication is a form of communication that is suddenly initiated and is dependent on a negative event occurring. Whether it is initiated straight after the event or is slightly delayed, that is, when the active crisis communication comes into play, is decided by the chosen crisis handling strategy. Its defensive or offensive nature has already been dealt with (see Section 4.3).

Crisis communication itself, on the other hand, has a defensive character. The initiative for this communication comes, not from the affected company or organization, but is caused by the event. This defensive aspect is the same independent of whether or not the organization was prepared for the crisis.

Crisis communication is also different from normal communication due to its increased quantitative and qualitative requirements. Quantitative requirements increase because, on the one hand, there is an increased need for information on the part of those interested in the organization, on the other hand, the circle of those demanding information is increasing. From that point of view, crisis communication is also mass communication, which is much more than media communication.

The greater qualitative requirements on communication are the result of the particular attention that is paid to the organization. This makes logical, precise and contradiction-free communication necessary, at least during the crisis (Mathes, Gärtner and Czaplicki, 1993).

Although the defensive character of crisis communication cannot be removed by preparation, being familiar with the particular quantitative and qualitative demands influences whether or not communication is classed as panic or planned communication.

Objects of the following discussions are the instruments of the communication policy with regard to the particular demands of crisis communication.

6.6.1.2 The reputation aspect

Reputation has an important function for a company even under normal circumstances. Depending on the organization's reputation, marketing activities, especially actions covered by communication policies, are assessed differently (Kaas, 1990). Reputation is not something fixed, it develops gradually. It is the result of the organization's past actions and communications.

If these past actions were similar and credible in their nature, a positive reputation is assumed. This credibility is an important asset. Nevertheless, its unique value only appears in critical situations. It can then help, like no other instrument, to reduce insecurity and accompany communicative actions with trust.

Considered more precisely, credibility is important for crisis communication in two ways: first, it exerts influence over the selection and assessment of information sources; second, it influences the way in which the recipient assesses information.

At a particular moment after the negative event, the media begins to investigate the topic and demand information. At the beginning of this information process, the affected company is the first of the information sources to be consulted. It is only later in the course of media coverage that a transfer process occurs, by which a wider circle of information sources is called on.

This transfer process can be accelerated by the affected organization. Implausible actions as well as implausible statements contribute to

227

journalists quickly making use of unofficial sources and other information providers. In this way, not only the opportunity of being the first to comment on events is wasted but emotional coverage is encouraged.

It is especially this emotional coverage that is a disadvantage for the company. If the company loses credibility in the eyes of media representatives, media reports concentrate more on inconsistencies within statements than on the actual content of the communication. In order to make this implausibility clear even to media consumers, the contradictions are portrayed in a polemic and exaggerated manner and possibly even contrived. Because this is a common consequence of implausibility or inconsistency in information policies, it must be paid great attention.

Moreover, credibility is important in the affected organization's direct relationship to the various spheres of activity. From this point of view, it has a longer and wider perspective. Longer, because it is geared towards both past experiences and the future effect of the information on the recipient. Wider, because it is a result of the whole spectrum of information, which is drawn upon to paint a picture of the circumstances (see also Section 1.5).

This offers opportunities because not every unfavourable media report is of consequence. At the same time, it makes clear the necessity for the affected organization to act circumspectly from a future perspective. Even longer after the phase in which the negative event is the object of media coverage and totally independent of this, credibility influences the success of the marketing measures now implemented.

If this credibility is missing in the various spheres of activity, constructive suggestions and changes have no chance of success. The remaining possibilities should be estimated as just as low. Mostly, they boil down to the purchase of more external credibility in which trustworthy institutions or people must be active on behalf of the organization. This is not only lengthy and costly but also very uncertain regarding its success (see also Section 6.6.2.4).

Seen as a whole, a positive reputation is a type of crisis insurance. It lessens consequences and contributes to the company's point of view gaining attention.

6.6.1.3 Possibilities and risks of unusual attention

A potential consequence of negative events is that the affected organization unwillingly becomes the focus of general interest. The accompanying communication processes are unusual for them and can incorporate both possibilities and risks.

One possibility is doubtless great attention. If this is the case in normal circumstances, that consumer interest is only achieved with difficulty by means of communication instruments, information is then demanded – without further help from the organization. Expressed in another way, the information market changes from a saturated market with a surplus offer, in which communication must be paid for, to a market with a surplus of demand.

If, in addition, it is taken into account that consumers only take notice of 2 per cent of general media and 5 per cent of advertising information due to information overload, one can have an idea of the value of this change (Kroeber-Riel, 1993a). The possibility, therefore, is a medium- and long-term increase in the degree of aided and unaided recall, which would otherwise be connected to considerable financial expenditure for the affected organization.

Because, however, it has to do with a negative event, an influence on image is also connected with this recall increase. The direction and strength of this change is determined by the relationship between product and event, previously described under image transfer, as well as by the organization's current actions.

Therefore, two cases are conceivable:

- The increased degree of aided and unaided recall is accompanied by a negative, that is, disadvantageous image change. In this case, it must be attempted to identify and lessen the negative connotations related to the event. If this is successful, it is possible to profit in the long term from the increased aided and unaided recall. This was the case, for example, when an aircraft belonging to Lauda Air crashed in Thailand. Responsible and circumspect behaviour in the crisis situation and after it meant that negative effects on company image were kept to a minimum. Fiedler (1994) even describes the measures taken created a winning sympathy for the company.
- Less frequent than the first case but just as possible are simultaneous positive image changes brought about by the event itself. For example, it was possible to demonstrate that the Austrian wine scandal influenced the image dimension: 'traditional wine country'

and 'variety of brands' positively (Peschke, 1986). These positive changes have to be identified and taken care of in the long term in order to be able to draw benefit from the incident. However, an immediate concentration on the reduction of the connotations related to the event, like in the first case, which accompany even this positive image change, should take place.

Other risks are rooted in the form of the communication process. Multi-stage communication processes not initiated by the company occur and replace the normal communication relationships. Once triggered, these cannot be controlled exclusively by the affected company. The independent communication processes make it difficult to estimate the effect that the marketing apparatus finally has (see also Section 1.5).

Almost always, if other social groups take part in this communication process, the three-actor model known from conflict research applies. Its peculiarity is that communication takes place on two levels, of which one is direct communication between the participants and the other is indirect communication via the mass media. The latter serves only to influence public opinion in the sense of its own standpoint and not to discuss objectively. High rhetorical abilities are an important prerequisite for the affected company in order to have a positive influence on this process.

6.6.1.4 The content of crisis communication

Crisis communication must take particular demands into account that result from the situation and are different from normal communication tasks. Especially, situations with unusual events are judged by the recipient to be complex. Therefore, the first contextual task of the communication policy lies in the creation of understanding and transparency. This explanation of the context essentially contributes to the credibility of the organization. If decisive information is not successfully conveyed, the objective facts and the rationality become less important and the organization's chances of influencing the information process are diminished.

Seen from a temporal point of view, the following sequence of contextual crisis communication focuses typically arise:

- In first place is the portrayal of the responsibility and dismay of the organization. Here, it should be underlined that the incident is taken so seriously that it is the highest level of authority that is responsible and manages the situation. This area as well as the following should be classed as especially time-critical. Assuming an active handling strategy is in use, only a few hours should go by before this initiative is introduced (other comments especially about concrete forming of press announcements and handling of press conferences at this point time can be found, e.g., in Berger, Gärtner and Mathes, 1989; Avenarius, 1995; WTO, 1998b).

- In a next step, decisions and measures introduced to cope with crises should be described. In this way, the company's own competence is underlined and contributes to the company being considered, also in the future, as the most important interviewee.
- Finally, it remains to explain further measures that are the result of current experiences and serve to avoid future repetitions. Because the event must not necessarily be attributed to the company's own sphere of responsibility, it is recommendable to emphasize the general problems, that form the background of the incident. In this way, the assessment of a shipping disaster, for example, turns out differently if it is seen within the context of the overload of shipping routes.

The content and moment at which information is made available is also determined by information obligations that a company must fulfil. In tourism, information relationships with customers prevail.

Tour operators in Germany, for example, take on particular responsibility for their customers (see also Section 2.1.2.4). They have a general information obligation to their customers and must make all information important for the realization of the trip available. A limit can be seen in the area that is attributed to general life risk. The phase between the conclusion of a travel contract and the start of the holiday is of particular importance. During this phase, the tourist should, without restriction, be made aware of all particular occurrences at the destination that could influence the holidays. These are, for example, changes in beach quality, natural catastrophes and oil pollution (Strangfeld, 1993).

Finally, it should also be taken into account that communication content can have legal consequences. Above all, in communication measures that admit mistakes or make apologies, it should be checked whether they lead to claims of recourse (Avenarius, 1995; for this reason Berger, Gärtner and Mathes, 1989, advise against it). Therefore, the use of such communication content should be avoided in the initial time-critical phase. Apologies should only be made under careful consideration in the medium and long term. On the one hand, it is completely uncertain whether they will be taken on positively by the recipient of the information. On the other hand, there is the danger that, if they occur when media representatives are present, a shortened reproduction outside the context will have the opposite effect to the action in mind.

6.6.1.5 Forms of crisis communication

Apart from crisis communication aspects as regards content, the fundamental forms of further communication must also be considered. This determining of the mixture of pictorial and textual communication, also important under normal circumstances, increases in significance in the present situation.

Considered in context, negative events only become discernible by the interposition of the media if they are not experienced on a personal level. If an incident becomes worth reporting, it is spread by print, acoustic or audio-visual media (for factors influencing news selection, see also Section 1.5). At the same time, it can be observed that audio-visual media is the more dominant, for which reason television is described as sensationalizing.

This circumstance can be traced back to various influences:

- First, the high proportion of pictorial information means that television makes information perception easier. Instead of a sequential information perception like with text information, information is perceived holistically by means of pictorial information, which requires less cognitive effort. This becomes especially clear if it is considered that an average recipient of information needs 1.5 to 2.5 seconds to perceive a picture of medium complexity whilst, in the same space or time, he comprehends only ten words (Kroeber-Riel, 1993a).
- Second, the recipient of the information develops a different relationship to textual information then he does to pictorial information. He trusts the latter more because he believes he has seen everything with his own eyes; therefore, pictures are subject to little logical intellectual control. This is also confirmed by empirical investigations, according to which, television was considered

by over half of those questioned to have a relatively high level of credibility (Berger, Gärtner and Mathes, 1989; Berg and Kiefer, 1992). Newspapers and radio followed at a distance, their relative credibility only being acknowledged by one in six (Berg and Kiefer, 1992).

■ Third, as well as being informative in nature, pictures convey a high proportion of emotional stimuli that can hardly be conveyed in words. This is where the danger of negative news coverage lies as the emotional effect on recipients occurs whether they are highly or low involved. This effect could be clearly observed, for example, in the conflict of Nestle baby food in which audio-visual media played an extraordinary role in conveying feelings (Dyllick, 1992).

■ Finally, apart from these aspects of quicker perception, greater credibility and more intense emotional activation, pictures also make it easier to remember an event. In concrete terms, this means that a negative event communicated by means of audio-visual media, especially if it is conveyed in the form of moving rather than static pictures, is remembered for longer.

If these findings are transferred to the appropriate employment of instruments, there is much to favour the use of pictorial communication even in times of crisis. In the past, important arguments, especially the availability of information channels and the flexibility of the necessary instruments, undoubtedly spoke out against its use. In the active phase, communication was restricted to verbal communication preferably in the form of press reports. However, new instruments, such as the Internet, outline possibilities of avoiding these restrictions. Pictorial information, even in the form of video sequences, can be made available early and without much preparation time. Extensive use should be made of these possibilities from the very beginning because they are an important crutch for credible communication.

6.6.2 Measures of the communication policy

6.6.2.1 Public relations, media and customer information

Crisis communication includes elements of public relations as well as customer communication. On the one hand, it performs a public relations function, the aim of which is to create a positive and benevolent atmosphere for the organization, principally among the wider spheres of activity. On the other hand, crisis communication also has concrete sales objectives that are normally reserved for advertising or sales promotion. The aim is to fulfil, in the most differentiated way possible, the tourists' increased need for information in the orientation, decision and holiday phase as well as in the wider spheres of activity.

These measures can be carried out with the inclusion of the media, in a direct or indirect manner.

6.6.2.1.1 Direct customer communication

Direct communication between the affected organization and interested parties offers many advantages. It allows individual needs and questions to be dealt with very precisely. That way it fulfils the necessity for a differentiated employment of instruments as already discussed (see also Section 6.2). In addition, this form of communication reduces the filtering and distortion of information by one-third.

Emergency telephone numbers are worth a particular mention when considering instruments of direct communication. As a rule, these are set up by the affected organization and serve as a point of contact for concerned customers. Depending on the type and scope of the event, other organizations or state institutions follow suit and themselves make emergency telephone numbers available.

As well as conveying information, this form of direct communication with customers helps to cope with emotional problems that often arise among with those directly or indirectly affected by the negative event. In addition, it ensures the accessibility or presence of the responsible organization. This demonstrates that the organization is still 'in charge' and controlling the situation (the fulfilment of both these needs makes an important contribution towards avoiding long-term damage to those affected; Butollo, 1990; WTO, 1994d). Another advantage is the possibility of questioning callers and assessing their concerns to draw conclusions as to further measures to be taken and the content of the communication (see Example 32).

At the same time, it should not be forgotten that an increase in direct communication with customers requires more flexibility on the part of the affected organization. This has to do with infrastructure measures as well as the availability of appropriately trained staff. There is also

Example 32 Call-in hotline questionnaire

The following sample demonstrates how such a telephone conversation could be structured.

To be filled out by Hotline Operators:

Thank you for calling. We appreciate your interest. How can we help you?

1. Identify caller's concerns

_____

_____

2. If they want general information, inform them.

The status of the situation is: _____

The (DISASTER) occurred at _____

(Time, place, area affected) _____

Damage includes:
Injured _____

Dead _____

Cost of damages _____

Facilities that are open include: (Provide list of resorts and attractions that are open.)

Facilities that are not yet open, but expect to be reopen within a week are: (Give list.)

Facilities that will be closed for an extended period are: (Give list.)

Would you mind if we ask you a few questions so that we may send you more information about our area upon further recovery? Thank you.

Name _____

Address _____

Phone (if appropriate) _____

Where did you see or hear about our Call-in Hotline?

_____

Do you have a confirmed reservation in the area and will you still be coming?

_____

Thank you for your call.

Source: WTO (1998b): *Handbook on Natural Disaster Reduction in Tourist Areas.*

a difficulty in that emergency telephone numbers are not only used by affected customers but also by those interested in what has happened.

The scope of this type of communication and the related lead times were important reasons why crisis communication concentrated so strongly on media communication in the past. More recent technical developments help to eliminate these disadvantages. On the one hand, GDS, which can transfer information to the tourist with the help of travel agencies, should be mentioned in this context. This still requires the intervention of travel agency employees but also aids the practice of the most individual information policy possible.

In times of crisis the use of the Internet appears even more appropriate. Information can be presented to an otherwise unimaginable extent and made directly accessible to everybody interested. This refers to background information that can place the event in a temporal and topical context as well as the actual reports. The latter can be made available directly, continuously, without delay and without the intervention of other media. Moreover, all the advantages of pictorial communication can be made use of. This applies both for static and moving pictures that can be made available in the form of complete video sequences (see Example 33).

Using hyperlinks intelligently to provide the static information available in a more dynamic manner once it becomes available is a further advantage of this approach. The amount of information provided during the moments following a negative event can thus be used to answer questions more individually than with any other instrument (the preparation of such websites even before a crisis occurs – the so-called dark sites – increases reaction speed). Naturally, the actual satisfaction of information needs depends on the appropriate portrayal of information that becomes available over the course of time. This, however, is more a problem of will than feasibility. If questions still remain, these can be answered individually in the form of e-mails.

A high level of dissemination and the constantly increasing degree of Internet usage make this a thoroughly appropriate instrument available for crisis communication. To assess this in brief, the Internet is in a position to make comprehensive and unbiased information available in the shortest space of time possible as well as being cost-effective and highly flexible. Besides, it provides the advantages that visual communication offers for the crisis communication.

Example 33   Luxair's webpages after the accident of November 2002

On 6 November 2002, a Luxair Fokker 50 flying from Berlin to Luxembourg crashed in heavy foggy weather conditions a few minutes before landing. It left twenty passengers dead, two persons survived (the captain and one passenger). It was the first accident for the company, which had been operating for more than 40 years within Europe. It was also the first time that such type of aircraft was affected.

Some 60 minutes after the accident, the company changed its presentation on the Internet. It replaced the homepage with its classical banners and promotion by a special page providing all the details and news of the accident. The page was simple and concentrated on textual information. The text the Internet journalist drafted was approved within minutes by the CEO and immediately made available world-wide. It was directed both at the customers and relatives of those involved in the accident as well as to the media. The page was permanently updated with new and more detailed information as soon as it became available. It also gave details and maps of the places where the various press conferences would be held.

Making this information available through the Internet reduced the number of those persons calling the emergency numbers although they had no relatives involved. It narrowed in that sense the emergency communication to those most important at that moment but also provided extremely detailed information to the normal clients of the company who had enormous interest in keeping themselves informed about the accident.

The Webpages, which had some 36 000 accesses during the first day, more than ten times higher than in normal situations, worked without problems during these difficult moments. Due to the reduction of unnecessary graphics on this page, the data volume remained only slightly higher than usual. The communications department of Luxair, which had the overall responsibility for this webpage, had one person permanently dedicated to update the page with information. At the same time ten persons were attending emergency telephone numbers.

> Two days after the accident, the emergency homepage was replaced by the classical companies' homepage with a prominent link to the former emergency homepage, which became as from then a subpage.

The Luxair Homepage during the day of the accident and the regular homepage

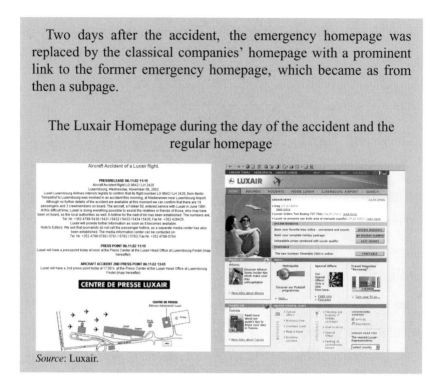

Source: Luxair.

6.6.2.1.2 Direct wholesaler communication

Communication with wholesalers – from the destination point of view, including, for example, tour operators and travel mediators – is characterized by a different desire for information and a different form of communication.

In the first place, it must be considered that tour operators have in many countries legally founded information obligations to their customers (see also Section 2.1.2.4). If the communication measures are to be of use, they must be prompt, comprehensive and credible. Above all, they must allow the tour operator to assess the situation as objectively as possible. An example is the fact that the influence of the various product areas is illustrated and explained in the same way as the measures introduced.

Apart from this type of information obligation, wholesalers are characterized by a particular sensitivity. Possible contractual obligations as well as greater economic risk make a quick and prompt decision necessary. Even in the active phase, affected service providers should practice a credible communication policy that has a medium- to long-term orientation.

Wholesalers are also characterized by the fact that they have a certain personal interest in keeping the consequences of a negative event to a minimum. They also often have their own ideas as to how problems can be handled. In order to consider these ideas and needs, the affected service provider should strive for dialogue-oriented communication. It is to be recommended that this dialogue be carried out by the highest management levels. This means that extraordinary decisions can be taken more quickly. In this way, credibility and interest in those measures introduced and those to be taken in the future are effectively documented.

These information efforts are appropriately accompanied by direct product assessments – the so-called familiarization trips. This applies for the active phase, if it concerns the assessment of potential damage, as well as for the post-active phase, if the measures already carried out are to be assessed (see Section 6.6.2.3).

6.6.2.1.3 Media communication

Mass media communication processes are characterized by various peculiarities, the observation of which is of significance for the affected organization's communication efforts. The principal influence variables of media coverage have already been discussed (see Section 1.5). At this point, therefore, those peculiarities that offer control formations for the affected organisation are mainly of interest.

In the first place, the importance of quickly making information available must be discussed (Berger, Gärtner and Mathes, 1989; Avenarius, 1995; WTO, 1998b). Journalists are always under pressure to explain. They have to explain what has occurred and illustrate its consequences to their audience. Therefore, if a journalist puts a question to an organization and it is not answered, he cannot simply leave it at that. Rather, he tries to answer the question himself using alternative sources. If he is able to do this, the organization has wasted a vital opportunity to put forward its own position and influence the communication process.

Because, however, not all questions are directed at the organization, it becomes necessary to introduce media monitoring in order to quickly determine which needs are current. The most sensible thing is to implement this monitoring process in the news agencies, as it is their information that is predominantly used by media representatives. If a quick reaction is assumed, this offers the organization the opportunity to present its own point of view before the news is published in the mass media.

Although general aspects of credibility have already been discussed, a further facet of credibility based on the personality of the spokesperson is of great importance for the communication. It is generally agreed that that this function should be undertaken centrally and, if possible, by someone at the top management level of the organization (Leaf, 1995; WTO, 1998b). At the same time, however, external aspects and the form of expression determine whether the person and also the content of the communication are seen to be credible (Berger, Gärtner and Mathes, 1989; Avenarius, 1995). For this reason, it should be determined at an early stage which person is to act as a representative for the organization in this situation.

Normally, the advantage of a relationship of trust already built up with responsible media representatives is pointed at. In this way, thoughtless and rash media coverage should be avoided in times of crisis. Furthermore, this should help to communicate the core messages to the media, which are rarely conveyed by press conferences in situations of this kind, so that they include them in their stories recognition sinks to around one-fourth of the otherwise normal perception (Avenarius, 1995). In practice, however, the organization is confronted with several adversities that brings the effectiveness of this behaviour into question.

On the one hand, a change of editorial takes place depending on the type of event. Coverage responsibility changes from the previously responsible editorial (e.g. economic editorial) to the editorial in charge of current affairs. Whilst it is still possible to have a relationship with the former, this would appear to be less probable for the latter because, under normal circumstances, the editor has no professional interest in the subject. On the other hand, with regards to electronic media, the number of independent television and radio journalists who sell their reports to broadcasters is constantly increasing in the same way as the change frequency of teams or their employees is increasing. Therefore, if a relationship of trust is to be established, it should be related to the organization rather than to a person.

The organization also has legal and economic ways of controlling the media. Legal possibilities include corrective statements, omission claims and damage claims, which mean that both material and immaterial damage can be asserted. A prerequisite for the implementation of such claims, however, is that the organization is able to prove a journalist's culpable behaviour and at the same time provide evidence that there is a contextual link between the report and the damages. As a rule, this is difficult. Economic opportunities available as a reaction are, on the other hand, numerous and include, for example, advertising boycotts as well as the use of rival media organizations. Whilst economic methods can be implemented without causing further sensation, the use of legal methods requires careful reflection. It must be considered whether unchallenged archiving is not preferable to the danger of lengthy negative coverage.

It can be concluded that the contact with the mass media requires a certain amount of practice and should not take place if the company is unprepared. An analysis of the principle peculiarities and mechanisms of media communication is recommendable even before a crisis occurs. This at least ensures that the situation will be dealt with in a prudent and targeted manner. However, this is not a guarantee of success. Consistent behaviour combined with a reputation acquired over a period of time are the most effective instruments for balanced media coverage.

6.6.2.2 Advertising

Advertising describes efforts to influence the behaviour of the recipient of information using certain methods of communication. Under normal circumstances, this is a known attempt to induce customers to buy or consume a product, that is, sales advertising. However, the intention of advertising, that is, to convey information and control behaviour, can aid every set corporate goal, including crisis management.

It can be assumed that certain advertising measures have been introduced before a negative event occurred. Consequently, it is the company management's first task to examine the coherence of these advertising decisions. This examination should be carried out under consideration of short- and medium-term corporate goals, which have changed because of the negative event, and the situation itself. The often voiced point of view that advertising should be essentially stopped cannot be followed as that way an important communication channel and, consequently, the chance to exert influence would be lost.

In the active phase, the aim of advertising is to convey information. (Three influential aims of advertising can be distinguished: topicality, emotion and information. That which brings attention to the product, that is, the topicality, is a result of the negative event and rules it out as an influential aim in this context. The release of emotional stimuli or the conveying of information about the product remain as influential aims.) This arises from the fact that, in times of crisis, the affected organization has to deal with information deficits as well as the negative event itself. These information deficits are apparent in the various spheres of activity and are not rectified by the media but, in many cases, intensified.

In such situations, advertising has the task of transferring information that would otherwise have no chance of being conveyed and would cause damage to the organization's credibility and image if absent or distorted.

Advertisements, promotional letters and leaflets are useful advertising tools due to their availability, suitability and cost. Radio and television advertising appear to be suitable in principle but are costly. Their effective use requires, therefore, a six to seven figure budget. For this reason, their practical use is restricted to very large tour operators and destinations:

- During all phases, advertisements in newspapers and magazines prove to be a useful advertising tool for conveying information that represents the company line. One advantage is their quick availability, which is only restricted by time needed for the writing of the content and the layout of the advertisement. Another advantage is their high coverage and cost-effectiveness. Of disadvantage, on the other hand, is the lack of opportunity for differentiation. Consequently, they are of special use for a content that can be the same for all readers of a newspaper or magazine.
- Promotional letters are, to a great extent, suitable for explaining the actual circumstances to, for example, those customers in the pre-holiday phase. They can directly inform the customer of product-political or price-political measures. Apart from the opportunities to select the target groups, the content of the communication can be individualized. This helps complying with the above-mentioned differentiation necessities for the information, the product on offer or the price (see Sections 6.2, 6.3.1 and 6.4.2.1). The usefulness of this advertising medium is only restricted by the necessity of keeping the contact addresses ready.

■ Leaflets and brochures can relatively quickly impart comprehensive information to potential and current customers as well as other more relevant spheres of activity. A differentiation of the content is only possible if the targeted persons, who are to be informed similarly, can be reached through the same distribution channel of information. These are, in principle, the distribution channels of the service promise as well as inserts in newspapers and magazines (for the distribution channels of a service promise, see Section 6.5).

To what extent the affected organization is able to achieve its influential goals in a crisis situation by means of informative advertising depends, above all, on whether the information offered to the target person in this situation is relevant and credible.

Whilst, in the active phase, tactical advertising has to even out bottlenecks, in the post-active phase, strategic influential objectives of product positioning are once again brought to the fore. This deployment of the advertising instruments does not have any crisis-specific peculiarities. It uses the same measures and instruments as under normal circumstances. It is worth mentioning here that strategic influential objectives could have changed as a result of the negative event. On the one hand, they could prove themselves to be fundamentally unsuitable and make a repositioning necessary. On the other hand, the aimed or held positioning could still be sensible, for which reason advertising measures must be directed towards the recovery of this position. Consequentially, before initiating activities in the post-active phase, a fundamental assessment of the actual and desired positioning must take place. If this is not done, advertising activities can cause lasting damage.

6.6.2.3 Sales promotion

The aim of sales promotion is the creation of unique, non-recurring additional incentives to purchase the product. They should immediately encourage sales. Apart from communicative measures, sales promotion includes other marketing elements that belong to price, product and distribution policy.

Sales promotion actions are frequently used in tourism especially to balance fluctuations in demand under normal circumstances. Sales promotion actions are also fundamentally suitable for crisis management.

However, it must also be noted that the generation of topicality for the product in the active phase is not the aim of sales promotion but overcoming the other sales problems is (see also Section 6.6.2.2). It is only in the post-active phase that the opportunity arises to view topicalization as an aim of sales promotion.

According to the target groups, the following cases of sales promotion can be differentiated.

The first level, consumer-oriented sales promotion, is aimed at the end customer. Seen from a communication point of view, this end customer can be informed by means of information material that is made available to him directly or via the travel mediator. Its content should – as already mentioned in the section on advertising – concentrate, in the active phase, on information deficits. These measures can be accompanied by the employment of price-political instruments.

An effective use of sales promotion can be achieved, for example, by guaranteed services. Different to a general price reduction, guaranteed services are thoroughly more effective and, at the same time, more economically interesting instruments. A prerequisite, however, is that the product has not suffered and that the criteria for an eventual reimbursement are clearly regulated. Under these circumstances and from the standpoint of the consumer, this active step could be viewed as credible. At the same time, the sensation of a product damage, which is somehow implied by each and every price reduction at these moments, can be avoided.

For a differentiated approach, above all, in the post-active phase, it is also recommended to use coupon advertisements and competitions in magazines and newspapers. If coupon advertisements are used to convey or request secondary information, their use is also to be recommended in the active phase.

The aim of trade-oriented sales promotion in the active phase is the maintenance of sales efforts on the part of the travel mediator; in the post-active phase, it is the recovery of previous sales figures. Seen from a communication point of view, this includes the preparation of information material with which travel agency employees can provide customers with correct information. This includes background information as well as information to help argue the case with customers. It is important that this is quickly made available because travel agency employees are normally the first refuge for customers. Financial incentives should also accompany these actions in order to support the particular strain of the additional information work (see also Section 6.4.3).

Apart from training, through which the sales assistant is prepared to handle specific problems, familiarization trips are of much use in the post-active phase. The latter offers the possibility to assess the product itself and to be comprehensively informed unlike any other instrument. Familiarization trips are always useful if product changes can only be communicated with difficulty as with events that trigger a slowdown in demand due to a perceived security situation.

Motivation and ability should increase with sales promotion aimed at the own sales personnel. The incentives are numerous and include both monetary and prestige benefits. These can be in the form of a competition or can be gained by fulfilling certain requirements. Training measures aim to prepare solutions for particular sales problems in the same way as trade-oriented sales promotion.

To what extent such measures are necessary for destinations, which address the staff of their tourism offices, and tour operators depends on the corporate culture. If there is already a high identification with the corporate goals, this type of sales promotion action has no additional motivational success.

These explanations make it clear that sales promotion is a useful instrument offering a broad variety of creating incentives. The specialty, different to the other instrument of the communication policy, is the generation of a direct incentive to purchase the product. Nevertheless, it should be noted that these incentives are created in such way that they are understood as a logical consequence of the negative event and help to overcome specific sales problems. In this way, it is ensured that, for all market segments, the additional incentive is understood and the organization's credibility is not harmed.

6.6.2.4 Sponsoring and product placement

Sponsoring is based on the principle of the exchange of services between the sponsor, who provides a previously defined sum of money or payment in kind, and the recipient. People, groups and organizations as well as events can be sponsored.

The use of sponsoring in crisis management can take on various forms. If we consider the person or group of people being sponsored, they should ensure the personalization of the product already under normal circumstances. If we go back to the person sponsored before the onset of the negative event, they can use in the active phase their persuasive effect and credibility to declare their continuing support for the product. These measures transfer trust, which is convenient for reducing the perceived increased risk.

More problematic, on the other hand, is the inclusion of people who only commence their activity after the crisis has already begun. Because the intention of the sponsor is obvious, this offers a starting point for public criticism. Therefore, late inclusions should only occur in exceptional situations. This includes the case when due to their own lack of credibility, people with high public standing become active for the organization (for the purchase of external credibility, see also Section 6.6.1.2) (see Example 34).

The sponsoring of events is an encouraging variant, for example, for destinations affected by negative events. Depending on the size and significance of the event, the accompanying media coverage gives rise to national or international interest. In this way, the destination becomes an indirect integral part of media coverage. Moreover, it offers the possibility to target specific market segments based on the appropriate thematic selection of the sponsored event. Much more important than this addressing of a specific segment is, however, the thematic selection from the point of view of communication content. If the participants or event themes have a beneficial relation to the desired communication goals, an effective indirect communication can, therefore, be produced. This is subject to little intellectual control from recipients because it is taken on in passing and, therefore, subconsciously.

Egypt has already taken this road many times and applied to hold conferences and sponsored cultural events in the country. The advantage of all these events was that the risk – in this case, the security situation – could be assessed and controlled. Therefore, providing the event is successful, positive news coverage is very probable.

However, if the risks do not appear to be controllable, the establishment of such exposed events should be avoided. This became clear at the sponsored American Society of Travel Agents (ASTA) conference in Manila in 1980, which was attended by 6000 American travel agency

Example 34 Prominent faces – helping to get up again

It is known that sponsoring helps promoting a product. Less often practised, because quite more risky, is the use of prominent figures when it comes to overcome negative events or even long-lasting negative images. Hillary Rodham Clinton, then a first Lady, now a Senator from New York, visited in 1999 the city of Palermo, the Sicilian capital (Italy), which had been struggling until then with the negative image of a Mafia stronghold. During her visit she did everything to underline that she believed that this city should be considered a secure tourist destination. The press echo proved the success of this visit for the destination with many positive articles on the 'securer destination' or 'The Renaissance of Italy'.

Another example of using prominent faces was the advertisement campaign Lufthansa started after the September 11 attacks on the United States of America. Understanding that the restraint of customers to fly was more emotional than rational, they used personalities with a high public credibility in their 3-month advertisement campaign. The company's strategy was honoured by a higher-than-average result.

Advertisements with the former President of Germany,
Prof. Dr Roman Herzog, the former Minister of Foreign Affairs of
Germany, Hans-Dietrich Genscher and the CEO of Siemens,
Dr Heinrich v. Pierer

Source: Lufthansa.

employees. A bomb attack against the Philippine President Marcos at this event caused long-term damage and a decline in visitor numbers rather than the intended promotion of tourism (Hall, 1994).

Ideally, these measures take place in the post-active phase once the product changes that might have been necessary are completed (normally, this is already ensured by the lengthy application periods that exist for this type of event). In this way, an undesired analysis of the negative events can be avoided as much as possible, but cannot be ruled out completely.

Product placement, that is, the placing of a product in a non-promotional part of a medium, is another instrument available within the communication policy. First, films are of great significance in the arrangement and establishment of realms of experience. Second, stimulation is, as a rule, carried out unobserved and by means of credible communicators. Examples of its successful use are the films 'Gandhi' for India and 'Crocodile Dundee' for Australia, the consequence of which was a lasting international tourism demand (Kotler, Haider and Rein, 1993). The main problem after negative events would be to find a producer with an adequate script who accepts this product placement. Only if the content is of quality, the film reaches the market segment aimed at and if it becomes successful it can be assumed that the film helps indirectly the destination. The considerable length of time it takes to produce such a film should also not be forgotten. Consequently, films are mainly of use for the post-active phase and especially for the emotional product positioning.

6.7 The marketing instruments within the framework of crisis management: a conclusion

As has been illustrated by the previous explanations, opportunities to form, combine and finally employ the marketing instruments in crisis management are numerous. In no way can these portrayals be complete. Rather, they help in the analysis of fundamental problems with which the marketing is challenged when negative events occur. This applies, in particular, for the composition, reaction time and effects of the respective instruments.

A first result of these analyses is that the high significance that is often assigned to media-oriented instruments should be reconsidered.

Exclusively or mainly concentrating on these instruments is not only unnecessary but also gambles away opportunities that arise due to other communicative instruments. Above all, the Internet presents a new form of communication that enables quicker reaction times, editorial control and pictorial portrayal possibilities in a crisis.

Another conclusion of considerable significance refers to the consequences of an active use of the pricing instruments in crisis management. Despite the quick success that can be achieved by reducing prices, an active use of this instrument is advised against due to the medium- and long-term damage it can cause. Leaving with price-political decisions the established framework of the price structure policy should be carefully weighed. It is important to take the 'scenery effect' into account, especially in the case of higher positioned products.

Interesting are also those possibilities that arise in the aftermath of a crisis as a result of guarantees, the sponsoring of events and the use of the extraordinary attention. But also the significance of the company's own personnel as a crisis management success factor should not be ignored and should be used early for appropriate training.

It applies for the employment of instruments in general that crisis management requires a well-considered, coordinated timing more so than normal marketing. By introducing measures too early or too late, the effect not only falls flat but, in unfavourable circumstances, the situation can actually be made worse. This should also be noted regarding differentiation.

The various reactions and needs of the different spheres of activity form both opportunities and risks. This refers to operative differentiation within the narrower temporal context of the negative event as well as the differentiated strategic targeting of spheres of activity. Short-term concentration on segments with higher risk acceptance appears to be especially promising. Nevertheless, limited and particular demanded resources in times of crisis management and the lack of time limit the differentiation. Above all, however, the increased general attention makes it difficult to keep differentiated areas separated.

Consequently, as has already been ascertained, it depends more on the reconsideration of the marketing instruments taking changed circumstances into account and their suitability for dealing with these successfully than on a fundamental innovation.

Bibliography

Adams, W. (1986). Whose lives count?: TV coverage of natural disasters. *Journal of Communication*, **36**, 113–22.

Ahmed, Z. (1996). The need for the identification of the constituents of a destination's tourist image: a promotional segmentation perspective. *Revue de Tourisme*, **2**, 44–57.

Ansoff, I. (1981). Die Bewältigung von Überraschungen und Diskontinuitäten durch die Unternehmensführung – Strategische Reaktionen auf schwache Signale. In *Planung und Kontrolle* (H. Steinmann, ed.) pp. 233–64, Vahlen.

Apostolopoulos, Y., Leivadi, S. and Yiannakis, A. (eds) (1996). *The Sociology of Tourism*. Routledge.

Ashworth, G. J. and Goodall, B. (1990). *Marketing Tourism Places*. Routledge.

Avenarius, H. (1995). *Public Relations*. Wissenschaftliche Buchgesellschaft.

Aziz, H. (1995). Understanding attacks on tourists in Egypt. *Tourism Management*, **2**, 91–5.

Backhaus, K., Erichson, B., Plinke, W. and Weiber, R. (1996). *Multivariate Analysemethoden*. Springer Verlag.

Bar-On, R. (1990). The effect of international terrorism on international tourism. In *Terror in the Skies* (A. Lewis and M. Kaplan, eds) pp. 83–104, ISAS.

Becheri, E. (1991). Rimini and Co – The end of a legend. *Tourism Management*, September, 229–35.

Becker, U. (1993). Risikowahrnehmung der Öffentlichkeit und neue Konzepte unternehmerischer Risikokommunikation. In *Risiko ist ein Konstrukt* (Bayerische Rückversicherung, ed.) pp. 343–63, Knesebeck.

Berg, K. and Kiefer, M. (eds) (1992). *Massenkommunikation*. Nomos.

Berger, R., Gärtner, H. and Mathes, R. (1989). *Unternehmenskommunikation*. Gabler.

Bieger, T. (1996a). *Management von Destinationen und Tourismusorganisationen*. Oldenbourg.

Bieger, T. (1996b). Anpassung von Destinationsstrategien an die Globalisierung: Erfolgsfaktoren und Hemmnisse für den strategischen Wandel. In *Globalisierung und Tourismus* (P. Keller, ed.) Vol. 38, pp. 427–450, AIEST.

Bierter, W. (1988). *Risikogesellschaft – Über den schwierigen Weg neue Sicherheiten und Gewissheiten zu erringen*. Syntropie – Stiftung für Zukunftsgestaltung.

Boltz, D. (1994). *Konstruktion von Erlebniswelten*. Vistas.

Boush, D. and Loken, B. (1991). A process-tracing study of brand extension evaluation. *Journal of Marketing Research*, **28**, 16–28.

Braun, O. and Lohmann, M. (1989). *Die Reiseentscheidung*. Studienkreis für Tourismus.

Bruhn, M. and Meffert, H. (1995). *Dienstleistungsmarketing*. Gabler.

Brunt, P. (1997). *Market Research in Travel and Tourism*. Butterworth-Heinemann.

Buckley, P. and Klemm, M. (1993). The decline of tourism in Northern Ireland. *Tourism Management*, June, 184–94.

Bundestagsdrucksache (1977). No. 8/786, Entwurf eines Gesetzes über den Reiseveranstaltungsvertrag.

Burtscher, J. G. (1996). *Wertorientiertes Krisenmanagement*, Diss.

Butollo, W. (1990). Krisen-Psychologie. *Süddeutschen Zeitung*, 15/16 September.

Carmouche, R. and Kelly, N. (1995). *Behavioural Studies in Hospitality Management*. Chapman & Hall.

Carter, S. (1998). Tourist's and traveller's social construction of Africa and Asia as risky locations. *Tourism Management*, **19** (4), 349–58.

Chakravarti, D., MacInnis, D. and Nakamoto, K. (1990). Product category perceptions, elaborative processing and brand name extension strategies. In *Advances in Consumer Research, Proceedings* (Goldberg, Gorn, Pollay, eds) pp. 910–16.

Chierek, M. (1996). Rechtsanspruch des Kunden auf einen bestimmten Carrier? *FVW International*, **4**, 24–6.

Clift, S. and Grabowski, P. (eds) (1997). *Tourism and Health: Risks, Research and Responses*. Cassell.

Cothran, D. and Cothran, C. C. (1998). Promise or political risk for Mexican tourism. *Annals of Tourism Research*, **2**, 477–97.

Datzer, R. (1983a). *Informationsverhalten von Urlaubsreisenden.* Studienkreis für Tourismus.

Datzer, R. (1983b). Einflußfaktoren auf das touristische Informationsverhalten. *Der Markt*, **85**, 6–17.

Derieth, A. (1995). *Unternehmenskommunikation.* Westdeutscher Verlag.

Des Kilalea (1987). Marketing to the affluent: natural treasure attracts repeat business. *Advertising Age*, **58**, S12–S13.

Dolnicar, S. and Mazanec, J. (1998). Destination marketing: reinventing the wheel or conceptual progress? In *Destination Marketing* (P. Keller, ed.) Vol. 40, pp. 55–87, AIEST.

Dörr, G. (1999). Buchungslage bei OFT Reisen. *FVW International*, **1**, 17.

Doswell, R. (1998). *Tourism.* Butterworth-Heinemann.

Doswell, R. (1995). *Tourism: Understanding its Development and Management.* Butterworth-Heinemann.

Doswell, R. (1997). *Tourism: How Effective Management Makes the Difference.* Butterworth-Heinemann.

Downes, J. and Paton, T. (1993). *Travel Agency Law.* Pitman.

Drosdek, A. (1996). *Credibility Management.* Campus.

Dunwoody, S. and Peters, H. P. (1993). Massenmedien und Risikowahrnehmung. In *Risiko ist ein Konstrukt* (Bayerische Rückversicherung, ed.) pp. 317–41, Knesebeck.

Dyllick, T. (1992). *Management der Umweltbeziehungen.* Gabler.

Eckert, H. W. (1995). *Die Risikoverteilung im Pauschalreiserecht.* Luchterhand.

Elliott, J. (1997). *Politics and Public Sector Management.* Routledge.

Fakeye, P. and Crompton, J. (1991). Image differences between prospective, first-time, and repeat visitors to the Lower Rio Grande Valley. *Journal of Travel Research*, **2**, 10–16.

Fasse, F.-W. (1995). *Risk-Management im strategischen internationalen Marketing.* Steuer- und Wirtschaftsverlag.

Felger, S. (1997). Über die weitere Entwicklung des Ägypten-Tourismus herrscht große Unsicherheit. *FVW International*, **28**, 67–8.

Felger, S. (1998a). Ägypten sucht Weg aus der Tourismuskrise. *FVW International*, **7**, 72.

Felger, S. (1998b). Spanien und Griechenland waren die Gewinner. *Deutsche Veranstalter in Zahlen, Beilage zur FVW International,* **28**, 26.

Felger, S. (1998c). Kommenden Winter werden Reisen mit NUR in Krisendestinationen deutlich preiswerter. *FVW International,* **17**, 14–15.

Fesenmeier, D. and MacKay, K. (1996). Deconstructing destination image construction. *Revue de Tourisme,* **2**, 37–43.

Fiedler, S. (1994). Kommunikation zur Krisenvermeidung und – vorsorge. In *Erfolgsfaktor Krise* (R. Gareis, ed.) pp. 211–35, Signum-Verlag.

Frechtling, D. (2001). *Forecasting Tourism Demand: Methods and Strategies.* Butterworth-Heinemann.

Freyer, W. (1995). *Tourismus.* Oldenbourg.

Freyer, W. (1997). *Tourismus – Marketing.* Oldenbourg Verlag.

Frömbling, S. (1993). *Zielgruppenmarketing im Fremdenverkehr von Regionen.* Lang.

Fuchs, M. (1995). *Erlebniswelt Bundesländer.* Diploma thesis, Vienna 1993, quoted after Mayerhofer, W. (1995). *Imagetransfer.* Service Fachverlag.

Führich, E. (1995a). *Reiserecht.* C.F. Müller.

FVW International (1996). *Dokumentation 1995/96. Deutsche Veranstalter in Zahlen, Beilage zur FVW International No. 28,* 28 December.

FVW International (1997). *Dokumentation 1996/97. Deutsche Veranstalter in Zahlen, Beilage zur FVW International No. 28,* 19 December.

FVW International (1998). *Dokumentation 1997/98. Deutsche Veranstalter in Zahlen, Beilage zur FVW International No. 28,* 18 December.

Galtung, J. and Ruge, M. (1965). The structure of foreign news. *Journal of Peace Research,* **2**, 65–91.

Gälweiler, A. (1992). Determinanten des Zeithorizonts der Unternehmensplanung. In *Strategische Unternehmensplanung* (D. Hahn and B. Taylor, eds) pp. 203–20, Physica–Verlag.

Gareis, R. and Rabl, W. (1994). Krisenbewältigung in Projektform. In *Erfolgsfaktor Krise* (R. Gareis, ed.) pp. 163–79, Signum-Verlag.

Gartner, W. and Shen, J. (1992). The impact of Tiananmen Square on China's tourism image. *Journal of Travel Research*, **4**, 47–52.

Gee, C. and Gain, C. (1986). Coping with crises. *Travel & Tourism Analyst*, June, 3–12.

Geitlinger, E. (1976). Unternehmensplanung in unsicherer Zeit. *Management Zeitschrift Industrielle Organisation*, **2**, 55–60.

Gialloreto, L. (1988). *Strategic Airline Management: the Global War Begins*. Pitman.

Glaeßer, D. (2001). Krisenmanagement im Tourismus – Was ist angesichts der aktuellen Vorfälle zu tun. In *Terrorismus versus Tourismus* (H. Bähre, ed.) pp. 9–15, Integron.

Glaeßer, D. (2002a). Crisis management – what has this crisis taught us, *Report presented to the Second Meeting of the Tourism Recovery Committee of the World Tourism Organization* (Berlin, Germany).

Glaeßer, D. (2002b). Crisis management in air transport and tourism. In *Air Transport and Tourism* (P. Keller, and T. Bieger eds) Vol. 44, pp. 121–42, AIEST.

Gold, J. R. and Ward, S. V. (eds) (1994). *Place Promotion: the Use of Publicity and Marketing to Sell Towns and Regions*. Wiley.

Gomez, P. (1981). *Modelle und Methoden des systemorientierten Managements*. Haupt.

Goodall, B. and Ashworth, G. (1987). *Marketing in the Tourism Industry: the Promotion of Destination Regions*. Routledge.

Graham, A. (2001). *Managing Airports: an International Perspective*. Butterworth-Heinemann.

Grewe, W.-G. (1970). *Spiel der Kräfte in der Weltpolitik*. Econ Verlag.

Gu, Z. and Martin, T. (1992). Terrorism, seasonality and international air tourist arrivals in Central Florida. *Journal of Travel & Tourism Marketing*, **1**, 3–15.

Gutiérrez, C. and Bordas, E. (1993). La competitividad de los destinos turísticos en mercados lejanos. In *Competitiveness of Long Haul Tourist Destinations* (AIEST, ed.), Vol. 35, pp. 103–211, AIEST.

Haedrich, G. (1993). Tourismus-Management und Tourismus-Marketing. In *Tourismus-Management* (G. Haedrich et al., eds) pp. 33–43, de Gruyter.

Haedrich, G. (1998a). Kommunikationspolitik. In *Tourismus-Management* (G. Haedrich et al., eds) pp. 379–403, de Gruyter.

Haedrich, G. (1998b). Destination marketing – Überlegungen zur Abgrenzung, Positionierung und Profilierung von Destinationen. *Revue de Tourisme*, **4**, 6–12.

Hahn, D. (1979). Frühwarnsysteme, Krisenmanagement und Unternehmensplanung. *Frühwarnsystem, ZfB-Ergänzungsheft* (H. Albach, D. Hahn and P. Mertens, eds) No. 2, pp. 25–46.

Hahn, H. and Hartmann, K.-D. (1973). *Reiseinformation, Reiseentscheidung, Reisevorbereitung*. Studienkreis für Tourismus.

Hall, C. M. (1994). *Tourism and Politics*, John Wiley & Sons.

Hall, C. M. (1995). *Tourism and Public Policy*. Routledge.

Hartman, C., Price, L. and Duncan, C. (1990). Consumer evaluation of franchise extension products. In *Advances in Consumer Research, Proceedings* (M. Goldberg, G. Gorn and R. Pollay, eds) Vol. 17, pp. 120–7.

Hätty, H. (1994). *Der Markentransfer*. Physica-Verlag.

Hauser, T. (1994). *Krisen-PR von Unternehmen*. FGM Verlag.

Heath, E. and Wall, G. (1992). *Marketing Tourism Destinations: a Strategic Planning Approach*. Wiley.

Hellenthal, M. (1993). *Policy Study of Traveller Safety – Confidential Report for the World Travel & Tourism Council*.

Hilton, D. and Slugorski, B. R. (1986). Knowledge based causal attribution: the abnormal conditions focus model. *Psychological Review*, **93** (1), 75–88.

Hindley, G. (1983). *Tourists, Travellers and Pilgrims*. Hutchinson.

Höhn, R. (1974). *Das Unternehmen in der Krise*. Verlag für Wissenschaft, Wirtschaft und Technik.

Hollinger, R. and Schiebler, S. (1995). Crime and Florida's tourists. In *Security and Risks in Travel and Tourism, Proceedings of the International Conference at Mid Sweden University*, pp. 183–215.

Holzmüller, H. and Schuh, A. (1988). Skandal – marketing. In *Umweltdynamik* (H. Frank, G. Plaschka and D. Rößl, eds) pp. 17–47, Springer.

Hultkrantz, L. and Olsson, C. (1995). Chernobyl effects on domestic and inbound tourism in Sweden. In *Security and Risks in Travel and Tourism, Proceedings of the International Conference at Mid Sweden University*, pp. 37–74.

Hurley, J. (1988). The hotels of Rome. *The Cornell H.R.A. Quarterly*, May, 71–9.

Janisch, M. (1992). *Das strategische Anspruchsgruppenmanagement.* Diss.

Jeck-Schlottmann, G. (1987). *Visuelle Informationsverarbeitung bei wenig involvierten Konsumenten*, Diss.

Johannsen, U. (1971). *Das Marken- und Firmen-Image.* Duncker & Humblot.

Jungermann, H. (1991). Inhalte und Konzepte der Risikokommunikation. In *Risikokontroversen* (H. Jungermann, B. Rohrmann and P.M. Wiedemann, eds) pp. 335–54, Springer.

Jungermann, H. and Slovic, P. (1993a). Charakteristika individueller Risikowahrnehmung. In *Risiko ist ein Konstrukt* (Bayerische Rückversicherung, ed.) pp. 89–107, Knesebeck.

Jungermann, H. and Slovic, P. (1993b). Die Psychologie der Kognition und Evaluation von Risiko. In *Risiko und Gesellschaft* (G. Bechmann, ed.) pp. 167–207, Westdeutscher Verlag.

Kaas, K. P. (1990). Marketing als Bewältigung von Informations- und Unsicherheitsproblemen im Markt. *Die Betriebswirtschaft*, **4**, 539–48.

Kahn, H. and Wiener, A. (1967). *Ihr werdet es erleben.* Molden.

Kaspar, C. (1991). *Die Tourismuslehre im Grundriss.* Paul Haupt Verlag.

Kaspar, C. (1998). Das System Tourismus im Überblick. In *Tourismus-Management* (G. Haedrich et al., eds) pp. 15–32, de Gruyter.

Kelders, C. (1996). *Unterstützung strategischer Entscheidungsprozesse.* M&P.

Keller, P. (1999). Estudio Global del Turismo de Nieve y Deportes de Invierno. In *1er Congreso Mundial de Turismo de Nieve y Deportes de Invierno* (WTO, ed.) pp. 41–70.

Keller, P. and Smeral, E. (1998). Increased international competition: new challenges for tourism policies in European countries. In *Faced with Worldwide Competition and Structural Changes: What are the Tourism Responsibilities of European Governments?* (WTO, ed.) pp. 1–24.

Kemmer, C. (1995). Resident and visitor safety and security in Waikiki. In *Security and Risks in Travel and Tourism, Proceedings of the International Conference at Mid Sweden University*, pp. 75–83.

Kemp, R. (1993). Risikowahrnehmung. In *Risiko ist ein Konstrukt* (Bayerische Rückversicherung, ed.) pp. 109–27, Knesebeck.

Kirsch, W. and Trux, W. (1979). Strategische Frühaufklärung und Portfolio-Analyse. *Frühwarnsystem, ZfB-Ergänzungsheft* (H. Albach, D. Hahn and P. Mertens, eds) No. 2, pp. 47–69.

Kleinert, H. (1993). Kommunikationspolitik. In *Tourismus-Management* (G. Haedrich et al., eds) pp. 287–300, de Gruyter.

Köhler, R. and Böhler, H. (1984). Strategische Marketing-Planung. *Absatzwirtschaft*, **3**, 93–103.

Konert, F. J. (1984). *Emotionale Erlebniswerte auf gesättigten Märkten*, Schriften aus dem Arbeitskreis Betriebswirtschaftliche Verhaltensforschung.

Konert, F. J. (1986). *Vermittlung emotionaler Erlebniswerte*. Physica.

Konrad, L. (1991). *Strategische Früherkennung*. Universitätsverlag Brockmeyer.

Kotler, P. (1984). *Marketing Management*. Prentice Hall.

Kotler, P., Haider, D. and Rein, I. (1993). *Marketing Places*. The Free Press.

Kotler, P., Bowen, J. and Makens, J. (1999). *Marketing for Hospitality and Tourism*, 2nd edn. Prentice Hall.

Krampe, G. and Müller, G. (1981). Diffusionsfunktionen als theoretisches und praktisches Konzept zur strategischen Frühaufklärung. *ZfbF*, **5**, 384–401.

Kreikebaum, H. (1993). *Strategische Unternehmensplanung*. Kohlhammer.

Kreilkamp, E. (1987). *Strategisches Management und Marketing*. de Gruyter.

Kreilkamp, E. (1998). Strategische Planung im Tourismus, In *Tourismus-Management* (G. Haedrich et al., eds) pp. 287–324, de Gruyter.

Krippendorf, J. (1980). *Marketing im Fremdenverkehr, Berner Studien zum Fremdenverkehr*. Verlag Peter Lang.

Krippendorf, J. (1991). *The Holiday Makers: Understanding the Impact of Leisure and Travel*, 2nd edn. Heinemann.

Kroeber-Riel, W. (1986a). Erlebnisbetontes Marketing. In *Realisierung des Marketing* (C. Belz, ed.) pp. 1137–51, Verlag Auditorium.

Kroeber-Riel, W. (1986b). Emotionaler Nutzen entscheidet. *AOK Management*, **3**, 8–11.

Kroeber-Riel, W. (1992). *Konsumentenverhalten*. Verlag Vahlen.

Kroeber-Riel, W. (1993a). *Strategie und Technik der Werbung*. Kohlhammer.

Kroeber-Riel, W. (1993b). *Bildkommunikation*. Vahlen.

Krummenacher, A. (1981). *Krisenmanagement*. Verlag Industrielle Organisation.

Krystek, U. (1979). *Krisenbewältigungs-Management und Unternehmungsplanung*. Diss.

Krystek, U. (1987). *Unternehmungskrisen*. Gabler.

Krystek, U. and Müller-Stewens, G. (1992). Grundzüge einer Strategischen Frühaufklärung. In *Strategische Unternehmensplanung, Strategische Unternehmensführung* (D. Hahn and B. Taylor, eds) pp. 337–64, Physica-Verlag.

Kulhavy, E. (1981). *Internationales Marketing*. Rudolf Traumer Verlag.

Kupsch, P. (1973). *Das Risiko im Entscheidungsprozeß*. Gabler.

Leaf, R. (1995). *Crisis Management, Report presented to the General Assembly of the World Tourism Organization* (Cairo, Egypt).

Lebrenz, S. (1996). *Länderimages*. Josef Eul.

Leimbacher, U. (1992). *Krisenplanung und Krisenmanagement*. Zentralstelle für Gesamtverteidigung.

Lennon, G. (1999). Marketing Belfast as a tourism destination. *Tourism*, **47** (1), 74–7.

Lettl-Schröder, M. (1998a). Gewöhnt an unberechenbares Auf und Ab. *Destination-Report Mittelmeer, Beilage zur FVW International No. 26*, 20 November, pp. 18–20.

Lettl-Schröder, M. (1998b). Ägypten wird weiter über den Preis verkauft. *FVW International*, **16**, 40–1.

Linde, F. (1994). *Krisenmanagement in der Unternehmung*. Verlag für Wissenschaft und Forschung.

Luhmann, N. (1991). *Soziologie des Risikos*. de Gruyter.

Mansfeld, Y. (1995). Wars, tourism and the "Middle East" factor. In *Security and Risks in Travel and Tourism, Proceedings of the International Conference at Mid Sweden University*, pp. 109–28.

Mathes, R., Gärtner, H.-D. and Czaplicki, A. (1991). *Kommunikation in der Krise*. IMK.

Mathes, R., Gärtner, H.-D. and Czaplicki, A. (1993). Krisenkommunikation Teil 1. *PR Magazin*, **11**, 31–8.

Mayer, A. and Mayer, R. U. (1987). *Imagetransfer*. Spiegel Verlag.

Mayerhofer, W. (1995). *Imagetransfer*. Service Fachverlag.

Mazanec, J. (1979). Probabilistische Meßverfahren in der Marketingforschung. *Marketing ZFP*, **3**, 174–86.

Mazanec, J. (1989). Consumer behavior in tourism. In *Tourism Marketing and Management Handbook* (S. Witt and L. Moutinho, eds) pp. 63–8. Prentice Hall.

Meffert, H. and Kirchgeorg, M. (1992). *Marktorientiertes Umweltmanagement*. Poeschel.

Meffert, H. (1993). *Marketing*. Gabler.

Meffert, H. (1994). *Marketing-Management*. Gabler.

Meffert, H. and Heinemann, G. (1990). Operationalisierung des Imagetransfers. *Marketing ZFP*, **1**, 5–10.

Meyer, M. (1987). *Die Beurteilung von Länderrisiken der internationalen Unternehmung*. Duncker & Humblot.

Meyer, W. (1981). Das Image von Dänemark als Urlaubsland. In *Reisemotive, Länderimages, Urlaubsverhalten* (Studienkreis für Tourismus, ed.) pp. 141–57.

Middleton, V. and Clarke, J. (2001). *Marketing in Travel and Tourism*, 3rd edn. Butterworth-Heinemann.

Mileti, D. and Sorensen, J. (1987). Determinants of organizational effectiveness in responding to low probability catastrophic events. *The Columbia Journal of World Business*, **22** (1), 13–21.

Moutinho, L. (ed.) (2000). *Strategic Management in Tourism*. CAB International.

Mühlbacher, H. and Botschen, G. (1990). Benefit-Segmentierung von Dienstleistungsmärkten. *Marketing ZFP*, **3**, 159–68.

Müller, H., Kramer, B. and Krippendorf, J. (1991). *Freizeit und Tourismus*, Berner Studien zu Freizeit und Tourismus, No. 28.

Müller, H. and Flügel, M. (1999). *Tourismus und Ökologie*. FIF.

Müller, R. (1986). *Krisenmanagement in der Unternehmung*. Peter Lang.

Murray, V. V. (1995). Rückentwicklung von Organisationen und Führung. In *Handwörterbuch der Führung* (A. Kieser et al., eds) Col. 1843–58, Schäffer-Poeschel.

Muthukrishnan, A. and Weitz, B. (1991). Role of product knowledge in evaluation of brand extension. In *Advances in Consumer Research, Proceedings* (R. Holman and M. Solomon, eds) Vol. 18, pp. 407–413.

N. A. (1995a). Hoher Boykott-Schaden für Shell. *Börsenzeitung*, No. 114, 17.6.1995.

Nelson Jones, J. and Stewart, P. (1993). *Practical Guide to Package Holiday Law and Contracts*. 3rd edn. Tolley Publishing.

Niehuus, M. (1996). *Reiserecht*. Dt. Anwaltverlag.

Nies, I. and Traut, U. (1995). *Reiserecht*. Beck.

Nieschlag, R., Dichtl, E. and Hörschgen, H. (1997). *Marketing*. Duncker & Humblot.

von der Oelsnitz, D. (1993). *Prophylaktisches Krisenmanagement durch antizipative Unternehmensflexibilisierung*. Verlag Josef Eul.

Opaschowski, H. (1995). *Freizeitökonomie*. Leske und Budrich.

Park, W., Lawson, R. and Milberg, S. (1989). Memory structure of brand names. In *Advances in Consumer Research, Proceedings* (T. Srull, ed.), Vol. 16, pp. 726–31.

Pearce, P. L. (1982). *The Social Psychology of Tourist Behaviour*. Pergamon.

Perrow, C. (1992). *Normale Katastrophen*. Campus.

Peschke, G. (1986). Der Skandal. In *Jahrbuch der Werbung*, pp. 21–3, Econ.

Peymani, B. and Felger, S. (1997). Angst vor der großen Stornowelle. *FVW International*, **26**, 1–4.

Phipps, D. (1991). *The Management of Aviation Security*. Pitman.

Pizam, A. and Mansfield, Y. (eds) (1995). *Tourism, Crime and International Security Issues*. Wiley.

Pizam, A. and Mansfield, Y. (eds) (1999). *Consumer Behaviour in Travel and Tourism*. Haworth Press.

Pohl, H. (1977). *Krisen in Organisationen*. Diss.

Porter, M. E. (1998a). *Competitive Advantage*. Free Press.

Porter, M. E. (1998b). *Competitive Strategy*. Free Press.

Priel, A. and Peymani, B. (1996). Angestrebtes Rekordjahr in weiter Ferne. *FVW International*, **18**, 50.

Pümpin, C. (1980). *Strategische Führung in der Unternehmenspraxis*. Schweizerische Volksbank.

Pürer, H. (1991). *Praktischer Journalismus in Zeitung, Radio und Fernsehen*. Ölschlager.

Raffée, H., Sauter, B. and Silberer, G. (1973). *Theorie der kognitiven Dissonanz und Konsumgüter-Marketin*. Gabler.

Reason, J. (1974). *Man in Motion: the Psychology of Travel*. George Weidenfeld and Nicolson.

Regele, U. and Schmücker, D. (1998) Vertriebspolitik im Tourismus. In *Tourismus-Management* (G. Haedrich et al., eds) pp. 405–45, de Gruyter.

Reilly, A. (1987). Are organizations ready for crisis? *Columbia Journal of World Business*, **22** (1) 79–88.

Ries, K. and Wiedmann, K.-P. (1991). *Risikokommunikation als Problemfeld des Strategischen Marketings*. Institut für Marketing, Universität Mannheim.

Ritchie, B. and Crouch, G. (1997). Quality, price and the tourism experience. In *Quality Management in Tourism* (AIEST, ed.) Vol. 39, pp. 117–39, AIEST.

Ritchie, J. R. B. and Goeldner, C. (eds) (1994). *Travel, Tourism and Hospitality Research: a Handbook for Managers and Researchers*, 2nd edn. Wiley.

Robinson, M., Evans, N. and Callaghan, P. (eds) (1996). *Tourism and Culture: Image, Identity and Marketing*. Business Education Publishers.

Romeo, J. (1991). The effect of negative information on the evaluations of brand extensions and the family brand. In *Advances in Consumer Research, Proceedings*, (R. Holman and M. Solomon, eds) Vol. 18, pp. 399–406.

Röting, P. (1976). Organisation und Krisen-Management. *ZO*, **1**, 13–20.

Ryan, C. (1993). Crime, violence, terrorism and tourism. *Tourism Management*, June, 173–83.

Ryan, C. (1995). *Researching Tourist Satisfaction: Issues, Concepts, Problems*. Routledge.

Ryan, C. and Page, S. (eds) (2000). *Tourism Management: Towards the New Millennium*. Elsevier.

Santana, G. (1995). Crisis management and the hospitality industry. In *Security and Risks in Travel and Tourism, Proceedings of the International Conference at Mid Sweden University*, pp. 148–67.

Santana, G. (1999). Tourism: toward a model for crisis management. *Tourism*, **47** (1), 4–12.

el Sayed, M. K. (1997). The case of Egypt. In *Shining in the Media Spotlight* (WTO, ed.) pp. 21–25, WTO.

Scherler, P. (1996). *Management der Krisenkommunikation*. Helbig & Lichtenhahn.

Scherrieb, H. R. (1992). Qualitäts- und Imagemanagement. *Revue de Tourisme*, **3**, 11–15.

Schönefeld, L. (1994). Krisenkommunikation in der Bewährung. In *Unternehmen in der ökologischen Diskussion* (L. Rolke, B. Rosema and H. Avenarius, eds) pp. 207–222, Westdeutscher Verlag.

Schrattenecker, G. (1984). *Die Beurteilung von Urlaubsländern durch Reisekonsumenten*. Service Verlag.

Schuh, A. and Holzmüller, H. (1992). Skandalbewältigung durch Marketing. *EcSt.*, **7**, 343–8.

Schulten, M. F. (1995). *Krisenmanagement*. Verlag für Wissenschaft.und Forschung.

Schulze, G. (1996). *Die Erlebnis – Gesellschaft*. Campus Verlag.

Schweiger, G. (1992). *Österreichs Image in der Welt*. Service Fachverlag.

Seyderhelm, B. (1997). *Reiserecht*. Müller Verlag.

Sharpley, R. and Sharpley, J. (1995). Travel advice – security or politics? In *Security and Risks in Travel and Tourism, Proceedings of the International Conference at Mid Sweden University*, pp. 168–82.

Sharpley, R. (1999). *Tourism, Tourists and Society*, 2nd edn. Elm Publications.

Shaw, G. and Williams, A. M. (eds) (1996). *The Rise and Fall of British Coastal Tourism: Cultural and Economic Perspectives*. Mansell.

Skriver, A. (1990). Vom Unterhaltungswert von Katastrophen. *E+Z*, **4**, 15–16.

Smith, V. (1998). War and tourism. *Annals of Tourism Research*, **25** (1), 202–27.

Smith, D. and Park, W. (1992). The effect of brand extensions on market share and advertising efficiency. *Journal of Marketing Research*, **29**, 296–313.

Standop, D. (1996a). *Die Nebenwirkungen von Produktrückrufen*. Beiträge des Fachbereichs Wirtschaftswissenschaften, Universität Osnabrück.

Standop, D. (1996b). *Sicherheitskommunikation und Konsumentenverhalten*. Beiträge des Fachbereichs Wirtschaftswissenschaften, Universität Osnabrück.

Steger, U. and Antes, R. (1991). Unternehmensstrategie und Risiko – Management. In *Umwelt – Auditing* (U. Steger, ed.) pp. 13–44, FAZ.

Stobbe, M. (1994). Interview, *Wirtschaftswoche*, **1/2**, 51.

Strangfeld, R. (1993). Rechtliche Rahmenbedingungen. In *Tourismus-Management* (G. Haedrich et al., eds) pp. 105–31, de Gruyter.

Stutts, A. (1990). *The Travel Safety Handbook*. Van Nostrand Reinhold.

Sömez, S.F. (1998). Tourism, terrorism, and political instability. *Annals of Tourism Research*, **25** (2), 416–56.

Sönmez, S. F., Backman, S. J. and Allen, L. R. (1994). *Managing Tourism Crises*. Clemson University.

Sönmez, S. F. and Graefe, A. (1998). Influence of terrorism risk on foreign tourism decisions. *Annals of Tourism Research*, **25** (1), 112–44.

Teare, R., Calver, S. and Costa, J. (1994). *Hospitality and Tourism Marketing Management*. Casell.

Timothy, D. J. and Wall, G. (2000). *Tourism and Political Boundaries*. Routledge.

Trommsdorff, V. (1975). *Die Messung von Produktimages für das Marketing*. Carl Heymanns.

Trommsdorff, V. (1990). Image als Einstellung zum Angebot. In *Wirtschaftspsychologie in Grundbegriffen* (C. Hoyos, ed.) pp. 117–28, Psychologie Verlags Union.

Tscharnke, K. (1995) *FVW International*, **5**, 181.

Tschiderer, F. (1980). *Ferienortplanung*. Paul Haupt Verlag.

Tversky, A. and Kahneman, D. (1974). Judgement under uncertainty: Heuristics and biases. *Science*, **185**, 1124–31.

Ulrich, H. and Probst, G. (1995). *Anleitung zum ganzheitlichen Denken und Handeln*. Paul Haupt Verlag.

Uysal, M. (ed.) (1994). *Global Tourist Behaviour*. International Business Press.

Vallois, F. (1995). *International Tourism: an Economic Perspective*. Macmillan.

Vellas, F. and Bécherel, L. (1995). *International Tourism*. Macmillan.

Vukonic, B. (1997). *Tourism and Religion*. Elsevier Science.

Wachenfeld, H. (1987). *Freizeitverhalten und Marketing*. Physica Verlag.

Wahab, S. (1995). Terrorism – a challenge to tourism. In *Security and Risks in Travel and Tourism, Proceedings of the International Conference at Mid Sweden University*, pp. 84–108.

Weiermair, K. and Gasser, R. (1995). Safety and risk in tourism. In *Security and Risks in Travel and Tourism, Proceedings of the International Conference at Mid Sweden University*, pp. 134–47.

Weinberg, P. (1981). *Das Entscheidungsverhalten der Konsumenten*. Schöningh.

Weinberg, P. and Konert, F.-J. (1985). Vom Produkt zur Produktpersönlichkeit. *Absatzwirtschaft*, **2**, 85–97.

Weischenberg, S. (1990). *Nachrichtenschreiben*. Westdeutscher Verlag.

WEU (1995). *Directives on Planning Options and Priorities to the Planning Cell*, 6. Unpublished draft, 10 April.

Wiedemann, P.M. (1994). Krisenmanagement und Krisenkommunikation. In *Krisenmanagement bei Störfällen* (H.J. Uth, ed.) pp. 29–49, Springer.

Wilkinson, P. (1993). *Policy Study of Traveller Safety – Confidential Report for the World Travel & Tourism Council*.

WTO (1980). *Physical Planning and Area Development for Tourism in the Six WTO Regions*.

WTO (1985). *Contractual Procedures and the Nature of Contracts for Tourist Services Between Tour Operators and their Counterparts in Tourist Receiving Countries as well as Users and Consumers of Tourist Services*.

WTO (1989). *Document TOUR/89-DI.9, Interparliamentary Conference on Tourism, Madrid*.

WTO (1991a). *Special Report on the Impact of the Gulf Crisis on International Tourism*.

WTO (1991b). *Medidas recomendadas para la seguridad en turismo*.

WTO (1993). *Sustainable Tourism Development*.

WTO (1994a). *Marketing Plans & Strategies of National Tourism Administrations*.

WTO (1994b). *Document SEC/2/94/BM*.

WTO (1994c). *Document SEC/2/94/HEUNI*.

WTO (1994d). *Document SEC/2/94/CTO, Crime and Tourism in the Bahamas*.

WTO (1994e). *Budgets of National Tourism Administrations*.

WTO (1995). *Plan of Action for the WTO/UNESCO Cultural Tourism Programme 'The Slave Route'*.

WTO (1996a). *Budgets of National Tourism Administrations*.

WTO (1996b). *What Tourism Managers Need to Know*.

WTO (1996c). *Awards for Improving the Coastal Environment*.

WTO (1997). *Tourist Safety and Security*.

WTO (1998a). *Tourism – 2020 Vision*.

WTO (1998b). *Handbook on Natural Disaster Reduction in Tourist Areas*.

WTO (2001). *Special Report No. 18, Tourism After 11 September 2001: Analysis, Remedial Actions and Prospects*.

WTO (2002a). *Special Report No. 19, Tourism Recovery Committee for the Mediterranean Region*.

WTO (2002b). *Special Report No. 20, The Impact of the September 11th Attacks on Tourism: The Light at the End of the Tunnel.*

WTO (2002c). *Special Report No. 21, Climbing Towards Recovery?*

WTO *Yearbook of Tourism Statistics.* Various Editions.

WTO/UN (1994). *Recommendations on Tourism Statistics.*

Zahn, E. (1983). Konzepte der Krisenerkennung und Krisenvermeidung. In *Erfolgreiche Führung kleiner und mittlerer Unternehmen* (E. Gabele, ed.) pp. 187–215, Bayerische Verlagsanstalt.

Zwyssig, M. (1995). *Die Berücksichtigung öffentlicher Interessen in der externen Berichterstattung.* Diss.

Index